MW00452587

CULTIVATING EXCELLENCE

The ART, SCIENCE, *and* GRIT

of HIGH PERFORMANCE

in BUSINESS

DARRYL W. CROSS, MBA

with

REAR ADMIRAL

WILLIAM V. CROSS, USN, RETIRED

RIVER GROVE
BOOKS

This publication is designed to provide accurate and authoritative information in regard to the subject matter covered. It is sold with the understanding that the publisher and author are not engaged in rendering legal, accounting, or other professional services. If legal advice or other expert assistance is required, the services of a competent professional should be sought.

Published by River Grove Books
Austin, TX
www.rivergrovebooks.com

Copyright ©2017 Darryl Cross

All rights reserved.

Thank you for purchasing an authorized edition of this book and for complying with copyright law. No part of this book may be reproduced, stored in a retrieval system, or transmitted by any means, electronic, mechanical, photocopying, recording, or otherwise, without written permission from the copyright holder.

Distributed by River Grove Books

Design and composition by Greenleaf Book Group and Kim Lance
Cover design by Greenleaf Book Group and Kim Lance
Image Copyright Ilya Akinshin and Africa Studio, 2017. Used under license from Shutterstock.com; Orla/Thinkstock/iStock Collection

Cataloging-in-Publication data is available.

Print ISBN: 978-1-63299-135-5

eBook ISBN: 978-1-63299-136-2

First Edition

I dedicate this book to my family. My father has always been my model for achievement, integrity, and humility. My mother was my first coach and instilled in me my character. My sister, Melanie, is the artist who inspires my creative side. Most importantly, my daughter, Kelsey, keeps me striving to be the best man I can be in the hopes that she is as proud of me as I am of her.

—DARRYL W. CROSS

CONTENTS

Author's Note   *vii*

Introduction   1

Prologue: The Potato King of Mars and the Rise of Maverick   5

1. The Art of High Performance   17

2. The Science of High Performance   45

3. The Grit of High Performance   63

4. The Functional Reserve   87

5. Holding a Whistle Does Not Make You a Coach   119

6. The Octane HighPer Coaching Model   137

7. Reflective Coaching   147

8. Fundamentals and Situational Planning   173

9. Simulation and War Games   187

10. Continuous Improvement   209

11. High-Performance Teams, Tribes, and Communities   231

12. High-Performance Culture Starts at the Top   241

13. The Way to Win   245

Appendix A   *249*

Appendix B   *251*

Notes   *287*

About the Authors   *291*

AUTHORS' NOTE

Nothing is more inspiring than seeing those who excel at their craft. It doesn't matter if it is music, art, sports, business, or writing code. Watching people who are great at what they do makes us happy. However, we were fascinated by why some people entered the ranks of the elite in their domain while other performers who appeared to have similar education, experience, and drive did not. Perhaps it was the luck of being in the right place at the right time. It could've been where they were trained and what schools they attended. Maybe some simply had divine gifts that others could never emulate. However, we had a feeling there was more to it.

In addition to having been a vice president of performance development and coaching for an international, publicly traded corporation, I, Darryl, am the head coach of a rugby union team and a certified master personal trainer. Through my experiences in sports and business, I started to notice similar patterns in both domains that illustrated why some people continuously improved no matter the challenges while others' progression stalled. We needed to know why. We decided to talk to elite performers in multiple domains to learn what accounted for the differences.

We talked extensively to a US Navy fighter pilot, a former commandant of the Marine Corps, a Navy SEAL and astronaut, a metropolitan police chief, and a professional athlete to get their perspectives. What all of them told us was truly surprising. They were extremely insistent that they were not unique. All of them had natural abilities, training, education, experience, and strong work ethics; however, everyone else they were competing against did too. It was HOW they were developed that made the difference.

Through these interviews and years of academic research, we discovered that exceptional coaching, delivered in a team-centric model, develops high-performance individuals. Through reflection with the performers, coaches develop individual plans that emphasize simulation, situational planning, and mastering fundamentals. Exceptional coaches also know that team members collaborate, challenge, and compete with each other, which brings out the best in each individual. The coach's ultimate performance tool is the team.

If you examine any domain or activity that has binary, or terminal, consequences, this is how participants must plan, prepare, and perform. When the margin of error is zero and the consequences of failure are severe, this is the only acceptable way.

Exceptional coaching produces performers with a balanced ability to see things in new ways, perfect their craft, and engage in deliberate practice to continuously improve their performance. We came to define this as the "Art, Science, and Grit of High Performance." We contend that all domains can benefit from this approach. If you want multiple high performers, use the methods that have already been proven and are non-negotiable.

In the end, we learned it was less about the people who excelled and more about their willingness to let others help them excel. The higher the tier, the more important this concept was.

We may not reach the pinnacle of our domain, but we have learned that each of us can unleash our full potential through the right model of development.

Let's get to work.

INTRODUCTION

"Excellence is never an accident. It is always the result of high intention, sincere effort, and intelligent execution; it represents the wise choice of many alternatives—choice, not chance, determines your destiny."
—ARISTOTLE

Why and how do world-class leaders and great performers consistently beat their competition?

There is no shortage of high performers in the world. In every discipline, field, industry, and enterprise, proven experts at the top of their game are trying every trick in the book to squeeze one more challenge and one more percentage of improvement out of one more year. Other leaders, who want to win just as badly, and possess similar levels of experience, ability, and work ethic, test them. The next generation of performers jockey to take their positions and start erasing their records and replacing those memories with their own achievements.

However, all of them cannot be the best. Despite the fact that any given high performer might be in the top 1 percent of the top 1 percent in terms of success, most fields are still dominated by a handful of performers year after year. They all want to excel. They all think they can. However, many of them become frustrated when thousands of hours of hard work, years of experience, and an expensive education do not lead to the winner's podium as often as they think they should. Thus, you hear this familiar signal of acquiescence from "the best" who are not actually doing the best they *could*:

"Some people just have a divine gift that I could never hope to achieve." They are wrong. The common thread of outstanding accomplishment in any domain—from business to sports—involves what we term the art, science, and grit of high performance.

There are certainly great differences in natural abilities, access to training and education, connections, and the luck of the draw between people in the general population. But we're not discussing the general population; we're referring to people who have already succeeded beyond most tests and challenges. They are already among the best. But only a few of the best will be known as elite. The elite see situations and challenges in new ways. They perfect their craft to the nth degree. They put in countless hours of deliberate practice to eliminate performance gaps and realize that reaching the summit in one domain does not necessarily mean leaping to the summit of another. All high performers quickly realize there is only so much they can do on their own. Those who believe they can self-manage their drive and progress find the tendency is to default into areas of strength, ignoring weaknesses and reinforcing their current level of mastery.

High-performing leaders and other elites need someone with an external perspective and the expertise and patience to provide feedback, guidance, and a constant push to keep forward momentum toward attaining the next level. If art, science, and grit are the common threads, the needle pulling these components together is an exceptional coach.

The very best performers rely on expert coaching for plans that continually enhance their performance. Properly coaching elite performers involves a collaborative relationship between professionals, where discovery-based questioning and real-world application lead to solutions identified by the performer. These leaders see their coaches as partners who help them find answers and waste no time listening to endless advice and platitudes about theory.

High-performance coaches and their elite clients rely on simulations and managed competition to demonstrate competency and identify fundamental abilities. This allows coaches to develop preparatory scenarios for situations their clients might encounter. Together, they eliminate performance gaps, tackling them head-on, instead of ignoring or working around weaknesses. Then, they do it again—and again, and again.

Good performers tend to rely on their natural ability, previous education, and past experience. They look backward—mostly through self-reflection—for guidance. In contrast, those who are the absolute best envision new approaches to challenges. Guided by expert coaches who help them get better at what they do every day, they advance and perfect technique, and practice deliberately. They look forward to how things could (and will) be, and they do so with the counsel of others.

While the difference between the good and the best may be only a few percentage points, those extra points become logarithmic in terms of rewards. This is why coaching is so very important to high performers. Coaching is the force multiplier that takes talent to an advanced level beyond that of their peers—peers who may have almost identical abilities, backgrounds, and environments. *The only difference between being good and the best is if—and how—performers are coached.* If high performance is to be translated into future, sustained performance, the act of coaching is the catalyst.

Sports records never stand for long. Business superstars are always looking over their shoulder at the new up-and-comers who want their offices and their titles. Astronaut Gordon Cooper once famously said to reports, "Who is the best pilot I ever saw? You're looking at him." However, someone is always the new "best pilot you ever saw"; the only sure thing is that yesterday's success will not be enough to stay on top tomorrow. Great coaching, therefore, depends upon our understanding of individual successes and the application of research- and results-proven principles, methods, and approaches to the future.

The key to high performance is domain agnostic. Whether coaching an athlete, astronaut, pilot, doctor, lawyer, CEO, butcher, baker, or candlestick maker, there is a way to prepare. There is a way to instruct. And there is a way to win. It is the coaching method that determines if—and how—you'll get to the win.

The purpose of our book is to help coaches get the most out of an individual's or an organization's performance. Once it is understood how and why some individuals excel, processes can be repeated, and success replicated.

You may have heard of some of these principles before, and you may even already agree that they should be a coaching priority. Though many organizations understand what they *should* do, they often do not understand *how*. The plan is simple, but admittedly, not so simple to do.

We will show you how.

THE POTATO KING OF MARS AND THE RISE OF MAVERICK

"An ounce of performance is worth pounds of promises."
—MAE WEST

"The price of success is hard work, dedication to the job at hand, and the determination that whether we win or lose, we have applied the best of ourselves to the task at hand."
—VINCE LOMBARDI

"Success is a lousy teacher. It seduces smart people into thinking they can't lose."
—BILL GATES

It seems counterintuitive, but the types of organizations that have the most trouble developing high performers are the ones already flooded with them. Successful corporations, agencies, teams, firms, and units rest on soft, cushy laurels in relative comfort—for the time being. Full of great people, outstanding products and services, winning strategies, sound tactics, and a great deal of momentum, they keep rolling forward. Why, then, is there need for concern? Ask any leader and you will hear these responses:

"Clients are asking for new, sometimes unreasonable, things."

"Our competitors are catching up."

"Our enemies have thought of new ways to beat us."

"We have to do more with less; we get less from doing more."

"Everything has changed. The world is completely different."

Successful individuals, teams, coaches, and leaders share a common perception: that conditions affecting their status are changing at an exponential rate. While this may be true in some cases, it is not necessarily the world that is changing rapidly—it is the number of high performers competing for the spoils. To illustrate, here's an extremely fictional, yet also very real, example.

BEST IN HIS WORLD

In *The Martian*, an Academy Award-nominated movie about the Ares III expedition to Mars, the protagonist (astronaut Mark Watney, played by actor Matt Damon) is presumed dead during a freak storm and left behind when the rest of the crew makes an emergency evacuation. The crew does not realize their mistake until they are long gone, and so Watney becomes Mars' sole resident. On the plus side, he is a botanist. On the minus side, things that humans eat don't grow on Mars—that is, not without extreme ingenuity, arduous work, and a whole lot of luck.

Watney, naturally, was quite motivated. He could have complained about the unfairness of that unexpected storm. He could have bemoaned his lack of tools and supplies. He could have decided to sit back and watch old videos until his food ran out. No spoilers here, but he doesn't do any of these things. He gets to work, eventually figuring out how to grow potatoes. Potatoes, on the surface of Mars! One of Watney's most memorable lines is this proclamation: "I don't want to come off as arrogant here, but I'm the greatest botanist on this planet."

While Watney mightn't win any *Iron Chef* cooking competitions with the resulting cuisine, it kept him alive, buying time for the astronaut to figure a way out of his predicament. (If you want to know how things turn out for Watney, you'll need to see the movie, but this short recounting demonstrates a number of lessons about performance and success under extreme circumstances that we'll come back to later.)

Mark Watney was right; he *was* the greatest botanist on Mars. In fact, even including the six-person crew of the Ares III, he was still the best botanist on the planet. And when he was left behind on Mars, he also became the best football player, singer, and artist. Lack of competitors elevated his every level of performance. However, let's alter the story.

What if another botanist were to show up? Ignoring the feasibility, suppose that each trained at NASA, studied botany at the University of Chicago, and desired to keep eating on a regular basis. Who would be the best botanist now? Would there be that much of a difference? Potatoes are potatoes, and these two Martian neighbors would just need to produce enough to survive.

Let's add ten more botanists. Mars would become a regular hotbed of botanists; they'd establish infrastructure and industry on the red planet. Perhaps they'd vary the crops and try new techniques. At first, survival is the goal. Add one hundred more botanists, and the survivors are now a colony. Botanists might not be the most exciting bunch of people, but now there's a vibrant Martian community. And, pretty soon, something else is naturally introduced: competition.

On Mars, with its limited resources, Spartan habitats, and few luxuries, there is a finite supply of rewards to go around. This breeds more competition. When struggling to survive, little things—an extra twenty-five square feet of living space or a living pod with a window—don't matter. Once you are no longer just scraping by, however, people with talent and skills want more.

At this point, somebody on Mars is going to create an ever so slightly better tasting potato. This new unique skill will allow them to trade or barter for the bigger living pod. Other colonists will try to match or outdo the new Potato King of Mars, and the race is on.

Watney was surely the best botanist on Mars when alone, but now he is one of over a hundred. His skills are the same. Mars is the same. What has changed is the number of viable competitors for the "Best Botanist" trophy and their competitive desire for resources, comforts, and pride. You could, though, group them all together and claim they're the best botanists on any planet in the entire solar system! (Well, unless you included Earth.)

Should that disparity count? This depends on the market for potatoes. If markets and potato buyers on Mars and Earth can be separated, different sets of winners and high performers will exist. The worry is about size—do these sets form a small playing field? When rewards are abundant and everyone does well, the level of competition decreases. However, when the scope of the playing field is expanded and there's a finite number of desirable rewards, competition emerges and amplifies. In the real world, each of us deals with this every day.

THE NEED FOR SPEED

At the height of the Vietnam War in 1969, the US Navy grudgingly recognized an inconvenient truth: The kill ratio of Vietnamese MIGs (a type of Russian-built fighter aircraft) to American fighter jets in air-to-air combat was only 7:1. That is, seven MIGs were being shot down in aerial dogfights for every one of the navy's fighters. At first glance, this might appear to be a good exchange, but it wasn't. A nearly inexhaustible supply of cheap yet highly maneuverable MIGs was being supplied by Russia and China; a relatively small number of much more expensive US fighters was stationed on aircraft carriers in the Gulf of Tonkin and at air force bases in South Vietnam and

Thailand. Therefore, the kill ratio needed to be at least 20:1 for the United States to win the strategic battle in the skies over Vietnam.

The navy and air force's frontline fighter at the time was the F-4 Phantom II, manufactured by the then-McDonnell Douglas Corporation. The airplane was designed at the height of the Cold War in the 1950s primarily as a supersonic interceptor of Russian bombers. Close-in air-to-air combat was no longer considered likely in the world of supersonic fighters and long-range, radar-guided missiles. Vietnam proved this assumption totally wrong.

Close-in dogfights between MIGs and Phantoms were commonplace, though sporadic. Since the Phantom was not designed for maneuverability, the smaller, more agile MIGs had a distinct advantage in dogfights. Only individual pilot skill and aggressiveness produced the initial 7:1 US advantage. However, North Vietnamese pilots learned and improved quickly, and something had to be done to improve the kill ratio. That "something" was the Navy Fighter Weapons School (commonly known as Top Gun), established to teach pilots new tactics for applying the Phantoms' speed and power to counter the MIGs' agility and stealth. The best of the best needed to get better.

The foremost task for 1969's nascent Top Gun was the selection process for both instructors and students. The navy realized that the value of the program would only be as good as the professional skill and reputation of the participants. Instructors were carefully screened and chosen as the navy's most experienced and capable Phantom pilots. They would teach new tactics in the classroom and fly as adversaries, or red teams, in specially designed airplanes made to look and perform like MIGs. The students were similarly screened as the best of the navy's junior fighter pilots and radar operators (RO): one pilot and one RO from each Phantom squadron.

Imagine the level of competition for selection to Top Gun within each squadron! Navy fighter pilots were already at the top of their peer group in multiple schools and screening tests. But only a handful of the best pilots in the world were qualified for and selected to Top Gun. There were rivalries, hard-nosed competitions, and the occasional heated exchange of words.

The experienced instructors won most of the initial fights in the training syllabus, but surprisingly not many of the later ones! When the Top Gun syllabus had been completed, graduated students became their squadron's tactical experts, responsible for teaching the rest of the squadron the tactics and techniques they had learned to win against the MIGs.

While those pilots and operators not chosen for this elite training were clearly disappointed, they remained totally supportive of the selectees. Top Gun graduates formed a band of brothers who fought together and forged strong bonds of trust and mutual respect. Most importantly, competition for Top Gun slots improved the knowledge and skill of junior officers in every squadron. The results speak for themselves—within three years, the kill ratio had increased to 22:1!

Competition, combined with teamwork, trust, and mutual respect, brought out the best in every pilot and RO, and created a sea change in performance against the MIGs. In the end, they were all on the same team, and this method of training, coaching, and testing made *all* navy pilots better. To this day, Top Gun is widely acknowledged as the ultimate model for success in training fighter aircrews.

⚜

Both of these stories illustrate a key point: Performance is always relative to the competition. This doesn't matter as much if an individual is pursuing a hobby for personal gratification or checking something off a bucket list. However, when keeping score, or the consequences of winning and losing are severe, *self-perception* and assessment of current level of performance becomes irrelevant.

It's why the best pilots in the world had to go back to school to deal with a new reality. It's why Olympic champions have to work harder *after* winning medals to win them again. It's why business executives, lawyers, and doctors must constantly improve and update their skills as practitioners and acumen as client service providers.

EVERYONE NEEDS A COACH

High-performance coaches know that in business, sport, the military, protective services, and every other segment of society, top performers exhibit three key characteristics that allow year after year wins, no matter what conditions or competitors emerge. They coach mastery of the principles we call the *art, science, and grit of high performance.*

High performers constantly work on perfecting these principles, and they learn how to balance all of the elements required to reach the top and stay there. They don't rely on past experience, diplomas hung on walls, or titles on a business card to insulate them from reality. They relish the arena, ask their coaches for help, and compete over and over again. All of them.

It may seem a strange dichotomy that performers who wish to excel and unleash their potential must be so dependent on others for help. From a young age, many of us are taught to only depend on ourselves and that success is up to the individual. In fact, you will be hard pressed to find world-class performers who have not relied on a coach and coaching to get where they are today. Individual protégés in music, sports, or the arts might be viewed as exceptions and may give pause about whether anyone can achieve high performance alone. But parents, teachers, peers, partners, and trusted mentors all had a hand in their achievement. Those individuals may not have worn a shirt with the word *Coach* stenciled on the front or been dedicated to what they were doing full time, but they were "coaching" throughout their protégé's development. The performer may take home the trophies, but the team comprised of those who "coach" them makes those trophies possible.

THE BINARY CONSEQUENCES OF PERFORMANCE

Can coaches apply these same principles of art, science, and grit in all other domains so that leaders can achieve greater success and market advantage? The answer, we submit, is absolutely *yes*!

Today's top performers live in a world where competition increasingly has *binary consequences*. One wins, and everyone else loses. One business gets the deal, and the others get nothing. Industries have dominant players, and the rest are absorbed. At the individual and organizational level, the world has become a much harder place. More educated, skilled, driven people exist in the market than at any other time in human history. They work for some of the most innovative, successful, and robust organizations ever. And many of them will be left behind.

This concept of binary consequences is not new. In sports, winners take all while losers, who finish just one hundredth of a second behind, fade from memory. Navy SEALs do not compete for second place on the sea, air, and land. No one tells an airline pilot, "Nice attempt at keeping that plane in the air. Better luck next time." In these examples, the individuals' performance—despite the fact that they train and prepare as teams led by exceptional coaches—is the focus. Society rewards and encourages individual performance, and this will not change in the foreseeable future. However, this should not be mistaken to mean that the development of individual greatness comes from solitary toil and effort. In all elite domains, leaders have a methodology for getting the best out of people. The primary reason for this—there is no other choice.

Disciplines such as the military, police, firefighting, and space exploration often deal with binary consequences, better known in these lines of work as *terminal consequences*. The penalty for substandard performance is, well, quite high. Therefore, individuals in these disciplines train differently. Their demeanor relating to skills development and retention is more serious. They obsess with planning for every situation and pressure testing through simulation. They compete with each other to prepare. They are tremendously dependent on coaching as a constant factor in their development and integration with teams of other high performers. This is why they are so prepared and able to constantly take on new, increasingly difficult challenges.

Your performers may not be running into burning buildings or dealing with killer space debris hurtling at 22,000 miles per hour. However, when you are coaching top performers, teams, and their organizations, you are dealing with increasingly high-stakes issues in their areas of operation. There are businesses that attract the most profitable work and grow unremittingly, and those that get just enough scraps to keep the lights on. There are firms that lose over and over and over again to seemingly equally matched competitors. There are individual performers who attended the best schools, spent twenty years learning their craft, and still underperform their peers.

Why is that? Is it luck? Is it a matter of being in the right place at the right time? Do some performers have a divine gift that cannot be replicated? Perhaps it is something else. Perhaps high performers should be preparing for a more competitive world in the same ways that groups who live with the threat of terminal consequences do every day. The consequences may not be as severe, but they are just as binary. It's a lot to ask someone to self-manage their way to realizing their full potential when they are already overburdened with actual performance. They need an alternative perspective, one that provides an honest look at what needs to change and improve. This is where coaching comes in.

HIGH PERFORMANCE DEMANDS CONSTANT VIGILANCE

Some self-proclaimed high performers think they no longer need to develop skills and challenge abilities. The summit of their careers, they believe, has been achieved and now they'll spend the years until retirement repeating those winning ways. In most cases, if they were honest with themselves, these self-determined summiteers would admit that ascension was due less to a unique ability and more to unique circumstances. Through luck, random choices, or rare environmental forces, they have reached the top without much assistance from others. However, it is the highest performers who have already made it into the top tier who need the most training, coaching, and ongoing competition to stay there. Only a fool expects lightning to strike twice and then, when standing in the exact same spot, bemoans that it doesn't.

Experience, expertise, and wisdom can be great strengths for some performers. For others, these characteristics serve as their greatest sources of weakness. It's clear from research and experience that leveraging competition and training under duress play a huge role in developing better people and better organizations. However, despite displayed bravado and confidence, some performers shy away from further difficult challenges or appearing on a public scoreboard once they've reached the upper tier of their domain.

A coach's role includes creating situations where teammates prepare, plan, perform, and compete against each other. But high performers must be able to come together and operate as a team when the real competition against actual competitors begins. Great coaching involves encouraging performers to compete against other, slightly better leaders, as well as the ultimate competition—a better version of themselves.

People at the top of their field must also balance creativity, perfection, and hard work. Some performers constantly search for a shortcut or unique approach to getting an edge. Some may try to incessantly perfect their craft in antiquated or less effective ways, still obsessed with those processes that first made them a star. Other hard driving performers will work themselves into the ground, counting those long hours as guarantee of a next big win just ahead.

All performers tend to favor one of the following behaviors:

1. Pioneers always seek a better way, but they do not put in the time and practice necessary to learn and perfect their approach.
2. Purists refuse to look up to see what has changed, and they are overly concerned with fine-tuning performance to the nth degree.
3. Plow pushers work until they drop, whether or not their approach actually works.

Under duress, all performers default to their comfort zone.

High performers who, year after year and despite changing conditions and competitors, succeed in any one arena are able to balance and shift fluidly between all three of the following behaviors:

1. They look up occasionally to see how things could be different or who is doing things differently.
2. They perfect their craft.
3. They work hard.

These behaviors define the art, science, and grit of high performance and are a high predictor of those who will always be on top of their tier.

THE ART OF HIGH PERFORMANCE

"What is art but a way of seeing?"
— SAUL BELLOW

"He who works with his hands is a laborer. He who works with his hands and his head is a craftsman. He who works with his hands and his head and his heart is an artist."
— LOUIS NIZER

"I adapted an antiquated style and modernized it to something that was efficient. I didn't know anyone else in the world would be able to use it and I never imagined it would revolutionize the event."
— DICK FOSBURY

"Creativity is just connecting things. When you ask creative people how they did something, they feel a little guilty, because they didn't really do it, they just saw something. It seemed obvious to them after a while. That's because they were able to connect experiences they've had and synthesize new things."
— STEVE JOBS

Imagine you'd managed to mistakenly find your way into a pasture and had upset the local bull that had proclaimed that grassland to be his. Your primary goal would be to simply run faster than the bull. If you were alone and without help, there would only be one option: run to the fence before the bull reaches you. Let's assume you got to the barbed wire or electric fence first, but the fence is five feet tall. Could you scale it? What about without touching any part of it with your body? Even with all the adrenaline in the world flowing through your veins, this sounds impossible!

When Dick Fosbury was sixteen years old, he challenged this idea. Now, to be clear, he wasn't chased by a bull. He wanted to make the Medford High School track team. In Oregon, back in the 1960s, 1.5 meters (approximately five feet) was the minimum qualifying height for the high jump in high school track meets.

Fosbury was a tall, lanky guy. He played basketball and ran track in addition to trying to clear that bar. However, those long legs and arms so advantageous in other sports were a bit of a liability while trying to defy gravity by going over a high bar.

There are not many rules for performing the jump. You must not dislodge the bar, and you must take off on one foot. Thus, methods to clear the bar proliferated over the years. The dominant techniques of the time had colorful names, such as the western roll, upright scissors, eastern cut-off, and straddle method. Each was a time-tested, standard method of accomplishing this relatively unnatural task. However, Fosbury had little success with any of the traditional ways. He could have spent years studying and perfecting one of the methods that wasn't ideal for his body and ability. He could have stayed well into the night, practicing over and over again each day until he finally improved. Or, he could experiment with getting over that bar in a new way. That is exactly what he did.

Starting in 1964, Fosbury started using his own technique: head first and backwards. Many of his coaches, teammates, and local sports media were quick to ridicule—but that did not last for long. As he perfected his technique, Fosbury began to win, breaking long-standing high school records. He continued to perfect his style while at Oregon State University, despite his coach's encouragement to use a more traditional style during meets. However, once Fosbury returned to his preferred method for clearing the bar, he broke collegiate records. Not only did his collegiate coach become a believer, but he then taught Fosbury's method to others.

By 1968, Fosbury had gained national attention, become the country's No. 1 college high jumper, and qualified for the US Olympic team. He continued to find ways to perfect his unique technique, which became widely known by the name we use today: the Fosbury Flop. In the end, his innovative streak, quest for perfection, and hard work paid off. Fosbury won the gold medal in the high jump with a mark of 7 feet 4¼ inches, a new Olympic and American record. Since then, the flop has become the dominant method used in the event. One day, there might be a new innovation that changes how high jumpers soar over the bar, but for now, the art of high performance as demonstrated by Dick Fosbury is the standard. It took him seeing things in a new way to make it possible.

What really made his technique feasible? Was Fosbury smarter than everyone else, more creative, or just lucky? Success might have resulted from a combination of these things, but other variables and factors played a role. First was the advent of the modern landing pad, made of soft foam and elevated three feet off the ground. Before the early 1960s, jumpers cushioned their fall by landing in sawdust or wood chips. A high jumper in those days could have tried Fosbury's technique—once. At that time, the flop was not a replicable approach due to the unforgiving effects of gravity and solid ground.

Second, Fosbury was not built like many other high jumpers. He was tall, long limbed, and generally lanky. Other high jumpers had compact bodies and tended to be built like sprinters with powerful legs. To help him clear the bar, Fosbury's new approach provided as much crucial time with his center of gravity under the bar as possible.

Third, Fosbury's coaches allowed him to experiment—partly due to his determination in perfecting his technique. He was working hard and hitting the heights, so why not let him try? All coaches, however, would not have been so accommodating.

When Fosbury first started his unorthodox approach, the head coach at his high school was trying to move him from one traditional technique (the scissor) to the western roll, the approach all of his other athletes were using. However, the coach could see that Fosbury was having troubles, and he saw he had an athlete willing to put in the time for experimentation. This was a critical moment in Fosbury's evolution. A misguided coaching technique, one that demanded compliance, obedience, or unending repetition, would have stifled Fosbury (and been the end of this story). However, his coach encouraged experimentation, allowing Fosbury to use one technique in practice and a different one during meets. As long as his results improved, Fosbury would be given latitude to try different approaches. Luckily, this latitude continued into Fosbury's collegiate years. Fosbury had an empathetic and visionary coach at Oregon State, and when he beat the school record in his first meet using the Fosbury Flop, his coach had seen enough. From then on, the flop became Fosbury's coach's primary method, which he continued to study and taught to others. Fosbury benefited from exceptional coaching—a partnership, not the authoritarian approach often brought to mind when most think of coaching.[1]

Fosbury changed his perspective due to changing conditions of the sport, available technology, and his own particular limitations. This response allowed him to devise a new way of overcoming a common challenge. By adapting and innovating, Fosbury became the best at what he did and set the standard for others to follow.

This is the art of high performance.

Innovation in the high jump, however, did not cease in 1968, nor was it defined solely by Fosbury. While Fosbury kept his hands to his side as he cleared the bar, others stretched out their arms. He ran a "J curve" in his approach, but others utilized a "C curve." A Canadian athlete named Debbie

Brill had even developed a similar technique (the Brill Bend), but she did not win Olympic gold; as a result, her innovation didn't capture the media's attention and remained little known. Innovation, we see, never stops when competition is involved. The biggest limiting factors affecting achievement, however, are often found in the competitors' own minds.

When high performers reach a limit of vision, it is sometimes because they are too close to the problem. Exceptional drive and work ethic have them so focused on performance that seeing things from a different point of view may be difficult.

However, a coach is more detached and able to see their current performance as it compares to past performance, other's performance, and upcoming environmental changes. Sometimes the performer is the innovator; sometimes the coach has the new approach.

> **In most cases, the partnership between performer**
> **and coach changes an idea or aspiration into action**
> **and technique that can be perfected.**

In case you were wondering, the new minimum qualifying height for the high jump at Fosbury's high school is now *six* feet.[2] His art is now everyone else's science.

WHAT IS ART, AND HOW DOES IT RELATE TO HIGH PERFORMERS AND HIGH-PERFORMANCE COACHING?

Ask a hundred people to define the word *art,* and you will get almost as many definitions. In fact, the phrase "I know it when I see it" is part of American cultural lexicon based on an interesting case, *Jacobellis v. Ohio* (1964), decided by the U.S. Supreme Court (review at your own risk).[3]

Art is a challenging concept to define, and it is made more complex depending on who's defining it. A non-artist may define it as a creation such as a picture, sculpture, or musical composition. A philosopher may define it as the process of creation itself. Artists may bristle at the thought of anyone trying to constrain the concept into a simple definition that trivializes creation, production, and the greater meaning of expression.

Art is also very dependent on the eye, ear, or mind of the beholder. To some people, the song "Welcome to the Jungle" by Guns N' Roses revolutionized the music scene. To lovers of classical music, or for example, Panamanian dictator General Manuel Noriega (who was chased out of an embassy after ten days of hearing it at deafening levels[4]), the song is garbage.

One definition of art could be "the expression or application of human creative skill and imagination." In this context, the definition does not require a person to be an artist as a profession in their particular area of influence. It simply requires someone (under the same conditions, resources, and constraints governing others) to see things in new ways and be able to produce something original that creates a new source of direction, value, or advantage for themselves and others. For the purposes of this book, however, we need a solid definition, and so we do our best to encapsulate it into a useable concept (though surely we'll offend many a scholar or artist in the process):

Creation or construction of an innovative product, process, idea, or application through seeing things in new ways and from new perspectives to yield unique results for appreciation, adaptation, or advancement.

Let's break down those words and concepts into some manageable pieces for discussion.

First, "creation and construction" are meant to imply *action*. While the word *art* might be sometimes used as a noun when considering the results of creativity, we refer to *art* as a verb, designating the act of creativity.

Second, this action must produce something. The results might be a new idea, one that influences how we look at things or address everyday situations. It might be new ways to use common tools, components, and resources in business or to tackle challenges. Perhaps the action simply changes the order of steps or approach to problem solving. Of course, what is produced can also be something tangible, like a painting, piece of music, or technological gadget.

Third, and critical, is the idea that art sees things in new ways and from new perspectives. Art is most often the result of an individual or group having an "Aha!" moment once they are removed from an issue and consider someone's else's point of view or a different angle without self-imposed limitations (i.e., how things have been done in the past). From great painters to athletes and entrepreneurs, this change is a key part of creativity that liberates the creator's ability to produce something new.

Fourth, the result must be unique. Specific variations might be very slight, but art is not something that is mass reproduced. While that might make those who find comfort in numbers and efficiency uncomfortable, numbers and efficiencies are the antithesis of true art. Perhaps the ability to capitalize on a new idea might be an issue based on reality, scalability, and economics in the future. During the process of creating art, however, that thought is a constraint to be avoided.

Fifth and finally, the result must have a reason for being. Appreciation by the public (and perhaps by the artists themselves) may be the reason a beautiful sculpture or musical composition was created. Think of the "artwork" created by a three-year-old child that is a unique representation of the family dog. It may look like a Picasso, but it won't sell like one. However, it is still art, and its value is based on the audience. Other types of art might help us adapt to a new reality or a change in the environment. Reacting to rule changes in sport, new government regulations in business, or the sudden availability of broadband Internet access to the general public are examples of how art can be created to adapt to challenges and opportunities. Advancement benefits individuals, groups, organizations, or society as a whole. Architecture in a metropolitan city is a great example: Beautiful, energy-efficient buildings full of natural light are works of art that benefit countless others. The designers used steel, glass and rivets, components available to anyone, but they created something unique.

In terms of sight, sound, and touch, art is not always traditionally beautiful. However, it is always unique, expressing different perspectives and visions of what could be and—until that very moment—had never before existed.

ART IS HARD TO DEFINE,
BUT YOU KNOW IT WHEN YOU SEE IT

Art solves complex problems. For businesses, how a company takes raw materials, financial investments, and people to create new products that will be accepted by the market and fit realities of the *next* ten years as opposed to the *last*, is art. For painters, it is taking a blank canvas and, using only brushes and standard colors, creating something never before painted. For athletes, it is looking down a swimming pool's lanes and finding ways to refine their specific tool (their body) to beat new competitors who are trying to do the same thing.

Another thing to keep in mind: art appeals to emotions and the heart, not necessarily to logic and the mind. That is why art is so hard to define and so dependent on the beholder as well as the point in history in which it is introduced. Business artists, such as Steve Jobs, have numerous failures and false starts because they introduced a product at the wrong time or the product failed to resonate with consumers. Grunge metal had its moment, but it is unlikely that musical moment would have been the same in the 1500s. Fosbury's artistic flop was perfect in the early 1960s, but it would have been disastrous before the invention of elevated landing pads.

Coaching can act as a governor and catalyst when managing the art of high performance. If a leader is constantly churning out ideas and approaches that never see action, the coach's job is to rein in the leader. If coaches notice there are no more gains being made with an existing approach, their role is to help the performer move on to another. The coach's role, though, is not to have all the answers. Reflection and collaboration between coach and performer might uncover new ideas and approaches. In the end, coaching provides the extra perspective as to what can be achieved next, whether by focusing on mastery or experimentation. If a performer is fixated on the tiny details, the coach's job is to find the bigger picture. Let's look to business for an example of how extra perspective—or lack thereof—can make the difference between success and failure.

THE GREAT SMARTPHONE WARS

Remember the smartphone wars that started in the mid-2000s? At that time, Blackberry, developed by Research in Motion (RIM), was the market leader with more than 50 percent market share. Its primary rivals were Motorola and Nokia. All were fighting to take the basic mobile phone concept and add email communication, a benefit that would extend the desktop computer to the palm of users' hands. This new product would be a communication device, and each business proclaimed their networks were more reliable, communications more secure, and devices the most advanced on the market. Then everything changed.

Apple CEO Steve Jobs appeared at the January 2007 Macworld conference and announced a neat little gadget: the iPhone. Certainly, Apple was not new in the innovation game; they introduced the first iPod (2002) and eventually dominated the portable music device market. Keep in mind, however, that Apple did not invent the category. Sony, maker of the Walkman, had been around for years and many companies pioneered digital music devices based on the MP$_3$ format long before the idea of the iPod crossed Cupertino's design desks. However, Apple did have a reputation for forward thinking and making improvements through creativity, design, and functionality. They not only had an idea where the market was going, Apple intended to drive the market in the very direction they wanted. The world didn't know it "needed" a device like the iPad or the iPhone until Jobs and Apple showed that it did.

We all know how this story ends. In just the first quarter of 2016, Apple sold 74.8 million iPhones. RIM now owns less than 1 percent market share and continues to trend downwards. Realistically, RIM is no longer a competitor in this market; it has its fans, but the Blackberry is loved only by a cult of users— much as RIM once characterized Apple users. Many business analysts now refer to iPhone, with an initial development cost of around $150 million, as the most profitable product in history. How did this happen?

RIM founder Mike Lazaridis was in denial from the moment the product was unveiled. The iPhone had a terrible battery life; it was a network bandwidth hog; there was no traditional clickable keyboard; and the device didn't come with the encryption security that the Blackberry did. In Lazaridis's eyes, the iPhone was a toy for people addicted to watching cat videos on YouTube. Lazaridis reasoned that RIM's users would not be interested in such triviality, and most of RIMs internal advisors backed that thinking. They would stick to their approach and strengths. People did not want access to the Internet from their phones; they just needed to get email when they weren't at their desks!

Admit it: That's hard to read when you consider how everyone uses smartphones nowadays. Remember, this was the leader of the largest company in the world, in its domain, expressing his opinions on what the market wanted. RIM's pillars of success were built on ease of typing (like users did on a QWERTY keyboard, not a silly glass screen), low network usage, long battery life, and rock-solid encryption. Adherence to these pillars, they claimed, would protect RIM from this invasive new competitor. This proves how little they understood about the art of high performance. Not only was RIM relying on their customers to make the most logical decision, they failed to notice what was happening in their business environment—how Apple was chang-ing the commercial landscape and customers' hearts.

Apple made exclusive marketing deals with AT&T to sell their product; additionally, they worked a technological deal to incorporate a full web browser and access to the entire scope of the Internet into their product. They developed an app store and used their iTunes service to further tie consumers to communications and entertainment offerings. Apple also embraced beau-tiful, intuitive design, building their product with only a single button on its face and creating an instruction manual from a few simple drawings and sentences. All of these innovations had nothing to do with what RIM viewed as the Blackberry's strengths. They eventually tried to counter with products such as their Storm device and alignments with phone service carriers, but it was too late; Apple had destroyed RIM. However, the war is not over.

Samsung, with its Android operating system, was 2016's leading smart-phone manufacturer until fourth quarter's iPhone 7 release helped catapult Apple into the top spot. This continuing skirmish shows that battles between any industry's top manufacturers will continue to rage, and none can afford to be overly fixed on a single rival. The other three manufacturers in the top five, all Chinese companies, are taking advantage of the adoption of smart-phones in new markets by new consumers. What will those customers want? What makes those markets different? How will laws, languages, and customs dictate how those markets evolve? Now it is Apple and Samsung's turn to remain relevant.

Some accept that art is a constant state of problem solving. Others think they can insulate themselves from change by overreliance on technical details and hard work. In time, most artists win and, although some artists don't, the concept of art is always victorious. *Staying* on top takes more than art, but art is the key to passing competitors on the way there. We will return to this concept in future chapters as we discuss how art must be complemented by science and grit if an idea, product, or application is to take hold.

❧

Many performers claim to have great vision or a respect for the "art" of their domain. Whether it is in sports, business, science, or any other area of expertise, very few people claim they are automatons going through familiar motions over the course of a career—no matter how complex those motions might be. Instead, they call themselves visionaries, innovators, or strategic thinkers. All of those terms assure the world (and themselves) that these performers are more than a hard-working machine. They think and see how things *could* be.

However, is that true? Why do certain people (who are immersed in identical circumstances as their peers) see clearly how things could be better, while others—with the exact same sets of data, resources, and experiences—cannot? If performers keep missing changes around them despite their identical immersion, they are most likely acting alone and not training in a team environment. They are not using a coach as a partner to help them see changes. They only see competitors when playing for keeps. Leaders at the top of their domains naturally miss changes in the world because they have their heads down. A coach's role is to keep those heads up and thinking through "what if?" scenarios—in other words, to encourage performers to think more like artists. But becoming an artist doesn't occur at the flip of a switch; that transformation takes time, effort, and a willingness to change.

True artists actually *do* see things differently; non-artists cannot see things from other perspectives without the proper training and identification of what is obscuring their view. Try this experiment to differentiate how artists and non-artists see the world. Submit the following challenge to a group of smart people: "Draw me a picture of a tree. You have twenty seconds."

You will get a wide variety of submissions due to various factors: the age of the people, skill level in drawing, what part of the world they are from, and their memories and activities—even from the moments before you asked them to put pen to paper. Imagine a possible picture in your head right now. Got it? Remember that image.

If you took a representative sample of the trees drawn by people close to where you live, from similar backgrounds and between five and fifty-five years old, you would probably get something like this:

Some variations will occur. Some people might have used green for the top of the tree. Some might have added more or less detail. A few might have taken the "art" term a little too seriously and drawn a frame to prepare for its proper place in the Louvre. However, it's amazing that, without any limiting instructions, non-artists from similar backgrounds and experiences almost always draw this same tree if they are given a short amount of time to produce the image. Why is that? Is it a lack of artistic skill, or is there something else?

We could cite many reasons for the mass production of similar tree images by different people. Some reasons are based on the conditions of the request. Some are based on the skills and experience of the artist. Some are based on our reliance on the familiar as a starting point to begin solving a challenge. Let's take a look at these issues as they pertain to this example:

- Conditions of the request
  - Short time frame
  - Lack of direction
  - Limited access to materials or resources

- ° Unclear reason for request
- ° Unclear meaning of value assigned to what is ultimately produced

- Skills and experience of artists (or the performer or leader)
  - ° Varied and unknown skills and experience level
  - ° Lack of preparation time
  - ° No reference point or model
  - ° Varying levels of participation
  - ° Varied underlying primary strengths (other than artistic endeavors)

- Reliance on the familiar
  - ° Comfort level with simple design
  - ° Need to conform
  - ° No express permission of liberation of ideas
  - ° No definition of importance of the task

Of course, if you gave your group twenty minutes instead of twenty seconds to complete the task, the results would be different. There might be more detail in the branches, lines in the trunk, or even a bird's nest in one of the branches. If you told the participants to draw a big tree or specified a particular type of tree, the pictures might vary more. If you supplied a wide palate of colors to choose from, art supplies, and space to work, you might get an even wider spectrum. You might even tell people there was a contest with a $100 prize for the winner! But in the end, the trees would—for the most part and for most people—still look the same, despite any differences in the request conditions.

Changing the variables related to the skills and experience of the artists might have a greater effect on producing a higher quality of tree art. If only the best sketch artists in the room participate, the samples might be worthy of a wall (somewhere). If a tree outside the window provided a model that everyone could see, the results might look less like a blob on paper. Also, if you allow advance preparation for the exercise, you could counteract the effects of a rushed time frame on the outcomes. While you might have improved the quality of mass production, the variation in output has not changed within the group.

The first two groups of reasons for tree art cloning are what we commonly refer to in sophisticated, scientific terms as "excuses." You might hear one or more of these from the participants:

"Well, I'm not an artist. What do you expect?"

"I would do better if we had more time. The conditions make it impossible to do anything of substance."

"I had no idea that this was so important. If I had, I would have put more thought into it."

"I didn't know you wanted anything except a basic tree. You never said that was important. You asked for a tree, and I drew you a tree."

"Why am I doing this? Aren't there experts that can handle this, so I can get back to my work?"

While we call the above statements "excuses," the participants do have a point. There *are* natural limitations placed upon them due to the nature of the exercise. It is the job of the leader of an exercise to set parameters, manage resources and participants, and direct efforts toward the desired goal. This illustrates how a coach can construct a great moment with monumental effect on the leaders that supports the value of the coaching. Leaders' performances are limited by how they see things. Leaders and conditions may have created limitations and boundaries in which leaders can operate. But effective coaching will show performers how to think through challenges differently and, while still respecting the limitations, improve. Thus, performers move from frustration and complaining to continuous betterment. Without coaching, people may throw up their hands and go back to the approach they know best . . . even when it yields no better results.

So why do people keep drawing only slightly better versions of the same tree?

This phenomenon is most likely due to the third group of conditions, *reliance on the familiar*. There is nothing wrong with the challenge; you asked for a tree, so people drew a tree. It is a simple task, so the non-artists rely on iconic imagery of the object to produce something quickly that is readily identified and not easily ridiculed by their peers. Non-artists may even resort to drawing a tree as they would've at age five, and you probably will not see much difference between that drawing from a business setting and what is hanging on the home refrigerator. However, true artists see things differently. They do not try to identify and classify objects. They look at their component parts and visualize how to use them in new ways.

Untrained artists, many of whom claim to be visionary and strategic, see icons or representations of objects. If you ask them to draw a hat, a car, or a tree, they produce similar styles and reproductions. This is very helpful when making signs that anyone can understand, describing how to accomplish a task, or quickly summarizing a position. However, falling back on the familiar is exceptionally self-limiting when creating art. The non-artists see a tree as a representation of what has already been seen. They identify the object and recreate it, making variations in the slightest of degrees.

When artists look at a picture, they see shadows, contours, colors, and much more. By seeing things as an unlimited collection of variables and components, there is no limit to what can be created. In fact, studies have shown that when artists and non-artists view the same picture, they focus on different things. Non-artists spend 40 percent of the time looking at familiar objects. They scan for faces, common items, and symbols. They seek images that make them feel comfortable, and then they re-create them. Artists, on the other hand, spend less time looking at any one spot in a picture; they scan all of it. They give equal attention to all aspects, even rotating the picture in their hands to achieve different angles. These two groups of people see the same thing very differently.[5] We should expect that those two groups of people would also have different suggestions of how to create something new and truly unique.

Whether coaching, leading an individual performer, or performing, you are probably not in the business of drawing trees. You do, however, make decisions that involve your personal achievements, the future of your enterprise, well-being of your team, and possibly an overall impact on society. Those decisions can be monumental, and the "trees" you are asking people to draw are actually thought-based exercises such as these:

- Methods learned over the last twenty years are having less and less of an impact. What should be done differently?

- Should so much be risked by trying a new idea or approach? What if we are wrong?

- How do we deal with losing key talent and clients to competitors?

- How do we address operational problems within our business that, if ignored, will bring us to an end in less than a year?

Of course, some people are naturally inclined to be artistic. Keep in mind that it would be insulting to attribute profound expertise in art as something that comes easily to some people. There are art schools, art professors, and artists (whose first famous work came after twenty years of effort) who would take great offense at that assumption. The eye, mind, and heart must be trained to ignore the familiar, to see the whole landscape, and to create a new vision of what only some of us can view.

In all domains, leaders can be trained to see like artists. But they must also be provided with an environment and culture that welcomes and rewards creative thinking. This might seem like common sense to those who claim they want their performers to gain a competitive advantage through creative thinking, but this is not always the case. Individuals, teams, and organizations frequently run into friction that stops them in their tracks.

ART IN THE BOARDROOM

Think of the last really important meeting you attended, one where a great deal was at stake. Try to visualize who attended and conditions in the room, down to the palpable stress in the air and any scuttlebutt or chatter in the days before the meeting. As the meeting got started, imagine that someone in charge asked the following questions:

> *"How do we address the fact that we charge 20 percent more for our service than our lower cost competitor? Our clients are demanding discounts, and this will be the end of us in less than a year if we don't fix it. We've got the next three hours to figure it out. I want solutions, and I want them now."*

In most cases, you are stuck with a certain set of people, products, services, facilities, and market conditions. There is no magic wand or knight on a white horse to gallop into the room. The "they" who must fix this problem are actually a collective "you." So, what happened next?

You might have experienced these results:

- Engineering people produced engineering ideas. Finance people brought finance ideas. Marketing people had marketing ideas.
- A parade of charts, PowerPoint decks, fancy graphs, and pictures of arrows going up and to the right.
- Fine-tuning existing offerings and pricing to jump-start an existing product and service line.

- ○ Promises to work harder and imperatives for managers to turn the screws to create a "performance culture."
- ○ Cutting expenses, especially those that are particularly costly and hard to manage—people.

If this sounds a little too familiar, do not despair. That's the point. These results are exceptionally common and based on one of the reasons for low performance defined earlier: reliance on the familiar.

Yes, the timelines are unrealistically limited. Yes, we are stuck with what we have on hand. But the true inhibitor of performance is the inability to see how what we have, under conditions similar to those experienced by our competitors, can be used in new ways to change the outcome and create instantaneous competitive advantages.

You could offer a 20 percent discount, but at what cost to quality and your people? You could tell everyone to work harder to find more clients who can pay higher fees, but where are they? Maybe a new strategy, brand, or service offering could be the answer. Perhaps you could even go study the problem a little more and find a way to massage the numbers into showing that everything will be fine (eventually).

Or, maybe, the performance inhibitor is trying to find a new way to jump over the same bar at the same height using the same rules that constrain everyone else.

ART HAS AN ENEMY, AND IT IS US

High-performing organizations need high-performing teams comprised of high-performing individuals to be able to improve at a rate faster than their competitors—and faster than the rate at which the environment changes.

Everyone is expected to work hard and have the expertise and experience required to be a valuable member of the team. Expertise and experience are easy to measure, compare, and manage and, therefore, they tend to be the first places leaders turn to for help improving. When things aren't going well, leaders shout for more hours, higher goals, and better people.

However, it may only take *one* person, in a moment of brilliance, who sees a problem in a new way to change everything. That moment is hard to predict or replicate. Therefore, the challenge is to create the conditions and culture to allow artistic and creative solutions to happen as often as possible. This means that the conditions and culture inhibiting such a setting must be addressed.

For example, much research and numerous books have been published about the dangers of "groupthink." Groupthink applies to people with similar backgrounds, motives, and insular perspectives who arrive at irrational or ineffective decisions. The term implies that each person comes to the given decision in a natural way and all voice the decision in unison, sign off on it, and send it out the door.

But groupthink is more than the simple act of everyone backing the same idea or decision. In 1952, urbanologist William Whyte said that *rationalized conformity* is the real issue within organizations making large-scale decisions about their future.[6] A group may use a thoughtful, academic, data-backed process to arrive at the "right" decision. However, this is an illusion of their own creation if that decision, and the process to reach it, was constrained and influenced by the desire to conform within established cultural norms. This practice has been justified through a flawed process, hampered by what researcher Irving Janis defined as groupthink's antecedents: high group cohesiveness, structural faults within the group, and stressful situation context.[7]

Groupthink destroys art by driving away those who would introduce new ideas. At the very least, it silences the majority from future creative input. Groupthink provides a false comfort of agreement under a nice warm blanket of precedent and past success. And that trait spreads like wildfire.

From a bigger perspective, groupthink is a symptom of a self-managed, performer-centric culture. It happens when collections of experts, who have a deeply rooted view of the world, get together and reinforce each other's beliefs—which happen to be remarkably similar to their own. There is no one to step outside the circle of belief. However, in a culture where coaching is valued, performers have better perspectives about alternative solutions to bring to the discussion; shared conversation is, after all, how they interact with those trying to improve their outcomes. Thus, being exposed to coaching as an external influence on performance can affect how individuals, groups, teams, and organizations arrive at answers. Coaching is a way of seeing the world from multiple perspectives, not just your own.

※

Many organizations claim to be innovative. However, think back to the last large planning meeting you had when many very smart, accomplished people started offering unorthodox solutions to a critical problem. You might have heard rebuttal statements such as—

"That may work for someone selling cars, but this is the XYZ industry."

"Our customers will not stand for that for one minute."

"That is not how we do things here. We are different."

"Oh, boy. Here comes Jane with her 'change the world' ideas again."

"I appreciate your enthusiasm, but we need something more realistic and short term."

"There is no way that will work with our current pricing systems. Are you suggesting we get rid of all our current programs and do this instead?"

Statements like these are not only symptomatic of a team influenced by groupthink but also illuminate how this issue has become a deeply ingrained part of organizational culture. Not only is the single idea being dismissed, the very concept of having new ideas is being challenged. To become a high-performance organization, leaders and coaches must work together to deliver results. Coaches can improve performance, but they must also have institutional support regarding direction. Leadership's responsibility is to make the key decisions and set the course; otherwise, organizations wind up with extremely well-trained and well-coached performers who are going the wrong way exceptionally well.

LEADERSHIP AS THE ULTIMATE ART FORM

Leadership could be called one of the ultimate art forms. A recent study by IBM of more than 1,500 CEOs emphasized that, in a world of great complexity and change, the ability to innovate, adapt, and see things in new ways was paramount to success.

> "CEOs now realize that creativity trumps other leadership characteristics. Creative leaders are comfortable with ambiguity and experimentation. To connect with and inspire a new generation, they lead and interact in entirely new ways . . . Creativity is the most important leadership quality. Standout CEOs practice and encourage experimentation and innovation throughout their organizations. Creative leaders expect to make deeper business model changes to realize their strategies. To succeed, they take more calculated risks, find new ideas, and keep innovating in how they lead and communicate."[8]

People change, times change, opportunities and challenges change. Some believe that leadership potential is something people are born with, and that it can be taught, or will emerge under the right set of circumstances. We, however, believe that great leadership—in any domain—is dominated by artists.

Leaders may have operational, financial, and human resource experts to get things done, but their ultimate job is to see things in new ways and bring the proper resources to bear. If coaches, performers, teams, and organizations are to flourish, art must flourish. And, it must start at the very top. Famous American artist Jackson Pollock illustrates this top-down concept.

A METHOD TO ART'S MADNESS

Anyone who has ever seen a Jackson Pollock painting immediately recognizes the style and frenzied imagery typical of his creations. Some might think the painter never did the same thing twice, and the fact he didn't was the essence of his brilliance and unmatched creativity.

While it would be correct to say that each of his paintings was unique, depicting concepts in ways never before done, his method and technique were actually quite regimented. Pollock started by laying his canvas out on the floor instead of placing it on a wall or easel.[9] This was one of the practices he used to create original works. However, Pollock became a legend because he successfully used this method again and again.

Pollock's product was always different. His inspiration came from who knows where. Predicting what he would produce next was almost impossible. One thing was for certain: most critics knew the work would be great. But what if Pollock had gotten bored with his famous drip-painting technique and then switched to making watercolors, using a traditional brush and easel, for the next couple of months? What if he then decided to try painting with the wooden end of the brush? After getting bored with that, he might have tried to go the mashed potato sculpture route.

While it is almost guaranteed that his resulting artistic creations would have been sights to see, would any of us know the name Jackson Pollock if he had adopted those other methods? Would he have become the master he was if he *always* employed a new way of doing things? Probably not. A good coach must always be diplomatic and careful not to stifle the artistic process. Eventually, however, they may need to say, "There are lots of amazing ideas here. We need to pick one and become great at it." A coach is a catalyst for execution, helping performers and leaders unleash potential. Art cannot express itself unless it is created, reworked, and refined.

⚜

There is a downside to becoming a person or organization in touch with and encouraging its artistic side. You can't *always* be looking for a new way to see things; eventually, work has to get done. Skills must be acquired to become proficient at key tasks. Work must be replicated or produced at scale. Even creative types need to become better at being creative, and that requires thousands of hours of practice. This is where the importance of coaching is key: the coach's role is to notice when it is time to create and when it is time to work. No matter what the approach, performers perpetually living in the creation phase will never improve. If they are always experimenting, they will never find the "next best way." This is not to be confused with *the* best way. Coaching manages the fine balance between thinking and doing. It's easy for performers to get lost in the process of creation and obsess over finding the perfect solution. Coaches manage this phenomenon from the outside, looking in, thus keeping the "artist" moving forward without restricting creativity.

⚜

What constitutes art is sometimes hard to describe. Often, quantifying its value and showing specific returns on investment is hard, and friction naturally exists between experts in "hard skills," where numbers and charts rule the day, and artists whose "soft skills" (perceptions, ideas, and experimentation) are the currency of value. This friction is actually a positive thing because it encourages a balance between what can be done and what could be done.

Creativity can also be inherently destructive, since it challenges—and sometimes validates—the status quo. Some citizens of the status quo often will resist, ridicule, and dismiss artists in any field as threatening and disruptive. If artists are right, everyone must change, or everyone must at least admit that their way of seeing the world is not absolute.

This is why true art is so rare. True art is based on individual perceptions, circumstances, and situations that are difficult to duplicate or explain to others. Even fresh revisions of true art are sometimes fought with great tenacity. However, leaders and performers who are artists—even if just occasionally—change the world around them. Their creations either become new standards of performance or cause everyone to adapt to these artists' performance. Thus, you can either become an artist or react to those who are. Your call.

ASSESSING THE ART OF HIGH PERFORMANCE

When assessing the art of performance, there are some areas to think about and questions to ask:

- When is the last time I stopped to consider how things have changed that might require me to adapt?

- Is my path the best approach for my unique circumstances, or is it simply the only way I know how to do what I do?

- Am I playing "catch up," adopting the standards and best practices of competitors?

- Am I getting better at predicting unforeseen circumstances by utilizing different perspectives?

- Do my colleagues, coaches, and organization encourage creative and innovative thinking, or do they see it as frivolous and flighty?

- Could I use my experience, education, and talent in ways that guarantee my future success even if all the circumstances around me change?

- If my craft had truly terminal consequences (lives and safety on the line), would I be more artistic in my approach?

⚜

Art is to be encouraged. It is essential to reinvigorate performance in response to new conditions or opportunities. It is not something to be left unconstrained and unmanaged. Thus, the support of art, innovation, and creativity must come from the top, and leadership must become one of the ultimate art forms. Think about true leadership—it is difficult to define, hard to quantify, and challenging to show an immediate return on investing in it. This sounds like art, and perhaps that is why there are thousands of books on the subject, each with a slightly different take. From our research and interviews with great leaders, art becomes a major differentiator in creating that sustainable, competitive advantage manifested in high-performing organizations, teams, and individuals. In any organization, environment, and domain, the ability to change perspective, see things differently, adapt, and innovate is what makes some people great. It is art that makes leaders, coaches, and individual performers consistently excel, even when the ground rapidly shifts under their feet.

Eventually, however, performers must execute and improve. Think back to Dick Fosbury and his high jump. What if he'd become obsessed with finding an even better technique every six months to get over that elusive bar? One day, some athlete or coach *would* probably figure out another new way.

But Fosbury was not in the "jump technique discovery" business. His business was winning medals, and once he'd found the advantage he needed, he perfected that medal-winning technique by spending countless hours practicing it.

The art of high performance is just one of the three essential components of creating sustained, exponential wins. *Perfecting the ideas created* and then relentlessly *doing the repetitions required to create momentum* are equally important components, which will be addressed in the next two chapters.

(2)

THE SCIENCE OF HIGH PERFORMANCE

"Perfect as the wing of a bird may be, it will never enable the bird to fly if unsupported by the air. Facts are the air of science. Without them a man of science can never rise."
—IVAN PAVLOV

"The methods and tools of science perennially breach barriers, granting me confidence that our epic march of insight into the operations of nature will continue without end."
—NEIL DEGRASSE TYSON

"Spaceflight will never tolerate carelessness, incapacity, and neglect. Somewhere, somehow, we screwed up. It could have been in design, build, or test. Whatever it was, we should have caught it. We were too gung ho about the schedule and we locked out all of the problems we saw each day in our work. Every element of the program was in trouble and so were we . . . "
—GENE KRANZ, FROM "KRANZ THE DICTUM"

Bumblebees should not be able to fly. A 100,000-ton, steel aircraft carrier should not float. Usain Bolt should not be able to run that fast. We know these statements are false primarily because we can see evidence to the contrary. The evidence doesn't make sense to us, but we accept the scientific possibilities rather than insist that, say, there is some vast conspiracy with a sole purpose of levitating bees to make us all look like suckers. Bumblebees can fly because their wings move in a cyclonic fashion, creating low-pressure air pockets that give them the ability to create lift. The USS *Dwight D. Eisenhower* (CVN-69) does not sink due *displacement*, a concept described by Archimedes' Principle.[1] Usain Bolt is so fast because, well, some people are just that fast. Or, is it much, *much* more complicated than that?

Just because we can't explain a fact or a concept doesn't mean there isn't a scientific reason for it. Therefore, unexplained facts and concepts shouldn't be dismissed as "just how things are." We should assume that there is always something we can learn that can be applied to us. High performers are obsessed with the science behind their craft, seeking incremental gains through incessantly studying the latest research, experimenting, and testing their hypotheses. Usain Bolt is a great example of this concept put into practice—on the track.

The 100-meter sprint is not a complicated event. Everyone starts at the same spot and at the same time. Sprinters run in a straight line until the end, and whoever gets there first is the winner. The nature of this event has not changed for thousands of years. Before that, 100-meter sprint events involved outracing mama bears after mistakenly wandering upon her cubs. Back then, you didn't have to be faster than everyone; you just had to be faster than the slowest person being chased by the bear.

If you break down the elements of a successful sprinter, there are only a few things to worry about: a good reaction time at the start and remaining upright until the end. Other than that, it's all about stride length and stride frequency. That's it.

The typical Olympic-level sprinter has a stride length of about 2.2 meters and takes about forty-five strides over the course of 100 meters. They train their entire lives to take forty-five strides for a time that, year after year, must become ever faster to beat the next up-and-coming competitor. However, do not let the simple math fool you; this is an exceptionally complicated science. Consider just a few of the variables involved in determining who wins and who loses:

- Reaction time at the start

- Body angle coming out of the blocks

- Force applied to first step

- Length of second step

- Time spent running at low angle from start

- Time to full speed

- Length of stride

- Frequency of stride

- Force production per step

- Ground contact time

- Deceleration rate

- Rotational torque

- Lateral movement of arms

- Sagittal movement of arms

- Amortization time per stride

- And so on . . .

In two people off the street, a single-digit percentage improvement in any of these variables would be the determining factor in who wins a 100-meter race. Olympic-level sprinters, however, have to try to get hundredths of a percentage-point improvement on *all of these factors* if they expect to win.

This should not be surprising to most people. Ask people about their chosen profession, sport, or hobby, and they will talk about its intricacies for great lengths. In fact, a sure way to get people who are very passionate about their chosen field all riled up is to start a conversation with "What you do doesn't seem that hard—all you have to do is . . . " They will then take great pleasure in giving you a free education in how little you actually know about the subject.

The science behind high performance is the willingness to research methods, experiment with approaches, and perfect the craft to the *n*th degree. Once high performers find the best methods available, they become students of their craft to the point of obsession. They consume books. They watch videos and listen to recordings of masters in action. They talk to those who have been successful, digging for every last detail hoping to discover a single nugget of wisdom or insight that can be applied to improve technique.

Think about someone like Bolt. He is obsessed with the science of his performance. He has coaches who study all of the details on his form, performance, and training regimen through real-time observation and slow-motion video analysis. Bolt and his coaches know he is one of the tallest and heaviest sprinters to ever compete at his level. His stature means he can't run like other sprinters. His tall body creates drag; his legs are longer; he has more mass to move down the track. Therefore, his coaches addressed the art of his performance to find a new way for him to get down the track faster than others.

Over the course of those hundred meters, Bolt takes forty-one steps instead of the typical forty-five. How? His stride length is twenty to twenty-five centimeters longer than the average sprinter. To counteract wind drag from his big sail of a body, he creates greater force production out of the blocks by employing a grueling weight-training regimen. In other words, he takes fewer and more powerful strides than his competitors.

Up to forty meters, most races with Bolt are a dead heat. After forty meters, it starts to look like he is in a class all his own. He is able to continue to keep accelerating and maintain top speed for longer than his competitors. In fact, one of the reasons he wins is he decelerates less quickly (after sixty meters, they *all* decelerate). His arms and legs become advantages, propelling him down the track when others are slowing down.[2]

The science of sprinting is not up for debate. There's no discussion of a different way to run down the track. A new competitor who is overly focused on the art of the sprint could look for new ways to do it: running backward, taking one hundred strides instead of forty-five, or any number of other variations. However, we know how this will most likely turn out.

❧

In sport, there is a winner and a loser. There is the thrill of victory and the agony of defeat (as so famously voiced by American sportscaster Jim McKay). In many other fields, there are also extreme variations in prizes between winning and losing. Now, let's step away from sport and turn to another field with binary consequences: space exploration.

Binary consequences are never quite so extreme as they are when you are sitting on top of a 66,000-pound, liquid-fueled rocket booster about to be accelerated into a suborbital trip around the Earth. That is exactly the fate that US naval aviator Alan Shepard chose when he entered the space program as one of the original Mercury 7 astronauts.

Shepard, the first American (and second human, after cosmonaut Yuri Gagarin) to enter space, was not new to dangerous pastimes. He'd served on ships as an officer in World War II and earned his wings as a F-4U Corsair fighter pilot after the war. He became a test pilot for the navy and qualified for many of their frontline aircraft, amassing over 3,600 hours of flying time over the course of his career.[3] After an arduous selection process, the first American astronauts were chosen from a field of 110 candidates narrowed down to seven top pilots. These pilots were known as envelop-pushing hot shots (in the air and in their personal lives). They were testosterone-fueled supermen who felt invincible, having walked away from dozens of close calls to prove it.

Though they accept great risk, pilots like Shepard are highly regimented performers. Every time they fly, they go though checklists with dozens—if not hundreds—of detailed steps to ensure theirs and their crew's safety. Once aloft, if anything should go wrong, specific emergency procedures are followed in a specific order and to the letter. When landing, flaps, speed, and angle of descent are all exactly controlled. These pilots are not "winging it." There is no patience for that type of uncontrolled behavior when it comes to professional aviators.

This need for exacting conditions and adherence to the science of their craft becomes even more pronounced when the pilot's speed increases to thousands of miles per hour. When piloting a spacecraft, the margin of error is nonexistent. In Shepard's case, he flew at a speed of 5,134 miles per hour (relatively slowly, compared to today's astronauts), which meant that every second, he would move almost a *mile and a half!* If Shepard had been relying on gut feel, or "figuring it out" based on his personal, artistic preferences, we would be remembering him in a very different way.

As a test pilot, Shepard's job was, within the parameters of science and proven performance, to try new things. As an astronaut, his job was to follow exact procedures that had been researched and proven by dozens of engineers at NASA—that is, unless something changed. And in that fifteen-minute, twenty-two second flight, a couple of things did go wrong. Shepard had to manually correct the reentry angle so he did not burn up in the Earth's atmosphere. He had to manually activate the retrorocket jettison system to ensure it operated properly. Even in these circumstances, he did nothing on the fly. Shepard used his skills and experience from thousands of hours of flying and practicing in the space capsule simulators to know precisely what to do in these conditions he had never exactly encountered before.

Unlike runners, business executives, or lawyers, astronauts have no second chances. There are two outcomes: return safely to Earth or die. High performers in disciplines with true *terminal consequences* (astronauts, military special operators, firefighters, law enforcement, and similar professions) train and behave differently. While they look at things in new ways to see things in new ways, they respect the science behind proven ways . . . and respect the science of high performance.

Performers in all domains should learn from this method of thinking. Even though normal business conditions are less physically dangerous, their outcomes are sometimes just as binary. Perform badly as a business developer, and you lose a multimillion-dollar deal. Perform less than satisfactorily as a lawyer, and a client goes to jail. All performers who reach the top of their domain deal with binary consequences. You may live to compete another day, but there will be collateral damage along the way. That will only last so long before it comes back to haunt you.

Eventually, we discover that there is a best way to do things. Science has proven it. We may vary our application based on the conditions given (tall body, wet track, nursing a hamstring injury), but the basic science will not be denied. Coaches ensure that high performers realize this and perfect their technique, approach, and preparation to find the incremental gains that allow continuous improvement. Likewise, there is a best way to perform heart bypass surgery. Proven methods to handle a complex merger exist. Properly writing computer code for specific platforms has a process. While standards like these naturally evolve and improve, they provide the essential format in which to excel. Performers, though they may find some creative moments along the way, must build upon past knowledge and proven experience. They cannot be searching for a *better* way at the expense of doing things the *right* way. This may seem in conflict with the art of high performance, but that is why this concept is a process to be carefully managed by performers, the coaches and, ultimately, teams.

❧

Consistent high performers are both consciously competent and consciously incompetent in their disciplines. No matter what their field is, they are constantly learning and perfecting their craft. They also realize that the environment does not stay the same, so they are constantly required to learn new skills. Those new skills have to be perfected, which requires a rededication to the science behind what works. To even be considered elite, these leaders also have to be able to do all of these things better than almost everyone else.

Many lawyers go to law school and become great litigators, but only a few are considered the best. Many business executives get MBAs from the top five business schools, but only a few are known as the elite. There were 10,768 athletes in the 2012 Summer Olympics in London, but only 961 medals were awarded. All of these high performers worked hard. Some had more natural ability than others. Some had better coaching and facilities. Some were just lucky. However, what they all had in common was they paid painstaking attention to every excruciating detail of performance in their never-ending quest for marginal gains in performance variables.

The concept of marginal gains was famously championed by Sir David John "Dave" Brailsford in his efforts to turn around British cycling's losing tradition: almost one hundred years of abysmal results on the international stage. Brailsford had been involved with cycling most of his career, first as a cyclist and then in cycling equipment sales, before going back to school to study sports science and psychology, where he began to learn new ways to increase performance beyond telling cyclists to pedal faster and harder.

Brailsford came on as an advisor to the national team in 1997 and, in 2003, became the performance director. This is when the British cycling community's results started to change rapidly. Within a year, in the 2004 Olympics, two British cyclists won gold medals—their best showing in almost a century. Was Brailsford just lucky? Did he happen to get the right athletes at the right time? The 2008 and 2012 Olympics put that idea to rest. In both games, Brailsford's team took home over 70 percent of the gold medals awarded. This achievement reflects consistent, growing performance—and it is no accident.

Brailsford had been a competitive cyclist in his youth, and he experienced firsthand that winning was not a matter of desire or effort. At that level, everyone was trying to win. They had the best equipment, and teams consisted of the best athletes in the world. The basics of racing had not changed, so Brailsford sought a new way: science. What if the British cyclists were able to improve their results by just 1 percent in *all* of the important variables? Would these gains in performance add up to more victories? Using his background in sports science and psychology, Brailsford determined to find out.

Of course, Brailsford looked at the most obvious areas, such as nutrition and pedal stroke technique, for improvement. Then, he kept going. He emphasized that cyclists wash their hands properly to minimize infection and sickness. He had them sleep with the same pillows when they traveled. He sought metrics on his riders' every aspect—their performance, equipment, and training regimens. He sought to improve every part of their performance by fractions of a percent. His goal was the "aggregation of marginal gains," which would add up to the edge his team needed to win. And win over and over again, because it was not enough to do the little things right; Brailsford believed they had to do the little things better in perpetuity. In 2012, he stated, "The whole principle came from the idea that if you broke down everything you could think of that goes into riding a bike, and then improved it by 1 percent, you would get a significant increase when you put them all together."[4]

One of any performers' biggest downfalls is the tendency to stop searching for marginal gains. They rely on their past education, expertise, or experience to maintain performance or reach the top of their craft. They shoot from the hip when they encounter a new situation. They begrudge the fact that competition nowadays "isn't like it used to be."

Of course it isn't. That is because everyone else is trying to get in front. They are accelerating. If performers are maintaining the same speed while others are aggregating marginal gains, even if maintaining a top, frenzied pace, it will not be enough to keep up. You are decelerating relative to the performers around you. Here's some historical background.

HOW PERFORMERS LEARN

The debate over the "science of learning" has been going on for thousands of years. Plato had his views on how to educate young learners, and they are very different from how we teach today. In those days, students who wanted to progress to subjects more in keeping with today's liberal arts first had to spend a period of ten years or more mastering mathematics. This was because Plato did not believe most people were capable of mastering such subjects. His heavy emphasis on cognitively challenging and regimented subjects served as a screening process for those who "deserved" further education. Teachers from this period viewed education as a process of opening the mind, not for developing practical skills.

Sophists, on the other hand, focused on the development of specific skills related to specific vocations. They were the fathers of today's professional and vocational education programs.[5] The Sophists believed that the study of rhetoric was the most important subject and its mastery could be applied to any other subject. They were hoping to create true *polymaths*, those who have complete mastery of multiple subjects. A polymath, a term first used in the seventeenth century, is what's known today as a "Renaissance man."

During the Middle Ages, the concept of education was codified in the establishment of a university system. Education in this era was designed to serve the needs of the church, and focused on topics such as architecture, geometry, and astronomy. The Middle Ages also saw specializations of faculty and institutions and, naturally, students of a specific universities started to become dominant in those areas of expertise.

Being a student in this period was especially challenging, because most people could not afford books. Let's not forget that someone had to build those universities, churches, palaces, and royal residences. While thinkers toiled in their universities, laborers studied in their craft guilds. There were no rhetoric courses, for example, in the carpenters' guild. As apprentices over the course of almost a decade, students learned how to make things with their own two hands, becoming a master if, and only when, they could accomplish the entire task without assistance and earn approval from masters in the craft. Tradesmen learned one skill, and they knew it backward and forward. Over the course of seven to ten years, they were challenged, admonished, and pushed to improve until they could not only perform on their own but also serve as master and judge for future apprentices. It would not do to have those castles and churches falling down on the heads of those in power. Punishment for such failures was, well, pretty severe.

Thus, universities became the model for mass education, the exemplar for conferring a general scope of knowledge to an individual for future application in a variety of fields. Guilds taught specific skills in a single domain, skills that would be replicated throughout the learner's lifetime. Ironically, this university model is what most people today think of as *science*, but the guild model is more

Continued on next page . . .

directly related to what we associate with scientific expertise and high performance.

As the Industrial Revolution swept the world, owners, investors, and managers became much more practical. While it might be nice to have a Renaissance man on the assembly line, a background in geometry, theology, and rhetoric did not produce more widgets. Practical skills get the job done (not thinking all day about how the job could be done). Mass production, war effort support, and the educational needs of the populace demanded changes in educational styles as it shifted from an agrarian to an urban society. All may need a general knowledge of the world and basic education, but people must have a concentrated area of specialization and expertise if they are to eventually become productive members of society. Therefore, the science of high performance shifted from generality to specificity and away from the development of the elusive *homo universalis*.

Over the decades, societal conditions have changed. There are now global economies, competitors, and conflicts. In the distant past, society's circle of influence may have just been a handful of friends and family. An individual's lot in life was predetermined by name, title, and caste. However, as opportunities increased and consequences became more severe, utilizing science advantageously in performance became more important. With this pressure came the advent of numerous attempts and learning theories designed to improve performance and predict success. Two theories of note were those championed by educational psychologists Benjamin Bloom and Robert Gagne.

Bloom believed that learning conditions and methods would make it possible for most people to break the distribution curve and perform in the top tier of a domain. However, the right conditions must exist! His theory became known as mastery learning and has been validated by numerous research studies. Mastery learning differs from traditional methods found in most school curriculums, university programs, and corporate training systems in that it is not a one-size-fits-all approach. Skills are broken into components to be mastered in relatively short periods of time (a few days or weeks). Pre-assessment determines each individual performer's current abilities and deficiencies. Performers are given specific instruction, or *correctives*, to improve in each task or skill. After the initial instruction, a second assessment is administered, which identifies improvement made and any corrective action needed. This assess-instruct-assess approach reinforces learning and allows performers to progress to the next level of difficulty.

Gagne's theory addresses learning hierarchies. Gagne was fascinated with the process of learning and performance, and he theorized that each skill was a collection of subskills that must be mastered before moving on to more difficult ones. If you cannot master a subskill and how it relates to other subskills, how could you ever grasp the more difficult skill? While a work-around or shortcut could be found, this means subsequent learning would be based on a false foundation. Skills are relational and, as an entirety, they form a system of performance. Learning one skill is independent of another skill; learning the first skill allows you to learn the next; until the first is mastered, the next skill could not be learned. Think about musicians or pilots and how certain skills build upon the next. In some professions, it is *really* important to have the right sequential order and not assume that learning one task, no matter how difficult, guarantees mastery of all the others and will achieve top performance.

Some of these skills are mental, and some of them are physical. Gagne also identified the difference between the behavioral aspects of learning (such as reacting to a stimulus or a set of stimuli) versus cognitive learning, where people are able to apply knowledge

Continued on next page . . .

and skills based on expected conditions and even unknown situations. Reinforcement and repetition is necessary if performers hope to progress, and subsequent tasks must be more challenging than the previous one. Because these new, harder tasks or skills are dependent on the mastery of lower skills and subskills, continuous improvement will occur with little regression.

Both Bloom and Gagne's theories are dependent on a few key items. There is a process to learning and an emphasis on fundamental skills and subskills. There is an emphasis on task analysis and the mastery of components. There is an emphasis on practice, assessment, and progression. To create individualized programs, give feedback and corrections, and keep performers moving forward, there must be teachers and coaches.

Though Bloom's research was based in the typical school setting and Gagne's theories are used in the military, the concepts each developed have direct applications to all performers. Not simply theories to be acknowledged or shelved for later consideration, these proven, scientific approaches to learning, skill acquisition, and mastery transition *performers* into *high performers*. Both theories have been validated and augmented by other researchers, and we've included elements of these approaches in our coaching model in this book.

This type of scientific performance enhancement is applied in all domains: elementary education, medicine, law, sports, the military, performance arts, and software coding. Anywhere the terms *virtuoso, master, superstar,* or *rainmaker* are associated with an individual, the science of high performance has been used to their advantage. Granted, some may have done so unconsciously, due to being in the right place, employing the right coach, or having the right resources and support at their disposal, and might not have realized their luck at the time. However, high performers consistently use the science of learning to become students of and master their domain.

Athletes film themselves running, swimming, and swinging a bat to hone slight variations in stride length, stoke efficiency, and rotational dynamics that could improve their results by fractions of a percent. Coaches utilize films and big data to analyze results, make corrections, and improve their chances of winning their next game. The military conducts debriefings, watches films of aircraft carrier pilot landings, and uses "After Action Reviews" to make improvements, no matter how small, to accomplish missions and save lives. Why shouldn't other domains benefit from this approach toward perfection and improvement?

Let's use a business example. A performer is trying to win a new piece of business worth hundreds of thousands of dollars. Closing this deal will not just be a big win for the company; it will make the quarter and help prevent changes in strategy or downsizing. It matters, and the consequences are binary (win/loss). A coach may identify areas to improve, conduct pre-performance briefings, create simulations to rehearse meetings, and review for further improvements before the actual performance. This behavior is the equivalent of filming a runner and grading a pilot—analyzing the fine details of any performer. Nothing should be left to chance or discussed only after the fact. Granted, there is a discomfort to being analyzed, judged, and graded on every detail. That is why so many people avoid such scrutiny, and why the few who don't greatly benefit.

❧

Some, however, go too far with research and analysis. Just as performers can become obsessed with seeing things differently and fail to move forward with any method, immersion into a particular aspect of the craft can be just as counterproductive. Some performers may even hide behind research and analysis to avoid performing at all, letting *perfection* become the enemy of *good*. Predictably, the smarter and more educated people are more likely to fall into this trap.

How does this manifest? First, we see analysis paralysis. Performers are so caught up in the data and resulting potential options that they never make a decision. Successful performers know that sometimes making a good decision and moving forward is better than constantly seeking a perfect decision that may never appear. Risk-adverse performers who have an extreme fear of failure are most susceptible to analysis paralysis. If you know someone who always wants an additional report, more data, or yet another pie chart before being "ready" to decide, you know the concept.

Second, there is the issue of ultrafine-tuning. Performers become obsessed with micro details to avoid the larger issues that might be affecting their performance outcomes. For example: a businessperson could spend weeks researching the best opening sentence to use on a sales call instead of actually making the calls to find out what works. Another example would be someone who is learning to become a racecar driver who won't do laps on the track until the perfect tires have been found. These performers avoid action by analyzing.

Third, obsessive studying is a crippling component. Performers are so immersed in studying the craft that they don't notice they are being left behind. A fixation on old techniques and irrelevant approaches that no longer apply to current rules, market, environment, and competition keeps these performers too busy learning how to win the last war. One day, they may be worldwide experts, but the technique they perfected is antiquated and obsolete. Performance excellence requires lifting your head up every now and then and adjusting your approach to avoid looking at everyone else's back. We're often taught that, to get ahead and become an expert, we must bury ourselves in books or spreadsheets for several years. However, the sheer fact that information was captured—printed on a sheet or sent in a file—means that material is getting older and more out of date by the minute. A lawyer who spends all day in the library will be studying old case law. A salesperson, staring at contact lists in the office, is missing new opportunities. An executive who constantly reviews past performance metrics is studying history, not improving business.

ASSESSING THE SCIENCE OF HIGH PERFORMANCE

- What key metrics should my coach should be using to measure performance?

- What subvariables are involved? Have I thought of all of them?

- What do the best performers do? Can these practices be modeled? Will a coach have to help me modify and then perfect that approach to suit my reality?

- Am I really a student of craft, or am I relying on replicating past success and hoping for the best?

- Do I allow a coach to observe, monitor, and critique my performance? Do I listen to the results?

- If the environment, market, or competitors have changed, have I adjusted my performance improvement approach? Have I taken the time to relearn what I need to know?

- Do I know more about each component of my craft than my competitors do, or do I think they are just "naturally better"?

- Are difficult tasks and challenges getting easier for me? Am I able to take on more difficult challenges than last year? Is my performance getting better?

- If my craft had truly terminal consequences (lives and safety on the line), would I be more scientific in my approach to improving my performance?

Top performers cluster at the top, as lower level performers have already been weeded out. The closer performers are to the pinnacle of their discipline, the smaller the margins of error are between winning and losing. Therefore, the importance of the science of high performance is hard to overstate. A single business conversation, extra stride, or flip of a switch at the right time means the difference between the thrill of victory and the agony of defeat.

THE GRIT OF HIGH PERFORMANCE

"Success is the result of perfection, hard work,
learning from failure, loyalty, and persistence."
—COLIN POWELL

"Nothing in this world can take the place of persistence. Talent will
not: nothing is more common than unsuccessful men with talent.
Genius will not; unrewarded genius is almost a proverb. Educa-
tion will not: the world is full of educated derelicts. Persistence
and determination alone are omnipotent."
—CALVIN COOLIDGE

"I love to see a young girl go out and grab the world by the lapels. Life's
a bitch. You've got to go out and kick ass."
—MAYA ANGELOU

Most people are not familiar with Olympic wrestling champions from the sixth century BC, but one in particular is worth modern mention. Milo of Croton was the equivalent of any modern sports superstar, winning the Olympic title six times in a row. He amazed ancient Greece with feats of strength and his reported ability to eat twenty pounds of meat and drink eighteen pints of wine.[1]

According to legend, Milo's journey to superhuman status began as a young boy, with the simplest of training plans. He started lifting a calf every day to develop the strength he wanted, but there was one key fact that made all the difference. Milo lifted the *same* calf every day until he was a grown man—and it was a grown bull.

Every day, Milo lifted that same calf onto his shoulders. As the calf grew, so did Milo. His legs became as massive as tree trunks. To compensate for lifting that heavier and heavier weight, his chest and back expanded. His confidence swelled as well. The calf got bigger and heavier, and what did Milo do with that calf after it finally became a bull and he could no longer use it as a training device? He made steaks.

Now, all of the stories about Milo of Croton may be hard to believe but, in some circles, he is known as the father of progressive resistance. By doing just a little bit more each day, he became powerful. Some people might think merely lifting a sixty-five pound newborn calf is an impressive feat. Keep in mind that calves gain approximately two pounds per day. A young boy lifting a calf is impressive, but it gets less impressive the older and stronger he gets. Milo wanted to be *impressive*. Now, think about which training program would produce better results after just one year—one that remains at a constant level of difficulty or one that progressively challenges the performer over time?

DEFINING GRIT

Much has been written about the concept of *grit* and its importance to success. Grit can be synonymous with *hard work, perseverance, determination, sweat equity, practice, discipline,* and *commitment.* Dr. Angela Duckworth, in her seminal publication, defines grit as "perseverance and passion for long-term goals."[2] Duckworth explains that the major advantage to having true grit is *stamina.* Performers with grit are willing and able to drive toward their goals despite hardship, frustrations, and failure, and in spite of a modest level of acceptable achievement. Lacking grit is a highly predictive indicator of unrealized potential. Performers who have natural abilities, access to education, and even introductory experience may remain at a novice level specifically due to lack of grit in key components of the craft in which they should excel.

Let's get one thing straight before discussing grit and success in any additional detail: Most above-average performers work hard, putting in countless hours and spending years learning their craft. However, unless that work, study, and practice is in the specific domain they are trying to improve, none of it matters. Athletes who run ten miles a day won't become great sprinters unless they work on sprinting. Lawyers with years of school who bill 2,500 hours a year to clients won't become better at developing new legal business unless they work on it. Carpenters framing in the hot sun for ten hours a day for ten years will not be great architects unless they dedicate themselves to doing so. Finance executives at large companies don't automatically know marketing strategy and sales, even if those areas seem less "complex" and mentally difficult than their own discipline.

When coaches suggest to high-achieving people that a lack of grit is why they haven't become experts in that activity, they react poorly. They will say, "Are you kidding me? Do you have any idea how many hours a week I put in at the office/track/job? I work my tail off!"

High performance is extremely domain specific. In fact, individual activities can be broken into components that can be broken into smaller actions, which must be integrated in the proper order and format to be effective. When discussing this application of hard work, education, and experience, a tried and tested training concept from the fitness world comes to mind: the law of specific adaptations to imposed demands (SAID). This law states that the body and mind adapt to the exact burdens placed upon it. Conversely, cognitive and physical adaptations unrelated to such burdens remain undeveloped. Therefore, if you practice surgical skills, you will become a great surgeon. Practicing those same skills, however, does not improve your bedside manner or how you run your medical practice. A sales manager who manages other sales representatives should not be surprised when her closing skills dissipate as her management and reporting skills increase. A business executive who spends too much time in the office will not develop the intuition and empathy necessary to predict clients' needs and properly prepare for the business's future.

Thus, grit is the specific key to unlocking potential. It is essential for high performance. As mentioned before, it is especially difficult, if not impossible, for high performers to be totally self-managed. Performing and coaching are two separate disciplines. A person can be proficient at both, but it is not possible to excel when sharing a common subject: personal performance. Successful personal performance must be coached, and that implies the involvement of others.

NATURAL ABILITIES

We all have natural abilities or predispositions, but they are not limitations on our fate; they are ingredients to success in raw form. There is no such thing as an overnight success; however, that doesn't stop people from saying, "That person is a natural. It must be nice to be that good at something like that." When that statement is made about someone who has reached a high level of proficiency, it is usually meant as a compliment. Frankly, it is an insult.

At best, it is a passive-aggressive statement dismissive of the blood, sweat, and tears necessary for achieving that level of competency. No one is a "natural" at making sounds out of a four-stringed, wooden instrument. No one was born to hit a six-ounce piece of vulcanized rubber with a wooden stick into a net while skating on ice. No one came into the world with a divine talent for calculating options on the stock market and exercising them with uncanny timing. Some people are born with traits that make them more musical, athletic, or business minded, but skills are not developed in the womb.

Society has long denoted certain families, classes, or backgrounds as more "apt" for certain types of work. This hereditary outlook, or predetermination, of individuals was the primary view for centuries about the limits of performance and prosperity people might achieve. While many people "felt" this was true (and used it to reinforce the upper tiers of society's ego), it wasn't until Sir Francis Galton wrote *Hereditary Genius* that this concept was positioned as official dogma.[3]

According to Galton's book, genetics determine body height, weight, and brain size and, therefore, mental capacities and performance abilities. For some people, the laws of nature would always be an upper boundary of ability and aptitude that could not be broken through. While anyone could be trained, these chromosomal limitations naturally restricted what some people could achieve. Today, Galton's views would, at best, be considered politically incorrect. One more thing of note about Galton: he invented the term *eugenics* (the belief that positive traits can be bred into the population to improve its genetic stock). Most of us would be very uncomfortable championing this concept, but it is very closely related to that insulting belief that "some people are just born to be good/bad at that."

A coach's role is to identify and evaluate natural abilities, and lack thereof, and build a performance improvement plan that reflects these realities. Hand in hand with that role is a need to educate and counsel performers as to the realities of skill development. Aptitude and achievement are different things. *Aptitude* is potential from inherent traits yet to be refined; *achievement* is accomplishment from using what exists to the best of ability. The coach manages the identification, evaluation, and improvement of performers, the two must work together to realize that no one is a "natural" in any given domain. This applies no matter the skill level—the same process for the protégé and the novice. While their final destinations may vary, the path to mastery is the same. Coaching is an integral step in that path.

EDUCATION

Are the proper curricula, classes, schools, and degrees essential to success and high performance? Basic training and formal education are critical to high performers. Though expertise does not always involve a classroom and a fancy document to hang on a wall, high performers have always trained, either through self-study or formalized instructions, on the basics before moving on to formalized concepts.

What do Elvis Presley, the Beatles, and Eric Clapton have in common (besides being some of the most highly regarded musicians of the modern era)? None of them could read music. This fact may infuriate graduates of Julliard and the Royal Academy of Music, but many rock stars achieve impressive careers without any formal music theory training. These musicians had an extensive education, but it didn't come from a tenured professor in a lecture hall. They learned on stage, on the road, and from each other, and no one can deny their musical achievements and influence.

Likewise, a thirteen-year-old can pick up a guitar, start listening to his favorite songs, and figure out a tune. Eventually, he may turn to YouTube for tips from more experienced guitarists and learn how to play hours and hours of music. Pervasive free content and available technology mean education is not limited to those with rich parents or access to scholarships.

However gained, education is essential to developing expertise in a domain. Some will find it easier to learn and progress due to natural traits and abilities. However, fewer and fewer barriers to achievement exist. Content is everywhere. Anyone can download top athletic performers' training programs from the Internet. Anyone can read the success stories about successful business titans on a tablet. Anyone can search YouTube for instruction on playing Mozart's musical pieces as originally written. Keep in mind that education, then, is not a barrier; learning offers no protection from competition.

In the past, access to greater education or better instructors kept performers on top of the heap in any domain. Limited people had access to the best knowledge, and it gave them an enormous advantage. Now that access to knowledge is almost universal, it acts as less of a differentiator. But once that minimum level of proficiency has been reached, what is done with that knowledge is what counts. This is when the coach steps in—when performers seek yet another degree, certification, or specialization, the so-called final thing needed for success. The coach determines whether their trainee is seeking education as a result of analysis paralysis while encouraging their continuous learning in conjunction with testing, experimentation, and performance refinement based on the trainee's current level of education.

EXPERIENCE

When asked whether or not performers are proficient at their craft, many rely upon past experience. This past experience reinforces their position of authority and achievement and, with each passing day, they become more certain of their opinion. After all, who would argue that a rookie racecar driver is better than one with twenty years of experience?

Many look at experience in terms of extremes. Someone new to a profession will not be as talented as one with decades worth of experience. The real question about the value of experience comes with less polar comparisons: Is a business executive with twenty years of experience better than one with fifteen? How about twelve? Six?

Do people who repeat the exact same task over and over again for twenty years become better at it? Think about this rudimentary task performed every day: brushing our teeth. Most of us have been doing it once or twice a day for our entire lives. Could you describe the "best" way to brush your teeth? After all, you've being doing it for decades. Shouldn't you be an expert by now?

We don't need to be enamel-cleansing experts to brush our teeth. We reach a certain level of proficiency (some more than others) and that is enough to automate the process of plaque removal. *Experience* does not equal *expertise*. We are simply repeating the exact same activity for twenty to seventy years. This single experience is repeated over and over again. Now, one of a coach's primary roles is to ensure that performers get better at what they do. Tasks should get easier, and more complex skills should produce greater rewards in the same amount of time. Therefore, any coach's most important statistic is the delta between current status and past status, instead of measuring current performance against a past standard. Improvement and rate of change are the currency of coaching.

Natural abilities can be augmented with education and then applied over a career through experience. Some of us look back at what we've been good at since we were children, admire framed documents on the wall, and count the years involved in performing in our domain. We equate these things with expertise. But, time and time again, research has shown this is not the case.

Think of performers who have all the "tickets," but are not the top in their field. They may equate this lack of success to bad luck, low opportunity, and fate. These factors may contribute, but the simple truth is that many performers enter a phase of automation and, despite time's passage, their performances then cease to improve.

DELIBERATE PRACTICE VERSUS REPETITIVE ACTIVITIES

How do performers avoid automation and encourage continued improvement? The key is *deliberate practice*. This differs from a series of repetitive activities in that it engages performers in activities, programs, and strategies designed to stretch and improve their abilities on an ongoing basis. Psychologist K. Anders Ericsson researched and championed this concept, arguing that the difference between average and elite performance is the time spent on deliberate practice throughout the performers' life. Natural talent, education, and experience will only take you so far. Ericsson is very specific that this deliberate practice spans a lifelong journey:

> " . . . expert performance is qualitatively different from normal performance and even that expert performers have characteristics and abilities that are qualitatively different from or at least outside the range of those of normal adults. However, we deny that these differences are immutable, that is, due to innate talent. Only a few exceptions, most notably height, are genetically prescribed. Instead, we argue that the differences between expert performers and normal adults reflect a life-long period of deliberate effort to improve performance in a specific domain."[4]

Deliberate practice is not repeating the same activities every day in the hopes that years of experience provide a positive, cumulative effect on performance. For example, the goal may be to complete a marathon, so runners create a program that begins with a mile at a slow to moderate pace. After several months of running a mile every day, these runners will have months and months of experience at running. According to their plan, this "preparation" will have them ready to complete that marathon.

However, as anyone who has run a marathon will attest, even the most dedicated runners would be no closer to completing a marathon than when they started, even after several years of employing this strategy. Sure, they are well prepared to run a mile. However, by never increasing distance or speed, their performance level has barely increased at all beyond the first thirty days of training—despite months or years of effort. They've engaged in repetitive activity, which reinforces the present level of performance. At best, these runners' plan is a delusional strategy for an unattainable goal. At worst, this kind of repetitive activity wears performers down and wastes time, keeping them from achieving other things and resulting in overuse injuries or disenchantment.

A marathon plan based in deliberate practice would also start with the fundamentals of running. However, each week, practice becomes more challenging. The pace gets faster. The distances get longer. Instead of the same type of run every day, new developmental exercises such as fartleks (aerobic capacity and recovery), sprint and hill work (speed and power), and progressive runs (toughness and resilience) are introduced. Each week during training, runners are pushed beyond their current ability level and areas of deficiency and, over time, prepared to complete that first marathon. For the next race, they'll have to work harder if they wish to not simply finish but run the distance faster.

Some runners can go faster and farther than others due to genetics. Years of running experience will help increase that advantage. However, only application of deliberate practice and progressive resistance will allow those natural performers to ever reach the peak of their capacity. Similarly, let's look at business executives. Imagine an executive who, over a career that includes a series of more and more difficult business deals, becomes a respected rainmaker. Most of us agree this course—rather than repeating similar deals of the same scale—would help an executive become a master at business, so it makes sense that any deliberate practice managed by a coach should follow the same approach. Learning doesn't only occur on race day or in the boardroom; we practice constantly and at ever increasing levels of difficulty before the big day.

YOU CAN'T DO IT IN YOUR SLEEP

Think of any skill, hobby, or profession. At first, learning the basics is mentally challenging. Then, performance becomes more comfortable as you begin to notice patterns, associate behaviors, and apply actions to expected situations. After a while, that skill, hobby, or profession feels automatic. You might even say, "I could do this in my sleep." This is the point where many people stop developing and performance stagnates.

For some tasks, however, that proficiency is all you need. Most people don't need to be the best tooth brusher in the world; they just need to be good enough to accomplish the task. In fact, brushing teeth may become so automated that it can be done while reading the morning news and humming to a favorite song on the radio. When it comes to dental hygiene, there's no need to go past this point of performance.

For those disciplines related to achievement, however, this isn't enough. Mindless repetition is exactly how some get stuck in an endless reinforcement loop of low- to moderate-performance. They reach a level of proficiency that becomes automated and thoughtless, which takes very little effort to maintain. They repeat these motions for years and wonder why their performance level never changes.

Continuous improvement and high performance requires avoidance of this automation stage of development. Research shows that people reach basic levels of achievement in most everyday activities after as little as fifty hours of repetition. A complete novice can learn how to drive a car without crashing or enough to hold their own in a conversation about physics when no real scientists are around.

There are three phases of procedural learning according to research by psychologists Paul Fitts and David Posner that all people go through when improving at a skill or discipline.[5] The learning process starts in the cognitive phase, where skills are broken into pieces and then brought together again. Next is the associative phase, in which skills are repeated and errors and inefficient components eliminated. Finally, learning enters the autonomous stage; the skill becomes second nature and can be maintained with minimal thought and maintenance. While their theory focuses on motor learning, it could be argued that all skill development follows this path.

Whether the skill is practicing law, flying a plane, or kicking a ball, all learners progress through these stages. The difference for high performers lies in what they do next. To continue to improve and move to the next level, learners must reinvigorate performance with deliberate practice. In short, you need to lift a heavier calf.

While law students know more about litigation after their first month of law school than the general public will ever know, this does not make them an expert. That's why you would not want such students in a murder trial. They are just beginning to learn their craft and have a long way to go. Three years later, these same students may be able to pass the bar exam and practice law. However, after the first year in business, they would soon fall behind as laws change and their skills would dull unless they engaged in hours of actual practice. Some lawyers could make a very good living repeating this process for the next twenty years; we could argue, though, that without new experiences and challenges, what they actually have is that first year of experience repeated twenty times.

Even the smartest, hardest working, and most dedicated performers can get stuck in an autonomic, basic level of proficiency. In fact, performance becomes so robotic that it's hard for performers to adapt and react to unforeseen environmental and situational changes. These stuck performers have the same solution for every problem, one that, eventually, becomes less effective and relevant.

To achieve expert skills, learners must constantly be in the cognitive and associative phases of development. When skills become automated, performers must move to the next challenge. Some will recognize when they've become mired in the muck of mediocrity, and these performers will try to move to the next level. But this can be an endless circle—all of us will remain in a stage of arrested development without ongoing deliberate practice; resistance must be progressive and constant. A heavier calf is always needed, and it is needed every single day. Deliberate practice requires performers to have GRIT.

Very few people will admit they lack the grit needed to get ahead. Even the laziest teenagers in the world will claim they are working hard at overcoming some unbearable life challenge. This attitude is amplified in those with natural ability, education, and experience. But grit associated with high performance is not the simple willingness to perform Sisyphean tasks. Grit is only defined by increasing levels of performance when it is combined with extensive, domain-specific, and deliberate, ongoing practice.

PERFORMANCE-BASED GRIT COMES FROM EXTENSIVE EXPERIENCE

It seems like common sense, but high levels of performance cannot be achieved without extensive experience. As much as stories about children playing piano concertos or four-year-old golfers hitting holes-in-one are entertaining, they are also exceptionally rare. Look deeper into these cases and you will still find these prodigies spending most of every waking day engaged in that activity. Thus, while the skill was learned at an early age, they have still put in hundreds, if not thousands, of practice hours. For some, the connections in the brain necessary for learning happen quicker . . . but they still have to occur in the first place. Without experience generated through practice, that learning just can't happen.

In past years, there has been a great deal of debate about the number of hours or years needed to become great in a particular domain. Author Malcolm Gladwell talks about the "10,000 hour rule" as a prerequisite to high performance, using musicians (like the Beatles) and computer geniuses, such as Bill Gates, as supporting evidence. There are also a number of detractors to this theory. Led by Princeton researcher Brooke Macnamara, a number of scientists believe the role of thousands of hours of practice might be overrated.[6] One of their main arguments is that environment makes a difference in those practice hours. Practice for performers in stable environments has greater significance than it does for individuals in more dynamic settings, such as business. Coaches also play a critical role, especially when working with people who are willing to put in massive time and investment toward becoming high performers. He or she may be the only person with the perspective and authority to tell performers they are not putting in the right kind of effort to become better. An extra one hundred hours of practice will only reinforce a current state of proficiency if it is not challenging. There is a place for reinforcing fundamentals, but the coach's goal is to ascertain whether this is being confused with hours spent toward improvement.

The fact is—extensive experience is one of *many* factors involved in high performance and it differentiates between various performers' achievements. Extensive experience and practice are the minimum investment all high performers must make toward eligibility in competition's highest levels. However, those investments don't ensure that anything is possible for performers who "just work hard enough." If that were the case, anyone willing to slog through hours of practice would be guaranteed the winning trophy at the end of a competition. Reality shows that only a few reach the winner's podium despite the fact that all competitors in the race worked hard and put in the time. There is more to achievement than practice and desire.

THE SO-CALLED SUPERSTARS

Back in 1973, ABC premiered a televised sports competition show called *The Superstars*. This incredibly addictive program showcased a collection of America's best athletes from various sports competing against each other in events outside their specialty. This program was a weekend favorite for many years, and the main reason was simple—seeing a different side to your favorite sports heroes was hard to miss.

Football players, such as Roger Staubach and Drew Pearson, from the Dallas Cowboys, took on baseball players George Brett and Darrell Porter, from the Kansas City Royals, in tandem bike relays, swimming, and war canoe races. Make no mistake, these were some of the finest athletes of their day.

In the spirit of friendly competition, *The Superstars* pitted that year's World Series champion team against the reigning Super Bowl champs. Even after watching the show only a few times, a pattern quickly emerged:

1. The competitors took the events very seriously. They were there to win.
2. They were terrible at most events. TERRIBLE.

Part of the show's fun was seeing fine-tuned, accomplished athletes flounder around in a pool to the point where someone might have been tempted to throw them a life preserver. They had trouble getting in and out of the boats. They had little stamina on the bikes even though they spent dozens of hours a week in high intensity, structured training sessions.

On February 14–15, 1978, the competition in Honolulu, which was tied three-to-three between athletes from the Dallas Cowboys and the Kansas City Royals, went into the final event, the tug of war. This last event, a test of brute strength and endurance, would decide the competition's winner. Based on what you know about football and baseball, which athletes do you think would've won? Most people would guess football players. They are the big, strong athletes! Most would believe that baseball players wouldn't have had a chance.

After a grueling *hour and fifteen minutes*, the tug of war ended in a draw. Neither team could pull the other across the line. Both were exhausted. Though they gave everything they had in the final, no one team could dominate the other over the course of two days, and they were declared co-champions.

PERFORMANCE-BASED GRIT IS DOMAIN SPECIFIC

A tie? How could this be? Why couldn't these professional athletes transfer expert-level skills, strength, and power to dominate their opponents? The reason is simple: they were performing outside their domain.

Grit is specific to domain. In general, hard work and discipline can have a positive effect on other parts of life, and they might even build overall mental toughness. If someone gets up at 5 a.m. every morning, goes for a five-mile run, and then eats organic fruit every day for breakfast, it proves willpower. They are probably more disciplined than their peers (and more likely to be more disciplined in other aspects of their life and career). Or that adherence to schedule might signal an obsessive-compulsive disorder, a desire to avoid dealing with the kids in the morning, or simply sincere enjoyment of exercise.

The point is that having the "grit" to get up in the morning does not automatically mean you are working harder and getting more proficient, whether on the track or at the office. That routine and those hours spent at productive activities simply means you have taken care of the day's arduous tasks before most people have gotten out of bed. Specific time devoted to and concentration on each of those activities you are trying to perform is required to improve performance. Coaching is about improvement; therefore, it is a coach's role to notice if time is being spent as a reinforcement activity or an improvement exercise.

People often talk about swimming competitions and participating athletes, saying things like "the 100-meter butterfly is that athlete's event, but he has a hard time with the 800-meter freestyle." Wait, aren't those both swimming events? Lots of water, silly goggles, and a skimpy suit? How could swimmers be good at one and bad at another?

First, let's start by noting that "bad" at the 800-meter freestyle means finishing a second slower than the fastest person in the world and multiple minutes faster than the average swimmer. Second, there are a massive number of variables at play that differentiate the two events: distance, strokes, energy systems, and body composition. Third, and most importantly, smart swimmers pick events that suit them best (or simply enjoy more) and then train for that specific event. Realizing that domain of expertise in any event is limited and specific, these swimmers work hard developing assets and traits that lead to continuously higher performances.

Non-athlete high performers could learn much from this example. A neurosurgeon, for example, needs to stay far away from the cardiothoracic cavity on the operating table. A top Wall Street lawyer should concentrate on deals and leave developing new million-dollar client opportunities to expert marketing and business development professionals. A small business owner should stick to running that dealership instead of figuring out the intricacies of tax code to avoid hiring an accountant.

The body and mind are subject to the law of SAID. Each person has limited resources and mental capacity to manage, and thus constant revision of what skills and characteristics are still necessary (and which ones are not) is crucial to improvement. This is why domain specificity—and using grit as a tool—is so important to improved performance. Golfers get "rusty" when they don't go to the driving range for six months to hit golf balls. They do retain some basic proficiency and, sure, they can get back to where they were faster than a true beginner, but those golfers lose the top of their game quickly. They atrophy. It is the natural state of things. Another aspect to consider—if you spend a few hours a week on other areas that could be useful to your present domain, that is not a new area of expertise; that's a hobby.

Smart, successful people sometimes think that performance in one domain creates success in most other domains perceived as "easier" or at the same level of complexity. This is the illusion of transferable omniscience, which can be a great roadblock for many would-be successful people. Those who want to be proficient in a new area should expect to put in the same amount of education, experience, and grit as they do in their current area. Many people have encountered self-proclaimed experts who sweep in and attempt to solve a complex issue in a domain where they have no formal training, experience, or background. If you are the chief marketing officer of an international organization, the last thing you want is a technology, finance, or legal expert telling you how to do your job. These "experts" may even say something dismissive, such as "I have a degree in advanced finance and computer science. I certainly think I can handle a silly press release."

Though a basic level of proficiency can be reached in a relatively short period of time, these folks need to be cognizant that this training and practice does not make an expert of them. Grit can help get you to the mountaintop, but it doesn't mean you can jump across to the next one without another climb. Trust me, it's farther away than it looks. Don't try it.

Domain-specific grit pairs well with a formalized coaching program. Coaches can help develop domain- and activity-specific programs to improve results, continually stretching performers and analyzing deficiencies to be addressed. They also bring best practices and research to bear, relieving performers of the need to conduct their own discovery, trial and error, or theory formation on the best way to do something. Coaches and teachers are why Sir Isaac Newton's theory of calculus—which took a lifetime to develop—can be picked up by a sixteen-year-old child in less than a school year.

High performers apply grit to their specific domain. They understand the specific demands they need to impose on themselves for improvement. And they use coaches to help them get there.

PERFORMANCE-BASED GRIT IS DELIBERATE PRACTICE

Thousands of hours of domain-specific practice and preparation are essential ingredients for incorporating grit into a coach-developed performance plan. However, the last ingredient, *deliberate practice*, is perhaps the most important. Without it, hours of experience and activity are simply consignment to hard labor without any reward at the end of the sentence.

Research has proven time and time again that, beyond initially learning a skill, *how* people practice is much more important than *how much* they practice. Challenging concepts, skills, and activities should build upon each other. That is why universities have prerequisite classes, the military has boot camp, and why law or business school doesn't allow you to pick which year's syllabus you want to start on first. You also can't skip steps and expect great results.

Deliberate practice acts like baking powder when mixing ingredients for a cake. Eggs, flour, and sugar are the key ingredients to baking a cake. Why add baking powder? Simple chemistry provides the answer; baking powder, a leavening agent, reacts with the moisture of the mix and the oven's heat to produce carbon dioxide bubbles. Baking powder causes the cake to rise.

You could still eat the cake without baking powder. While it will probably still be edible, it won't taste (or look) *great*. You can complain that, after all that effort shopping, mixing, and baking, a silly teaspoon—one little thing!—makes such a difference between success and failure. That is the science, so get on board with it. (Incidentally, don't open the oven too soon. Heat loss causes those bubbles to rapidly contract and your cake will fall!)

Much like baking a cake, the ingredients and process involved in performance-based grit are essential. In our grit recipe, eggs, flour, and sugar represent natural ability, education, and years of experience. Skipping steps is like skipping baking ingredients. Failing to add deliberate practice is like cooking without reactive agents and generates barely acceptable results. Abandoning skill development too early equates to opening the oven door at the wrong time. Adding cayenne pepper to an angel food cake shows the importance of domain specificity (leave that ingredient to your Tex-Mex cuisine).

Just as with cooking, science makes the difference when combining all the elements and steps. Mixing practice and repetition in the right amounts and order is the difference between putting in time and putting better results on the scoreboard. On a positive note, both take the same number of hours, so you might as well engage in deliberate practice to continuously reach the next level of performance.

❧

Deliberate practice is distinct from experience-based practice in the following characteristics:

1. Skills are broken into chunks of subskills to be mastered.
2. Strengths and weaknesses are identified.
3. Exercises and training tasks are designed to progressively address
   strengths and weaknesses.
4. Progression necessitates mastery of subskills specific to the
   whole task.
5. High levels of concentration are required for limited time periods.
6. Practice must be adjusted constantly to accommodate new levels of
   mastery and the next level of expertise.
7. High performers sustain deliberate practice throughout their
   entire career.
8. Coaches and teachers share best practices and monitoring, providing
   feedback and designing performance programs.

❧

To reach higher and higher levels of performance, performers must stay in
the cognitive and associative phases of learning as long as possible. Once
the skills become autonomous, development levels off and can even decline
over time. For many skills, that is acceptable. World-class performance is
not always needed. Want to become great at tying shoes or folding t-shirts,
to the point of setting a world record? You certainly can. (Yes, those records
are tracked.[7])

However, when you are trying to become great within a domain and
associated subdomains, this is not the case. An accumulation of repetitive

activities over time will only take you so far. Imagine a sales professional, a natural extrovert, who earns a business degree, goes through formal sales training, and begins managing a territory. Some initial success will be had and deals closed. Once a year, this professional may attend mandated corporate training sessions and read a few books picked up at the airport. This professional resists instruction on improving and engaging in deliberate practice with a coach because "I already learned that" and such education is "only for amateurs." Fast-forward twenty years: that sales professional is most likely still struggling to make quota every quarter and giving excuses for marginally adequate performances (bad economy, bad products, bad boss, and so on).

How could this be? After twenty years, that professional should have more than *40,000 hours* of sales experience. According to the 10,000-hour rule, this person should be a virtuoso! Think about all the middle-aged salespeople you have met in your life. Are they all great, or are some phenomenally better than others? Many sales professionals are not much better than they were in their first years, having reached a point of automated performance, and there they'll stay unless something changes. For those in professions where generating new business comprises three to four hours a week (a part-time job!), there is no way you will ever become proficient in sales without a massive change in performance improvement strategy.

Let's revisit deliberate practice in terms of those 100-meter sprinters. To master a sprint, you must break the race into each of its components: the start, the mechanics of the first few steps, acceleration, fatigue, and so on. If you are slow out of the start that is one area of concentration. Problems related to slowing down too much at the end of the race? Exercises would be designed to address these issues separately. Because you can only train so much at one time without burning out, practice on these various skills must be carefully managed. Once all components are improved, your time will improve. And then the coach must modify the training plan to move you up to the next level. This continues until the end of your career, because other younger, faster sprinters keep showing up at the meets.

As with the sprint, business requires extreme levels of concentration for success with deliberate practice. This type of high-intensity activity cannot be maintained for very long, nor should it be. If business professionals can multitask through a practice session without much difference in their results or concluding mental state, they should consider whether the activity practiced is helpful. A quick test—ask yourself why you stopped practicing during the last session. Is it because you became bored or thought you had finished the required amount of time? If so, that was merely time-based, not deliberate, practice. Were you mentally fatigued, to the point that the value of the training session was affected and you had to stop? If yes, then you were probably engaged in deliberate practice. If you are not sure, a coach responsible for managing and monitoring progression can tell you.

Deliberate practice applies to all domains in sport, business, performance arts, and leisure activities. Using the same sales techniques you learned your first two years of your career for the next ten years will not get you to the President's Club awards dinner.

Using the same approach to build your business or professional practice that you did ten years ago will have less and less effect over time. There are three key reasons for this.

First, a leaders' lack of deliberate practice will eventually automate their skills, making control over conscious execution more difficult. This skill automation becomes so engrained that leaders and performers struggle to change.

Second, skills become less relevant, as the competition and environment is constantly changing. In short, performers are being left behind.

Third, leaders who lack an outside performance manager (such as a professor, teacher, or a coach) are not going to succeed. Though most people embrace these guides at an early age, many abandon the model once out on their own.

ASSESSING THE GRIT OF HIGH PERFORMANCE

- Am I engaged in deliberate practice or simply going through the motions?

- When I finish practicing, am I done because I am mentally fatigued or because I am bored?

- When I practice with someone else or as part of a team, do I work harder?

- Do the coaches I work with find ways for me to challenge myself more than I do when training on my own?

- If I am not getting the results I want, is my default solution "putting in more time and working harder"?

- Are my training activities and methods at the same level of difficulty as they were years ago?

- Am I putting in the required amount of time to truly get better at a new skill compared to other disciplines I have mastered?

❧

Self-managed improvement is exceptionally hard to do, and performers need to resist the urge to do it all themselves. Grit is not about putting in the time, being disciplined, and mindlessly pushing that metaphorical boulder uphill.

Improving results requires hours of repetition of key tasks, based on performers' individual strengths and weaknesses, in a specific domain as part of a structured program. Grit is personal, but coaches who can ensure engagement in deliberate practice, in a highly concentrated state, with harder and harder challenges, should guide potential experts toward constant improvement.

Automation, equilibrium, and eventual atrophy are the natural progression of all things. Grit is human beings' conscious effort to fight that state. The less time to engage in deliberate practice, the more reason there is for shorter, more intense sessions. High performers must get more done in a shorter period of time and that requires an *increase* in discipline (how often and at what consistency) and intensity (how hard and in what period of time). Having the best coaches and trainers available helps high performers make the most of their time.

Grit is all about reaching potential. Reaching anyone's potential is a gradual and endless process. That is why most people quit. That's why we shouldn't.

THE FUNCTIONAL RESERVE

"If you break an individual record, it's because of the greatness that comes before you."
—ABBY WAMBACH

"Adversity causes some men to break; others to break records."
—WILLIAM ARTHUR WARD

"There is always someone better than you. Whatever it is that you do for a living, chances are, you will run into a situation in which you are not as talented as the person next to you. That's when being a competitor can make a difference in your fortunes."
—PATRICIA "PAT" SUMMITT

"The will to win, the desire to succeed, the urge to reach your full potential . . . these are the keys that will unlock the door to personal excellence."
—CONFUCIUS

We have defined art, science, and grit and how these concepts, when balanced properly and used effectually, positively impact performance. The concepts seem simple:

- See things in new ways.

- Study and perfect the craft.

- Put in necessary hours of deliberate practice.

In the top tier of any discipline, ability and experience are a given. Once in the top 10 percent of your domain, everyone is elite. So, what holds some people back? Why do some never reach their true potential? Perhaps the answer is incorrect focus—many people are too intent on realizing a *potential* instead of focusing on the *actual* performance.

Almost everyone has heard a story about people in extreme circumstances who perform superhuman feats, such as mothers lifting a car to save a trapped child. These amazing feats demonstrate hysterical strength, and though they have never been truly verified or scientifically proven, we all understand the concept. Someone performed well beyond what was thought possible. Whether adrenaline, pain suppression, or mental focus caused the increase in ability, these superheroes raised their *actual performance* (what is perceived to be their maximum) closer to *potential performance* (true maximum). The gap between these two performances is known as *functional reserve*. Though it sounds like a complicated term, you see this almost every day.

Imagine that you decide to run a 5K race for the first time in ten years. Your goal is simply to finish. As you progress through the run, you regret taking on this challenge, and this regret grows with every sidesplitting step. The finish line is only a few hundred feet away; you feel you are about to collapse, but you think you can make it. All of a sudden, out of the corner of your eye, you spot an older friend inching past, ready to finish ahead of you! That friend will always have that faster finish on you. Suddenly, a burst of speed emerges from your legs. You run faster than at the beginning. You beat your friend by only a few feet, but you won.

You did not magically become a better runner or more aerobically efficient. You changed your performance level to meet the challenge. You made a decision to dig deeper and push harder. You ignored pain, doubt, and self-limitations.

You tapped into your functional reserve.

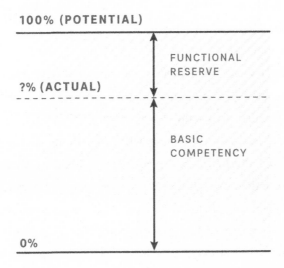

We have discussed how performers' natural abilities, education, experience, and deliberate practice will take them to a certain level of competency in each domain-specific skill. There is always a point where a level of comfort or satisfaction about where performers actually are *or* uneasiness and reticence about progression that prevents them from moving beyond that point.

You may find a heavy weight in the gym and say, "I can't lift that." You might be given a complex piano piece to learn and think, "I could never play that." You could finish your MBA, but declare, "I could never handle those kind of hours and pressure" when big companies recruit you. Thus your performance remains at a level that might be well below your capability.

In some cases, this self-talk is justified. If the discipline doesn't hold that much significance, reaching a basic level of competency is sufficient. For example, if you want to maintain general health, you don't need to try out for the Olympic team. However, you may need to tap into your functional reserve to generate *some* results. Likewise, you may not want to log one hundred hours a week working as a big city executive, but your functional reserve may be called upon when your business needs to thrive as markets and competitors change.

As we learn new skills or subjects, we gain proficiency rather quickly. Within fifty hours of learning and practicing, acceptable levels of performance can be reached. This is the ceiling of our self-limitations but the floor of our functional reserve. Deliberate practice, experience, and education can help break through this barrier, but eventually the limits set are mental. High performers create their own glass ceilings—they can peer upward to the true top but resign themselves to lower levels of what can be achieved.

Like other elements of high performance, functional reserve is also domain specific. A leader may reach the pinnacle of his profession but lack other elements (e.g., business development, staff management, or client service) necessary for success. A triathlete may be a great runner and cyclist, but the swim portion scares her and holds her back. A musician plays astonishingly well with an orchestra but has convinced himself he could never solo in front of an audience.

A performer in any discipline using art, science, and grit can improve in two ways—via true potential or actual performance.

While both approaches are important for continuous improvement, high performers should concentrate on improving their actual performance beyond what they thought was possible, or decreasing their functional reserve. This is by far the fastest way to results.

THREE WORLD RECORDS IN SIXTY SECONDS

The 1996 Olympics in Atlanta had plenty of amazing stories to add to the annals of human achievement in sport. However, one event came down to a battle between two athletes, Naim Suleymanoglu of Turkey and Valerios Leonidis of Greece. The sport was Olympic weightlifting. Their battle for the gold medal was one for the ages and demonstrated how competition brings out the best in any performance.

Olympic weightlifting consists of two lifts. One is *the snatch*, where lifters pull a weight from the floor to above their head, locking the arms, in one explosive motion. The other lift is *the clean and jerk*; the weight is brought from the floor to the chest and then pressed upward and arms locked in a separate motion. Each athlete gets three attempts at a weight in each lift. There are no negotiations, shortcuts, or tricks—the weight goes up, or it does not. The winner of the event is the lifter with the highest combined total weight for both lifts. In the event of a tie, the lifter with the lower body weight wins.

Suleymanoglu was a decorated champion and known as the best in his weight class. Pound for pound, he was arguably the strongest man in the world; Suleymanoglu was barely five feet tall and weighed less than 140 pounds.

On the night of July 22, 1996, thirty-six people from all over the world started the contest with the first lift, the snatch. Suleymanoglu won this half of the competition, lifting more than anyone else. Leonidis finished just 2.5 kilograms behind him, and so the second half of the competition—the clean and jerk—promised to be entertaining. But no one watching had any idea of what they were about to witness.

Part of Olympic weightlifting strategy is deciding how much weight to attempt. Go too light, and you may waste one of your attempts if a competitor decides to go heavier. Start too heavy, and you may never get a single "good" lift in three attempts and be out of the contest. Suleymanoglu decided to start with 180 kilograms (393.75 pounds), just 3 kilograms short of the world record held by his rival, Leonidis. This bold move set the tone for the evening. Bringing the weight to shoulder level, Suleymanoglu paused before powerfully propelling the weight over his head for his successful lift. Stone faced, Leonidis attempted the same weight. He easily equaled Suley-manoglu's total. However, he still lagged in the overall competition by those 2.5 kilograms.

Suleymanoglu was aware that Leonidis's next move would be to surpass him by eliminating the total weight deficit. He decided to load 185 kilograms on the bar. That weight would surpass Leonidis's world record. With great power and determination, he broke the world record in the clean and jerk AND the total weight lifted world record for his weight class with that successful lift. Leonidis, now losing by 7.5 kilograms, decided to load 187.5 kilograms on the bar. He completed the lift, setting another new world record in the process. Three world records had been set in less than sixty seconds. The contest was now tied for total weight lifted.

For his last lift, the Turkish superman loaded 187.5 kilograms on the bar. A totally silent audience perched on the edge of their seats as he exploded into the lift; as he propelled the bar over his head, the crowd erupted in cheers. Suleymanoglu's spectacular accomplishment had set the evening's fourth world record in total weight for a competition. To equal that total weight, Leonidis would have to load 190 kilograms onto the bar. If he succeeded, Leonidis—whose body weight was one pound lower than his rival's—would be declared the winner.

Despite his dedication, training, and mental focus, Leonidis could not lift the weight. Suleymanoglu was declared the winner and awarded his third Olympic gold medal. The difference between gold and silver in total lifted weight: 0.7 percent.

Leonidis, exceptionally gracious in defeat, admitted the better athlete had won that day. He said in reflection,

"You push yourself hard, and he pushes himself harder. And, that is why when we met before the awards I said, 'Naim, you are the best.' And he said, 'No, Valerios, we are both the best.'"

❧

Suleymanoglu and Leonidis were already at the top of their potential performance levels. After training for decades under the supervision of coaches, the difference between what they *actually* lifted and what they *could* lift was quite small. Each was well trained, confident, and fearless. However, there was still something to give, as evidenced by the fact that both weight lifters broke personal *and* world records within minutes of each other.

Stop to think for a moment what "world record" really means. It means that no human being who has ever lived on this planet has ever achieved that feat. This includes the person who just broke the record! Before the Olympics, Leonidis held the world record in the clean and jerk. Both competitors broke the record at the event. Had they been physically incapable at the last meet? Had they not cared? On this day, did their muscles suddenly become more powerful?

Competition made the difference. It allowed competitors to both tap into functional reserves and squeeze out those last kilograms of effort. Yes, they were capable of doing so the day before the event, but the feat was accomplished that day. That performance then became their new minimum standard. You can permanently shrink the functional reserve when you combine the methods associated with the art, science, and grit of high performance.

PROBLEMS WITH ONLY "IMPROVING YOUR POTENTIAL"

When people see diminishing gains in performance, the natural inclination is to either accept their current level of achievement or find ways to improve their potential. For those who decide to try to keep improving, they often start scouring multiple resources for answers in new methods, examples, and programs. They may seek out training courses and expert instructors; they may search for other successful people whose patterns and activities they can model. They set lofty goals as a target. All of these tactics will help improve their potential.

If the reason for a lower level of performance is related to a large functional reserve, however, these efforts will make little difference.

While these efforts might raise potential slightly, self-imposed limits of achievement will not have been addressed. Thus, the functional reserve has actually become larger and no real improvement made.

Let's turn to the world of auto racing to illustrate this concept. Think of NASCAR, Formula 1, or any other high speed, dangerous motorsport and choose a famous (or your favorite) driver. Now, imagine you have been offered a great opportunity—you get to go onto the track with that driver in the backup car. You will have the same equipment, setup, pit crew, and fuel that the professional driver has. There is one simple goal: Keep up.

You and your driver take the track and begin racing around at 200 mph, you are closely following that driver. Actually . . . this is not realistic. You would probably be well behind the professional driver, going half the speed, taking the turns much slower, and sweating through your racing suit. At first glance, this difference doesn't make sense. The car, fuel, tires, track, conditions (and everything else) are the same. The car has three pedals and one steering wheel, and there is but one direction to go on the track. It's a relatively straightforward task. Thus, if the performances don't equate, the only variable responsible for this inequality must be the driver.

Most would agree that this conclusion seems reasonable and quite obvious; a novice would not perform as well as a professional driver. The average person hasn't been formally trained, has little to no experience running laps at top speed, and probably lacks the natural reflexes and coordination. The average person could set goals to drive faster, model a great driver by watching races, and even go through some basic training by reading books and watching videos, and perhaps even go to a track to learn from an expert. However, that average person is still quite a long way from matching an expert racecar driver on the track.

Taking away their skill and experience as a driver, average people have three self-limiting issues holding them back: reservation, complacency, and fear.

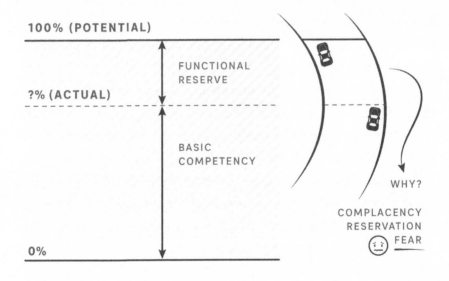

Reservation, in this instance, can come from many sources. Performers may be unwilling to look foolish or expose any weaknesses by doing something new. Perhaps they made statements in the past ("how hard could driving in a circle be?") that their performance might then prove erroneous. Ignorance can be bliss. If they are not fully engaged, it might take some time and persuasion to overcome these fears and get them to try at all. They may continue to do things the "old way" or "their way," ridiculing the challenge. This can occur in a business context when a new strategy or sales approach is rolled out. A business professional with reservations may wait to see how clients respond, find comfort in more analysis, or hold back to see others' performance first.

Complacency can be defined as satisfaction with the status quo based on performers' position as it relates to others. In other words, if you were racing a group of average people and you were in the lead, you wouldn't pay as much attention to the professional. Continuing with a business example, financial goals or new sales strategy quota may be viewed as completely unachievable. That goal can never be reached, so why even try? In fact, as long as those business executives are slightly ahead of people like themselves, in their minds, they are doing well. The goal has changed—not being the worst has replaced doing their best.

Fear is pretty simple. As an inexperienced racecar driver, you are afraid of flying off the track and slamming into a wall at high speed. As a business executive, that fear might be subtler, but it can be still as painful as crashing into that wall. Fear of looking foolish, being rejected, or exposed as less talented than you'd like colleagues to believe is enough for many people to avoid situations beyond their comfort zone. If a new sales approach evokes fear, it is easy to stick to the old way and denounce the new. While the fear is reduced, performance is reduced as well.

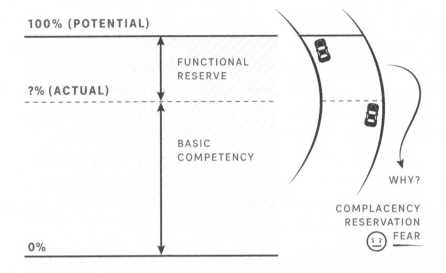

Let's continue to think about this concept in terms of performers such as executives, salespeople, consultants, or lawyers, who might be great in one field yet lacking in another. To improve, they can set goals, model the best performers, and read a few training books. In fact, this is what most high performers in one domain do when trying to gain expertise in another. They figure that mastery over one means the other related domain couldn't be that difficult. The thinking is, if they just apply themselves and try a few times, they will figure it out. However, what we have learned about domain-specific expertise tells us this is almost never the case.

Let's say you are a lawyer who's handled extremely complex legal matters and are held in high regard for having an exceptionally talented legal mind. The market slows and you are suddenly struggling to find clients. You figure that setting a goal (generating another $250,000 in new business), modeling a fellow rainmaker (someone with an exceptional ability, who's created good fortunes for themselves and others), and taking a couple of training courses will have you all set. But will it? Is that what it takes when success is measured on that kind of scale?

Raising potential is a long, arduous process that takes years of deliberate practice, perfection of the craft, and seeing challenges in new ways. Most don't have the time in our careers to wait until we can harvest the benefits of such efforts. Goal setting, modeling, and basic skills training raise potential performance, but they do not address the functional reserve that is governed by reluctance, complacency, and fear. The best tactic is to address those issues first. In short, get more out of what you already have—realize your potential—instead of theoretically increasing performance.

THE BENEFIT OF "IMPROVING YOUR ACTUAL"

The fastest path for reaching higher performance is getting closer to true maximum potential by improving *actual* performance. Even if your maximum is not where you you'd want it to be, shrinking the gap between actual and maximum (the functional reserve) is the best way to gain momentum and start delivering compounding results. To do so, performers must engage in activities that eliminate detrimental conditions of reservation, complacency, and fear.

These conditions are internally based, self-imposed, and self-limiting. Because they can be justified and rationalized, performers so hampered find them very hard to overcome. This is where the high-performance coach comes in.

REPETITION, TRAINING UNDER DURESS, AND SIMULATION

Coach and performers must work together to decrease functional reserve before raising potential. They do this by incorporating different methods. *Repetition, training under duress,* and *dynamic simulation* are essential to decreasing functional reserve and raising potential. As we discuss each one of these methods, we'll refer back to the racecar example to help improve your performance on the track!

Repetition seems self-explanatory. Performers who wish to become great at something have to practice in a deliberate fashion. This is not just to gain skill but to maintain skill. Police officers visit the shooting range throughout their careers. Violinists play musical scales. Professional basketball players shoot free throws. *There is never a time when, once a skill has been acquired in any domain, it becomes permanent, even at the highest level of achievement.*[1] Skills atrophy so they must be maintained through practice. For some reason, some experts in traditional business settings do not follow this reasoning. Once they receive a degree and begin their career, they do not see the need to practice learned skills on a perpetual basis. You can protect that framed and mounted diploma or certificate under glass, but expertise has no similar preservative. Lawyers who do not go to court slowly lose their trial skills. Sales managers who spend their time on paperwork become rusty at dealing with customers. Accountants who end up managing departments and people have a harder time scanning income statements and balance sheets as they once could.

Let's imagine a senior business executive at a manufacturing company in the United States. Her job is running floor operations smoothly and handling logistics that ensure raw material availability. It is a complex job and, after twelve years, she has a sixth sense about anything that could cause a disruption to an almost perfect level of efficiency and productivity. Due to her success, this executive has been asked to set up a new factory in China. Since locals will run the new factory, her new job is training workers and their managers. She will be gone for eighteen months.

When this star executive returns home after her stay in China, how long before she gets back into the swing of things at her previous position? If you were someone who believes practice is not necessary to maintain skills and expertise, you would say she is ready the moment she gets off the plane! However, most would admit she would probably need some time to return to the high-performance level she previously enjoyed. She may perform well immediately, but not *as* well. Even in her present state, she may still be better than most performers, but she was the *best* at what she did. That is what made her so valuable. While she was in China for those eighteen months, she had little or no exposure to any new conditions, competitors, or challenges in the US market. Her knowledge and expertise is out of date, and it will take time to get caught up. So, while this star performer is very likely to regain her past level of expertise, it will not return instantaneously. Ironically, as she gets closer and closer to her past performance in the United States, the nuances of the Chinese job will atrophy. And, like her new proficiency in Mandarin, her skills will continue to dissipate over time without practice.

This is a natural reaction—the body and mind commit resources and priority to those skills and traits needed at the present time to survive.

The previous examples deal with maintaining high levels of skill proficiency, and we have discussed how deliberate practice develops higher levels of performance. The repetition needed to remedy wide gaps in the functional reserve must address both the initial development as well as the maintenance of high-performance levels. Repetition for the expert maintains; repetition for the novice begins the learning process and builds the foundation and fundamentals necessary to progress. For both experts and novices, repetition builds confidence.

Think back to the racecar example. If you could take the car out for a few slow laps on the track with a coach in the passenger seat, you'd feel more comfortable. Say the coach asked you to go five miles per hour faster with each lap. You'd feel more at ease, and you'd be getting better. Your skills aren't dramatically improving—your ability to access them has grown. *With repetition comes confidence and higher actual performance.* In our star business example, she won't take long to get back to the top of her game. But what if we were talking about a new employee at the company? Can a few days of training mean he never has to worry about practice again? At the very least, practice is needed to maintain basic proficiency. If you want an employee to improve over time, repetition is needed for their skills to become second nature and provide a foundation upon which to build. Repetition is always important, but it is even more so during a skill's beginning learning. The rate at which skills atrophy is directly related to the length of time spent acquiring them. If that employee hasn't been doing a skill for long, it won't take him long to lose it.

Training under duress is an uncomfortable environment for most people. In this case, *duress* is not used as the traditional legal term, meaning people are forced or coerced into doing something they don't want to do. *Duress* used in the context of training refers to an external force beyond what is typically comfortable or normal for the participants. The external force could be a time limit, a new challenge, or a competitor. The only "threat" involved is the risk of underperforming. Therefore, training under duress is a positive methodology, though not necessarily enjoyable (and, therefore, very appropriately named). Let's imagine that a partner at a professional service firm is trying to become better at acquiring new, complex clients. The coach decides there has been enough instruction and calls the partner to the front of the room for a role-play scenario, in which a client visit goes wrong. Instead of going through the conversational motions, the partner has to deal with unexpected variables: a computer crashes, an argumentative client, time is cut short, and being graded against fellow partners. Working through the scenario under these very realistic changes illustrates the difference between training and training under duress.

This type of training is more complex than simple repetition of tasks and gradually increasing difficulty. A coach uses training under duress to place performers in challenging situations, scenarios that involve chasing or being chased. Now, we are not talking about being chased by a bear (even though that would be a pretty effective technique for pushing any performer's true limits of speed). We are also not talking about chasing the unattainable, such as running after a plane hurtling down a runway in an attempt to develop speed. Obviously, there would be no hope of ever keeping up.

Coach and performers must develop training goals that are challenging enough to be difficult, yet realistic enough to achieve. The coach may change training variables, such as time, conditions, repetitions, intensity, duration, and competitors, to accomplish this. The coach may ask performers to complete tasks in thirty seconds that previously required thirty-five. Performers might race against a peer for the best overall time or complete tasks while already mentally or physically fatigued. The coach may decide to keep the same exercises but require more repetitions of the task in the same amount of time. The point is to push performers beyond their comfort zone and out of the automation state. Some are disciplined enough to do this on their own from time to time, but maintaining duress training as a permanent part of a performance program is difficult. Performers need to be pushed to set personal records—and to attempt doing so—as often as possible.

Training under duress exposes weaknesses and faulty fundamental skills. It helps to identify areas for improvement and provide benchmarks to monitor progress. Using the previous example, duress resets the business partner's future bar of minimum performance. When a coach manages this type of training properly, performers gain confidence that they can take to harder future challenges and believe that their weaknesses can be addressed and conquered. When these performers meet a difficult client in the real world, they are not flustered into making bad decisions. They have "been here before," and it is no big deal.

Let's go back to the racetrack again. Your driving coach has provided a cash reward if you beat your best lap time. The coach recruits three of your fellow novice drivers to race against each other for nothing more than bragging rights. He amps up the challenge by pumping the audio from thirty racecars into your radio headset and heating the car's interior to more than one hundred degrees, simulating a real race. You drive, chasing the clock, dealing with peer pressure, and attempting to overcome difficult conditions in the hope you will drive faster. And your skills *are* incrementally improving (along with your ability to access those skills).

Dynamic simulation is the most complex method to devise situations, environments, and conditions that create realistic representations of competitive events. Dynamic simulation is a combination of repetition and training under pressure in a real-world context and can come in many forms. Businesspeople use role-playing, a simple way for employees to practice thinking on their feet in response to another person or competitor. Navy SEALS use multiple integrated laser engagement system (MILES) gear[2] to simulate battle, storming buildings, and engaging in team-based competitive war games. Airline pilots use flight simulators to practice basic landings (but they also practice an engine going out or severe wind shear—when you fly airplanes for a living, it's much better for everyone if you experience those situations first in a simulated environment).

Dynamic simulations have to be realistic. There must be a genuine possibility of losing. All actors must be doing their best. It's crucial that the immersive environment makes participants feel as though they are *really* there. By closely re-creating actual conditions, coaches teach performers to perform under pressure in uncertain circumstances and apply knowledge in ways that could never be simply memorized. Research has shown that simulation allows pilots to recognize situations, apply past knowledge, and adapt to changing environments more successfully.[3] The technique can work for pilots and anyone else who wants the same benefits.

Let's hop back in the racecar again. Imagine you have gone to the track for the past two Saturdays and, each time, you completed twenty laps. You have raced some similarly skilled competitors and tried to beat your best lap times. Now, the coach has plans for a race simulation. Perhaps after five laps, he calls on the radio to say you "blew a tire" and need to come in for a pit stop. He makes use of a few professional drivers planted in the race field, who push and test you in close quarters racing. By this time, would you be performing better? If you are, it's not because you became an expert racecar driver in a few sessions. It's because you tapped into that functional reserve, decreasing the gap between actual and maximum performance, and began raising your potential.

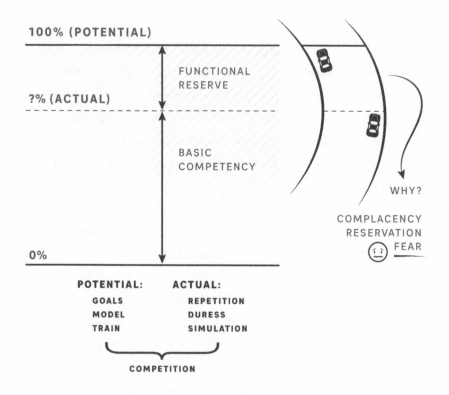

THE GREENIE BOARD

A twenty-four-year-old navy fighter pilot is landing a $50 million F/A-18 jet on an aircraft carrier on a particularly dark night. There are no moon and stars. In the middle of the Pacific Ocean, hundreds of miles from land, the flight deck heaves and rolls with the heavy seas. The pilot is low on fuel and has nowhere else to go. From the plane's cockpit, the dimly lit flight deck—a half a mile away—looks like a postage stamp floating in a sea of black ink.

The jet approaches the ship. At 150 mph, the pilot makes continuous throttle and control stick adjustments to stay on the proper glide path while honing in on the centerline. The landing zone is a small portion of the flight deck, measuring about two hundred feet long and fifty feet wide. To complicate matters, the landing zone is moving forward at 30 mph, and the zone is offset 9 degrees from the direction of the ship's heading.

The arresting wires are stretched across the deck to catch the tailhook that's hanging from the back of his jet. If all goes well, the jet will be brought to a jolting stop in about 200 feet. If the landing's a little too short, the pilot knows he could crash into the ramp (the flight deck's back of the portion). A little too long, and the hook flies over all four wires as the pilot slam the throttles forward to gain enough flying speed before reaching the end of the angled deck, some 250 feet away. The precision, speed, and consequences of the endeavor have his adrenaline flowing, breathing rapid, and focus absolute.

But after landing, the pilot's job isn't finished. Most carrier pilots consider the most important part of a carrier landing to be what comes *after* the flight: the landing grade.

Each and every carrier landing is recorded and shown in real time on a closed-circuit TV system in every ready room and command center on the ship. Pilots from nine different squadrons are watching and evaluating the pilot's performance. Moreover, each landing is assigned a grade by the landing signal officer stationed on the flight deck. Once assigned, grades are posted—by pilot name—on the ready room wall on the "greenie board," a large, conspicuous placard aptly named for the color of the assigned grade. Green means "good," yellow is "fair," and red denotes "poor." It takes only a brief glance to ascertain who has the most greens and who has a rare red. This board is stark notice of peer standings among carrier pilots. Is it a motivating factor for higher performance? You bet!

It would appear that competition is an inherent part of any carrier pilot's life, but mention the word outside the ready room and you'll often get a mixed (and even emotional) response. Pilots respond in a variety of ways, ranging from "the only competitor should be yourself" to "cooperation is more important than competition" and "competition is what brings out the best in me." While all of these are valid, experience in the military and business domains argues that *optimum performance is most often fostered in an environment of cooperative competition.* How good you can be can only be ascertained when measured against how good others can be at the same task.

THE BEST WAY TO IMPROVE POTENTIAL
AND ACTUAL: COMPETITION

Competition exists all around us. You see it many different ways. As soon as the boarding group is called at the airport, people start to nudge forward, attempting to reach the front of the line, even though all groups will eventually leave the ground at the same time. Friendly neighbors try to outdo each other at backyard barbeques and children's birthday parties. Coworkers fight for new work titles, even though there's no compensation or reward (other than the pride in receiving it). In nature, plants compete to reach water and sunlight, and animals use their plumage and fangs to assert dominance within a group.

As a method of improving performance, competition is the one thing that can address both sides of the functional reserve by raising the actual *and* potential maximum of the individual, team, or organization. As we discussed earlier, actual performance will always improve faster than maximum performance . . . but there is no reason you can't raise each at the same time. Managed competition allows performers to do just that.

Competition simultaneously utilizes all the methods mentioned before. Performers can set goals to achieve specific results, model winners, train, and practice. Mental imagery and ambition increase potential; hours and hours of active play or preparation, performing against challengers, and simulating real-life situations raise actual performance through execution and refinement.

Certain circles sometimes see competition as negative. By definition, *competition* is the opposite of *cooperation*. However, research has shown that, when tested in individual and team cooperation or competition experiments, performers do better and enjoy team-based competitive environments more than solo training or practice.[4] This explains the worldwide popularity of team sports and why organizations act collectively to dominate rivals (business competitors, recreational sporting teams, debate clubs, etc.). Competition occurs naturally and can be very healthy, despite any negative connotations of the word. For example: A company holds an annual meeting or retreat for all its executives at a fancy hotel, and organizers decide to randomly place attendees in golf foursomes for a recreational outing. Even with no prizes, rewards, or incentives, competition flourishes—between and within the teams. By the end of the week, foursomes have picked team names and mascots. They're trash talking. Some foursomes organize time to go to the driving range together and give each other a hard time for not improving, saying things like, "Kathy, you really need to work on your putting! I don't want to lose to that foursome from the NYC office! We will never live it down!" These are not professional golfers, and there is nothing at stake (except pride). However, the presence of competition brings out the best in people. Take away random selection and substitute a legitimate, need-based reason to form an actual team, and competition works even more effectively.

The takeaway here is that competition does not always have to occur on "game day" or have permanent winners or losers. The efficacy of using competition for *training and development* is that it prepares people for the real-life competition in their domain, where results are permanent. Healthy, collaborative, managed competition is a common tactic that pushes all members of a group to excel.

⚘

Players on a soccer team, such as Manchester United Football Club, compete for starting positions that lead to fame and lucrative endorsement contracts. Violinists in the London Philharmonic Orchestra compete for first chair and the right to solo. Law and medical students compete for grades and class standing, which lead to placement in the best law firms and hospitals. These types of competition bring out the best (and the worst) by allowing performers to test their capabilities in real time against a motivated competitor who wants to win.

Competition is effective even when the performers are all elite members of the same team with a common final objective. Competitive cyclists train for their country or sponsor as a team, taking turns drafting off each other and pulling the peloton during training. Navy fighter pilots attend Top Gun (Navy Fighter Weapons School) to find the "best pilot," but when they return to their respective squadrons, each serves as surrogate instructors to prepare fellow pilots for combat.[5] Sales managers in a Fortune 500 organization use "stack rankings" to motivate sales reps to better one another's generated revenue, which in turn enables the company to make its numbers.

MANAGED COMPETITION

For a competitive method to improve performance, proper management is key. This requires standards and experts who know how to create competitive environments and ensure the right behaviors and outcomes are encouraged. Managed competition exhibits the following characteristics:

- Rules: The competition must be perceived as fair and not predisposed to a particular winner or conclusion. Limitations as to what is allowed must be evenly applied to all competitors. "Win by any means" encourages participants to focus on finding ways to beat the system, not improving their performance.

- Appropriate classes: Group competitors into tiers of relative performance levels so that each has a realistic chance of winning (or losing).

- Limited duration: Set an ending for the competition, whether it's based on time, score, accomplishment, or another objective resolution.

- Definition of winning: Everyone should understand how the victor is decided and how to periodically evaluate rankings.

- Valued rewards: Offer a prize that appeals and is worth winning; it doesn't matter whether the motivating factors are intrinsic or extrinsic.

- Referees: Referees must be independent participants who ensure the competition is fair and rules are being followed, and who penalize those who disregard the rules.

- Coaches: Coaches are, by definition, biased experts who help specific individuals adjust to competitors, changing situations, or the environment to improve their chances of winning.

❦

Competition as a development methodology is highly effective but highly complex, with a great many moving parts that require agreement and coordination. Creating their own competitions would be very difficult for an individual performer to do, especially if it involved competing with others. Naturally, they would try to stack the deck in their favor! Therefore, performers must involve many other people if they wish to concentrate on improving. So why not let the experts manage and simply concentrate on the competitive process?

Perhaps the most important additional person to become involved is the coach. Coaches may or may not have been high-performing experts in the domain. They do not need to prove they were as good or better than the person being coached. That is not their job. Their role is to apply the art and science of helping others get better every day. Coaches use tools, such as repetition, to test abilities, develop programs, and monitor progress. They observe strengths and weaknesses, modifying their approaches based on the performer's realities and nature of the competition. They fine-tune skills through drills, form, and practice. Coaching's domain is its own domain of expertise, and having been a former star performer does not equate to coaching expertise.

Designers who create competitions, races, simulations, war games, and other such events are experts in scenarios that mimic real life or entail transferable activities that improve specific skills associated with actual circumstances and situations. This work is a massive undertaking, one that is most effective when new variables and possible outcomes are constantly added. Keeping performers guessing and adapting is key to success. Enlisting help from outside experts and utilizing market trends and competitive forces helps make competitions real, but it is ultimately the coach who makes final decisions regarding best formats and challenges to improve the desired performance. If the competition is too easy, overly hard, or completely unrealistic, that falls on the coaches' shoulders—it's their responsibility to make sure performers get better at what they do every day.

Other competitors are essential to truly test performers in a way that goes beyond their comfort zone. This seems like an obvious statement, but many performers feel uncomfortable competing once they've achieved a high level of expertise. They do not like to be challenged and resist situations where they may be exposed (they're not quite as good as they think—or want others to think—they are). This attitude is usually easily spotted; reluctant competitors argue with the rules, relevance, or composition of the competition. People who resist competition will argue they are disciplined, hard working, and will handle it on their own. All performers need fellow competitors who are also trying to win so they can get the most out of their efforts and continue to improve. We all improve when we are chasing someone or being chased. Whether it is the fastest time on the track, the number of business appointments you set, or being the top of your academic class, keeping score between you and peer performers matters.

We know that some people (even leaders and high performers) shy away from competition, but when they do, it is a disservice to the individuals, teams, and organizations that claim to desire high performance and the spoils that come from it. We all live in the arena. Sometimes the stakes are inconsequential—like being first in line to get into a concert or a recreational softball game at a picnic. Sometimes they are very high—if you are a professional athlete, firefighter, or a pilot. However, we all live in an arena where our competitive nature allows us to perform better than we thought possible. It is important to harness that power if we want to reach our maximum performance. We belong in the arena, and that "arena" includes where we train and prepare for the real thing. We cannot only seek the glory of the arena. We must embrace its difficulty and use it as a tool to realize our potential. It is the act of winning *and* losing that makes us better. As Theodore Roosevelt said—

"It is not the critic who counts; not the man who points out how the strong man stumbles, or where the doer of deeds could have done them better. The credit belongs to the man who is actually in the arena, whose face is marred by dust and sweat and blood; who strives valiantly; who errs, who comes short again and again, because there is no effort without error and shortcoming; but who does actually strive to do the deeds; who knows great enthusiasms, the great devotions; who spends himself in a worthy cause; who at the best knows in the end the triumph of high achievement, and who at the worst, if he fails, at least fails while daring greatly."

Performance improvement and enhancement comes from time spent in the arena. Don't miss your chances to spend as much time there as you possibly can.

⚜

As we have discussed in great depth, many variables can explain why certain performers excel and others are destined to moderate success, no matter how hard they work, study, or practice. This variation can sometimes be explained by a lack of natural ability or access to the right resources.

However, high performers in multiple disciplines have common traits. They see things in new ways, but they do not try to reinvent themselves or their field so often as to never be able to achieve mastery. They master their craft but realize that, when situations, conditions, and competitors change, they must as well. They are willing to put in thousands of hours of deliberate practice to get ahead, but they are smart enough to lift their head up every now and then. And—they use coaches to make sure they are practicing the right things in the right way. They balance art, science, and grit because these three elements are essential to continuous improvement in a competitive and constantly changing environment.

High performers realize they cannot automatically transfer expertise from one domain to the next. When someone from one domain *does* become successful in another, it is because they applied the same process to become an expert in the new domain as they did in their primary domain. Be wary when you look at a successful person and say, "That person is naturally great at everything!" Perhaps, they are actually great in the *process* of becoming great at everything.

High performers work hard when times are hard. Like cyclists trying to gain a lead on competitors during a long road race, they accelerate while going uphill. Anyone can go fast while going downhill or flying along a flat stretch. Sustainable gains and separation between competitors are made when going uphill. This applies to athletes, pilots, astronauts, military special operators, business executives, lawyers, or anyone else who deals in binary or terminal consequences. The old maxim "when the going gets tough, the tough get going" proves true.

High performers build momentum through exponential wins. Their frequent achievements compound, enabling them to do more and more each time. Their personal records become new minimum standards. Because they realize that today's record is something others are now trying to break, lack of movement is a guaranteed path to eventual mediocrity.

It's one thing to hear about theories, research, and philosophies about what it takes to be the very best. It is quite another thing to hear true stories about people who have done so. No one is born a great astronaut, but John Glenn became one. No one inherently knows computer code, but Bill Gates learned how to develop it into something unique. Sheryl Sandberg did not dream about social media as a child (it really didn't even exist yet), but she became Facebook's chief operating officer.

These are not super humans or lottery winners. These are people with natural gifts, early support networks, and a drive to excel beyond even the top 1 percent of performers in their domain. They are truly the elite. If there is a common theme among all of these people, it is that all of the people they competed against were also some of the best in the world at what they did. They had already made it through many, many rounds when the weaker candidates were weeded out. As they reached the final tier of competition, there were not many competitors left (if you view it as a share of the general population). They were not among the top 1 percent or higher of all performers in the world. However, even in this rarified air, there were still scores of performers who had dedicated their lives to being the best. Not all of them made it.

BEING THE BEST SOMETIMES MEANS
ONLY QUALIFYING FOR AN AUDITION

When the teams in the National Football League come back each summer to practice as a unit, it is known as training camp. Every July, all thirty-two teams in the NFL are permitted to have ninety players in camp who are fighting to secure a final spot on the fifty-three-man roster before the first regular season game. That means that over 40 percent of the athletes who were so talented that they were asked to try out to play professional football will probably have to go find something else to do with their lives after two decades or more of preparation, playing, and winning.

It might not seem unusual that not everyone makes the team. After all, it is the pros we're talking about here. Only a few can make it, and fewer still can have a prolonged career in such a violent, cutthroat profession. However, keep in mind that the 2,880 players that start on Day One of training camp have already been labeled as the best of the best. According to 2014 statistics, there were 1,122,024 high school football players. By the time these players moved to post-secondary education, only 90,136 continued to play at any level in college.

This means that only 8 percent of kids good enough to suit up on their high school team could expect to make a college team.[6] It also means that only 3.2 percent of those players in college would be asked to come to training camp in a typical year *if* they were the only people invited. In reality, veteran football players already take many of those spots on the ninety-man roster! Most teams only make 20 to 25 percent of their spots (about 720) available for recent college graduates.

Do the math. That means only 0.8 percent of the 90,136 players good enough to play college level football will even get *a chance* to make a professional team, and most of them will lose their spot to veterans and other rookies.

Likewise, think about an aspiring student who wants to become a bigtime lawyer practicing in one of the most prestigious law firms in the world. If you think about any profession in the world that attracts the very best candidates, this is one of them. However, there is still no guarantee that that student will be able to enter the elite ranks. For example, the top law firms in New York City recruit classes of summer associates to become future lawyers at the firm. Starting the summer of their second year of law school, summer associates are handpicked to serve at the firm doing actual work for actual clients. Those who perform well will be offered a full-time position after they graduate at salary levels that reach $160,000 per year. Not bad for twenty-five-year-olds who have never practiced law a day in their lives!

However, keep in mind that these summer associates are already in rarified air. They are most often from the top 10 percent of law schools in the country. They are also among the top 10 percent in class standing at those law schools. These candidates are the top students at the top schools who were good enough in their undergraduate studies to be selected into these schools in the first place. And, according to certain top firms, 90 percent of their students are not considered because they do not make the cut.

What about trying to join Special Operations groups in the military? If someone wants to join a SEAL team in the US Navy, there are high barriers to entry. First, they have to get into the navy itself, so there are various requirements to make sure people are fit to serve before they are accepted. Then there is a minimum eight-week boot camp as an enlisted sailor, longer if you enter as an officer. Every year, the navy recruits about 40,000 new people to join the service, and about 50 percent at one time or another express an interest in joining one of the teams. That means they are placed in a pool of slightly more than 380,000 other eligible candidates.

This number plummets quickly. While half of new recruits may say they are interested (while still wearing their civilian clothes and with a full head of hair), their perspective and expectations change quickly once they are in the service. They still show quite a bit of interest, but due to limitations based on their physicals, aptitude, and other requirements, only about 6 percent of all active duty sailors end up even eligible to apply.

Even if you are among the 6 percent—which means you are more qualified than 94 percent of all other sailors—you are still not among the elite. Think about that for a moment. If you grabbed a group of one hundred people who were good enough to serve in the US military for a living and were better than ninty-four of them, you still are only barely qualified.

To enter the pipeline, you must complete eight weeks at Naval Special Warfare Preparatory School, twenty-four weeks at Basic Underwater Demolition/SEAL (BUD/S) Training, three weeks of Parachute Jump School, and then finish twenty-six weeks of SEAL Qualification Training. If you fail any required tasks at any of these schools and do not meet their standards, you are done. So-called high performers had better be ready for the reality that only about 25 percent of the people who start the training can finish it. Let me repeat: only one-quarter of the top 6 percent of individuals in the most effective military force in history will finish the training and pass through the minimum selection criteria to become part of the elite. Then they have to do what it takes to stay there.

❧

In the end, it is up to performers to perform. They have limitations, but they have choices, too. It is they who get the thrills of victory and endure the agonies of defeat. Therefore, given the same pressures of time, environment, competition, and finite resources, the performers who succeed most noticeably will be those who don't forget to look up every now and then (art), refocus and perfect their approaches (science), and practice more deliberately (grit).

Finally, let's not forget that high performers need others to help them perform their best. Whether this is in the form of competitors, coaches, or dependable teammates, no one truly reaches the winner's podium (and stays there) alone. High performers use managed competition to constantly reset their expectations and do more than they ever thought possible.

Throughout the rest of this book, we will talk about how high performers use coaches and teams to improve their results. We will also introduce the proven methodologies of training that ensure the highest levels of achievement in any domain.

HOLDING A WHISTLE DOES NOT MAKE YOU A COACH

"The best way to inspire people to superior performance is to convince them by everything you do and by your everyday attitude that you are wholeheartedly supporting them."
—HAROLD S. GENEEN

"Each person holds so much power within themselves that needs to be let out. Sometimes they just need a little nudge, a little direction, a little support, a little coaching, and the greatest things can happen."
—PETE CARROLL

"Most people get excited about games, but I've got to be excited about practice, because that's my classroom."
—PATRICIA "PAT" SUMMITT

"There are two ways to do something: the right way and again."
—ANONYMOUS NAVY SEAL INSTRUCTOR

The blessing and curse of working with people who are the best at what they do is that, many times, they are not doing the best they can do. Many of us leaders, managers, and coaches are charged with making these people perform at a higher level. Leaders inspire confidence, managers guide results, and coaches develop people. While all three roles are necessary to run a productive organization or team, it's the coach's role to develop better performers.

We've explored characteristics of high performers and how they need to balance the elements of art, science, and grit particular to their domain and craft. They also need coaches to help them.

PAT SUMMITT'S COACHING GENIUS

If you are an NCAA women's basketball fan, you know the University of Tennessee's Lady Vols. This team has won more NCAA national championships than any other women's program in any sport. The Lady Vols have also made it to the national semifinals, the Final Four, twenty-four times in thirty-eight years. Suffice to say, a betting person would put money on this collegiate powerhouse to add yet another trophy to the case in Knoxville, Tennessee.

This statistic becomes more impressive when considering that, in college basketball, players leave every four years. Teams are constantly changing, which means that the stars, chemistry, and flow you count on one year can completely change the next. Teams that build dynasties have one thing in common: great coaches. At the University of Tennessee, that coach was Pat Summitt.

Summitt, a great player in her own right, started at University of Tennessee-Martin and later became co-captain of the United States Olympic basketball team. Her lasting impact—on players, the sport, and coaching as a profession—came after she retired as a player. However, Summitt's road to greatness wasn't a smooth one.

Summitt was a twenty-two-year-old graduate assistant when she was suddenly thrust into a major university head-coaching job. The existing coach had quit. Summitt was barely older than some of her players, and the job was far from glamorous. She washed uniforms, drove the players to games in a van, and even slept in opponent's gyms from time to time. Her first two years were full: she coached, completed her master's degree, and prepared to play in the 1976 Olympics. Summitt was a driven person, and her players soon found out what that meant for them.

After winning the silver medal in the Olympics, Summitt dedicated herself to full-time coaching. Within two years, she had begun running up impressive winning records, soon establishing the Lady Vols as a perennial powerhouse.

Over the course of her coaching career (1974–2012), Summitt set records for most Final Four appearances, most tournament wins, and most total wins (to name a few). She is also notable as a coach who made sure that every single player who completed her eligibility also completed her college degree.

All of them.

No one is this lucky. This success over decades, with hundreds of players, and against dozens of opponents comes from an established philosophy, system, and process thoughtfully designed to maximize individual performances. All of her players were highly recruited; they were some of the best at what they did. After they joined her team, Summitt had to make them the absolute best at their game and improve upon that performance daily. That is the essence of coaching.

When it comes to people's feelings, Summitt's personal style has been compared to that of General George Patton. She used icy stares, headshakes, and a raised voice to make her points. She had only to point to the rafters of the basketball arena where all the championship banners hung to remind her players that adhering to her system and methods were the key to success.

Summitt insisted on mastering fundamentals and countless drills. She planned for every situation and scheme the Lady Vols might face from an opponent. She simulated real-life game conditions. She insisted that players reflect on what they were doing well and identify their deficiencies, demanding continuous improvement to fortify those strengths and eliminate weaknesses rather than accommodate them. While she was obsessed with winning, Summitt included losing in her philosophy:

"I have a love/hate relationship with losing. I hate how it makes me feel, which is basically sick. But I love what it brings out. It forces our players and coaches to improve and to make better decisions. Only through adversity do we arrive at a more complete perspective and understanding of the game."[1]

Even though Summitt's job was winning basketball games, she understood failure's proper place in the big picture of life. She insisted her players sit in the first three rows of their classes and said that a class was always more important than a game. She believed that her players' dedication to bettering themselves over the course of their lives was the most important aspect of her coaching role.

Summitt also understood that her own learning was never complete. She constantly reviewed other college and professional coaches' styles. She adopted their defensive schemes, practice drills, and offensive plays. She realized that, to get the best out of her players, balancing the art, science, and grit of her own performance as a coach was crucial.

After thirty-eight seasons, Summitt retired in 2012. She'd been diagnosed with early onset Alzheimer's, and on June 2016, the disease took her life.

Summitt's legacy is secure in many ways. She has records that many believe will never be broken. She helped hundreds of players get degrees and grow from awkward teenagers to successful women who would be ready to meet the challenges of career, family, and life. Perhaps her biggest legacy will be from what she did for coaching. At least forty-five of her former players, about a third of the total players Summitt coached, have become coaches themselves, sharing their knowledge from youth to professional leagues.[2]

These former players will be passing on pieces of Summitt's style and philosophy, helping others achieve greatness just as Summitt helped them realize their potentials.

Coaching lasts. Great coaches last forever.

THE GOOD, THE BAD, AND THE AVERAGE

Take a moment to recall the worst coach you ever had. Do you have the mental image? Most of us picture someone with a whistle, wearing bad polyester pants, and barking out orders and random barrages of criticism. This coach believed bad performances were best remedied with punishment: wind sprints, withholding water, or publicly ridiculing offenders in front of their teammates. Most will never forget them . . . but not because they made anyone better athletes.

Now, think of the best coaches you ever had. You probably remember their name, and thinking back on them causes you to smile. Playing for them might not have been a walk in the park, but there was a method to their approach. Toughness and support were administered equally. They demanded the best from you and were able to get it. You regarded these coaches as mentors and positive influences on multiple areas of your life. They made you a better performer, a better person, and a better influence on others.

Coaches have this lasting impact. Out of the many people who populate a child's life, teachers and coaches tend to be the ones remembered. We are readily influenced and most vulnerable in these formative, early years (and in formative phases of our adult lives). Whether we encounter coaches in sport, business, or other areas, they positively—and negatively—push us, maximizing or snuffing out potential. When you think of the bad coaches, your memory of how they looked, what silly things they said, and how they acted may be almost cartoonish. When you remember the great coaches, you remember the lessons, support, and sense of confidence derived from unlocking capabilities that would characterize your entire life.

Bad coaches only want wins. Great coaches want to create winners.

Now, think about an average coach you have had, someone who wasn't that bad or great. Perhaps that coach was adequate, sometimes even very good. Can you remember a name, recall a face? Probably not. These "simply OK" coaches performed their task but left no lasting impact. At that point in life, mediocrity may have been acceptable. Once we focus on areas that ARE important, however, there's no room for merely adequate. We must have great coaches.

Great coaches are the difference between generating a win and becoming a perpetual winner.

LEADING, MANAGING, AND COACHING

Leaders are neither born nor made. At too many organizations, leaders seemingly appear out of thin air. Young go-getters with promise become hard-working members of a team. They start down a progressive path of promotions and create a reputation, mostly on their own, based on results, work ethics, and skills, becoming known as people with great potential. The boss asks them to serve on some key committee or task force, and they are then known as a rising star. Then, one day, the boss's boss needs someone to be in charge; someone should step forward. The rising star doesn't notice that everyone else immediately took one step backward. Uh oh.

Now this up-and-comer is head of a team, division, practice group, or geographic area and suddenly responsible for delivering products and services, supervising others, and building a growing and profitable business. These responsibilities simultaneously require a leader, manager, and coach. While that rising star was being promoted based on individual contributions, none of this work prepared them in any way for being responsible for another's performance. *Being a great individual performer does not mean success as a leader, manager, or coach.* When you are in charge, you have to master all three domains (leadership, management, and coaching) and you may have to leave your old domain (whatever got you the promotion in the first place) behind.

Many people will mistakenly blend leadership and management or debate the proper definition of each. Vineet Nayar, founder of the Sampark

Foundation and former CEO of HCL Technologies, stated that the difference is that "management consists of controlling a group or a set of entities to accomplish a goal. Leadership refers to an individual's ability to influence, motivate, and enable others to contribute toward organizational success. Influence and inspiration separate leaders from managers, not power and control."[3]

> **Leadership inspires confidence. Management guides results.**
> **But coaching develops people.**

People in charge are expected to produce new business, increase revenue, and secure higher profits. Many leaders fall into the trap of thinking that by managing results they are concurrently coaching their people to develop and sustain business. Thus, they assume a command and control approach that emphasizes the inspecting and auditing aspects of management without any of the guidance of true coaching.

Successful coaching is dependent on the proper approach and attitude about creating better performers. Coaching is particularly hard for rising stars to accept. They must suddenly rely on the efforts of others instead of the yoke they used to proudly wear on their own backs.

WHY DO HIGH PERFORMERS NEED COACHES?

It is a fair question—why in the world would the greatest talents in their domain need a coach? If they are the best in the world, what can a coach or anyone else possibly add to their status?

Let's first address this question by defining coaching:

Coaching is the art, science, and grit of repetitively helping others become better than they were yesterday.

"Coach" is a verb. It implies action and present tense. It's also a noun. However the word functions in language, "coaching" isn't happening if the person being supported isn't improving. In fact, don't get too tied up in the title; "coaches" may also be called mentors, teachers, advisors, instructors, and even parents. The defining characteristic of coaching is whether the performer improves. Progress comes from interactions between a performer and their coach and as a result of the coach's planning, counseling, and monitoring of the performer's results.

Frankly, it would be hard to find a performer or leader at the top of any field who has not used (or is not currently employing) a coach. Even the best reach plateaus where they become content and confident in their achievements. Plateaus can quickly lead to complacency and arrested development. Research has shown that avoiding complacency is an essential component of success. Coaches accelerate the process of learning new skills, offer critical and candid feedback, and show performers what is needed to perform at their next level.[4]

RESISTANCE TO COACHING

However, some performers do not want candid feedback or to be pushed. They have reached a comfortable level of performance and are content to remain there as long as possible. Insecure performers may feel they are already operating at a level beyond their actual ability and fear incompetencies might be "discovered." Another reason why some above-average performers are resistant to coaching is that they feel they don't need help. Having completely mastered one domain, these performers assume the other domain couldn't be as difficult. Finally, in some organizational cultures, performers who reach out for help may be perceived as weak and unable to maintain success on their own.

While all of these are understandable reasons to resist formalized, persistent coaching, it is almost unheard of for performers to reach the top of a specific domain without a coach. When you are already in the top tier, the difference between where you are and where you want to be is infinitesimally small. The coach's job is to monitor and manage that gap for the performer.

We've talked about Usain Bolt, the fastest sprinter to set foot on planet Earth. Glen Mills, a legend in Jamaican speed coaching for decades, has been Bolt's coach since 2004. Bolt looks to him for guidance both on and off the track. "He has always made the right decisions for me," said Bolt. "He is a guiding light in my career, and he has shown me the way to improve myself both as a person and as an athlete."[5]

About fifteen months before winning her first Olympic gold medal, swimmer Katie Ledecky's coach, Yuri Suguiyama, completely overhauled Ledecky's stroke. He'd noticed that her unique body mechanics, including a better than average hip rotation, would support a "gallop" stroke. The gallop stroke, more common among male swimmers, is so named because one arm takes a longer stroke than the other. Suguiyama also helped her revise her kicking style. This responsive coaching pays off; Ledecky has *never* lost a major international meet.[6]

Eric Schmidt, Google's former chief executive officer, was once told by one of his board members that he needed a coach. Schmidt was already the leader of arguably one of the world's most successful companies, so he was taken aback by the suggestion. At first, he saw the suggestion as an affront to his achievements and a suggestion that he was not doing as well as he should. Later, he realized that this was not a punitive suggestion. It was a tool to make the best even better. After a reluctant start, Schmidt acknowledges that everyone needs someone to watch, observe, ask questions, and see themselves as others do.[7]

Contrary to what some believe, top business performers actually *do* want coaching. Seeking it out, though, might not always be their idea (21 percent of the time, someone else suggested coaching). In a 2013 Stanford University study, almost all CEOs said they were open to being coached; only 33 percent of them, however, actually were.[8]

There is clearly a disconnect regarding coaching that appears to be discipline related. Domains such as performance arts, sports, and other team-related activities have culturally accepted the idea of coaching as an acceptable method for performance enhancement. Business, finance, law, and medicine are usually less likely to utilize coaching due to the individually oriented aspect of these professions. In all cases and no matter the discipline, coaching resistance is usually based on three things: culture, receptiveness, and coaching quality.

Culture is extremely important to coaching success in any organization. If seeking help and requesting feedback is looked upon as weakness, they will be shunned. Elite performers find the top to be an exceptionally lonely place, and they are often expected to be responsible for their own success. However, no one would argue that it is against the best interests of the board, management, employees, customers, stockholders, and vendors for the top performers to be successful. If coaching has been shown to improve the performance of everyone, including the elite, the culture must embrace it.

Therefore, steps must be taken to make coaching an acceptable and even mandatory practice for all top performers—and *not* when one is failing. Coaching should be introduced during high-growth mode, and it should include as many performers as possible. It can also help performers accelerate uphill during hard times. Thus, coaching is of the utmost strategic importance for any organization that seeks the greatest return on all investments.

Receptiveness to coaching is critical. Ironically, many top performers have reached elite status thanks to an elaborate network of coaching and support. Their parents spotted their natural gifts and then hired tutors or private coaches. They later went to specific schools or training camps due to the faculty or coaching staff. People constantly pushed and provided them feedback until they "made it" to the big time. Then, suddenly, they stopped needing coaching (in their opinion). To stay on top, these high performers started relying on past accomplishments, raw talent, and status (their selection by a great organization, being surrounded by outstanding performers, and so on). They are no longer "coachable."

Professional coaches often lament potentially great performers who, because of their resistance to coaching, will never reach their potential. These players lack *coachability*—a willingness to take feedback and critique from others and then act upon it to improve performance.

Expert August Turak boiled coachability down to five key characteristics:

1. Humility
2. A bias towards action
3. Purity of purpose
4. Ability to surrender control
5. Faith in the unknown[9]

The common thread here is that performers must accept that they cannot do it all on their own. Coaching and performing are two different domains, and no one can competently manage both while simultaneously being the subject.

Organizations have a responsibility to encourage coaching, just as the individual has a responsibility to be coachable. The coach has a responsibility, too: to work in the best interests of the performer and deliver improved outcomes. When great performers have the proper resources and still fail to improve, that's not a performance problem. It's a coaching problem.

Many of the problems related to poor coaching come from leaders and managers who *think* they are coaching but are not actually affecting their followers' performance in a positive manner. Ineffective coaching is usually found in a few common manifestations. Perhaps you'll recognize someone in your organization (or even yourself) in these descriptions.

SIX FALSE COACHING PERSONAS

Preachers

These leaders stand in front of an individual or group and proclaim the direction to be taken, importance in following, and gains derived from following their vision. They state the expected results and communicate full confidence that all will carry their own weight. Preachers expect that the power of their words, indefatigability, and boundless charisma will inspire effort. The shared end goal is the motivation for success. However, as soon as the preacher leaves the room, no one knows what to do next.

Good coaches inspire. They place a vision of success in performers' minds. Performers take a leap of faith to follow coaches into new ways of thinking, acting, and winning. Like good coaches, preachers appeal to the heart, and this is a critical part of success. However, inspiration and vision alone do not equal coaching.

Drill Sergeants

Drill sergeants believe that no one will work as hard as needed unless they are constantly being pushed. In many cases, Drill Sergeants believe people are soft and that they won't find the business the team needs nor work as hard as they did when they were younger. The default position is that the key to success derives from more effort and greater difficulty. Drill Sergeants usually tell people to try harder and put in more hours.

Good coaches hold people accountable for their effort and intensity. They check that performers are doing what is required for them to improve. From time to time, Drill Sergeants push people beyond their self-limitations. However, driving people into the ground day in and day out is not coaching.

Reminiscers

These coaches talk about how they used to do things. They expect everyone to basically become their clone, mimicking what worked for them in the past as they rose through the ranks. They believe if everyone would just do things that worked before, success will appear in the future. You will hear phrases such as "back in my day" or "when I was getting started" included in a long-winded trip down memory lane. Not only did this coach walk to work uphill both ways; the Reminiscer lived in a simpler, more genteel time while doing it.

It's true that past successes and wisdom can help a performer who needs coaching. However, unless this type of coach happens to own a time machine, much of that advice is irrelevant. Good coaches know that current competitors are totally different, rules may have changed, and what worked thirty years ago in almost any domain is not as applicable today. Looking back to the past and sharing what helped someone succeed gives perspective. However, it is not coaching.

Backseat Drivers

This type of coach never fully lets go of any opportunity to direct other performers. No one will do the right thing without their guidance, so Backseat Drivers micromanage every part of performance. They make performers memorize processes and scripts and get upset when those are not followed to the letter. They frequently act as "player-coach," skeptical that winning can happen without their direct involvement. In sport, when people are not performing well, they want to run onto the field and show "how it's done." In business, they take over and handle all the difficult discussions and meetings because the stakes are too high to trust an employee to do it correctly.

Good coaches, who are experts in a domain and channel that knowledge into coaching, are great assets to any performer. They fully realize their role is not to be the best performer. The coach's role is to help others succeed, which cannot happen when performers are never trusted to learn and improve on their own. Being able to perform at a high level can generate respect from people, but it is not coaching.

Monday Morning Quarterbacks

Monday Morning Quarterbacks spend most of their time critiquing efforts and results after the fact. They point out what people should have done or what *they* would've done in a similar situation. These armchair critics only see what went wrong and may obsess over specific details; often, because these items were never mentioned in planning or preparation, those mistakes may seem overblown to the performer. Most coaching attempts come across as negative feedback and may be accompanied by some form of punishment, revoking of rewards, or verbal lambasting.

Frustration often arises when the coach doesn't believe that performers or employees are doing exactly as instructed. This coach neglects to see that performers had not been properly prepared for certain situations or did not know how to adjust when the situation did not follow the coach's "perfect" plan. Exceptional coaches know that feedback and reflection are critical to improving performance. They also know that, when feedback and reflection *aren't* linked to an ongoing enhancement plan, it is not coaching.

Bean Counters

These cerebral coaches spend all of their time tracking metrics, numbers, angles, hours, dollars, trend lines, and any other science- and math-based measurement they can get their hands on. They champion a manufacturing approach to generating higher performance: volume, intensity, six sigma (quality improvement), or lean (eliminating wasted steps).

They use formulas, technology, and modeling to predict performance improvement. They grade past efforts. They communicate in very specific and precise ways. This type of coach tells a sprinter to come out of the blocks with body at a 44-degree angle and shins at a 24-degree angle and expects performers to know exactly how to do it. When the performer fails to follow through, they're frustrated. They figured out the perfect method—why won't the performer just do it?

❧

Technology and hundreds of years of research have allowed coaches to share best practices and techniques. They must not forget they are dealing with *people*, not robots. Humans have variances to deal with, emotions to manage, and limitations to how much they can do. Perfection of technique, eliminating wasteful effort, and modeling the ideal effort have their places. However, when focus is on detached measuring and monitoring of facts instead of on tools to help people improve through a systematic, incremental approach, it is not coaching.

Many performers and organizations instantly envision people who fit these personas. Some of them are closely related to each other.

Bean Counters and Monday Morning Quarterbacks are obsessed with numbers, plans, scripts, and smooth trend lines. They despise variance and surprises. All performers, in their minds, are interchangeable, if only they would all just follow the plan. Reminiscers and Backseat Drivers cannot let go of being a performer; they want to do it themselves and don't understand why performers can't simply copy their efforts. Their own past success is their only blueprint for the success of others. They may not count the numbers, but they have a gut feel for what works. Preachers and Drill Instructors think people need to be inspired and pushed or they won't do anything for themselves. They believe that people have to be extrinsically motivated and rewarded if they are to ever achieve greatness.

One common characteristic of all the false personas is an insistence on managing one aspect of the process of performance improvement instead of viewing it in a holistic manner. Ineffective coaches are just monitoring the desired end product (success) and, when there is a gap in achieving that success, they have just one or two intervention techniques to manage the process (development).

The ideal coach should be able to use some of the traits of the above personas and incorporate a variety of techniques and methods at appropriate stages. It is perfectly acceptable to be tough on people when needed, but this cannot be the only method. Sharing past experiences is helpful, but they are not always applicable to new situations. There may be times when you have to step in, but if you always do so, you have become the performer and not the coach! Remember, the word "coach" should not be viewed as a noun. It is active. And what we are stressing here are the actions of the coach. Successful coaches continuously improve the individual performer. If responsible for a team of performers, they may have an overall infrastructure that supports all of them. But that infrastructure does not eliminate the need for each performer to be coached in a specific way. If coaching is handled properly, success will be the natural manifestation of efforts.

WHAT MAKES A TRUE COACH?

Most leaders talk about end results and vision. They may offer a general path for "how to get there," but this path is often lacking step-by-step details. It would be like people trying to convince their neighbors during the

California Gold Rush (1848–1855) to pack up everything they owned and head to California to seek their fortunes. They would talk about the possibilities, the limitless rewards, and chances for a better life for their families. "Head West, young man!" is their call to action. But a true leader would also accompany them all along the way because, after a few weeks in a wagon, enthusiasm would be sure to wane. A leader keeps people going by focusing on what is ahead.

Managers spend the majority of their time inspecting and auditing. Inspecting involves monitoring activity and approaches, while auditing is reviewing performance after the fact. A manager in the gold rush example would calculate miles per day, average repair times, food consumption, and return on investment per settler. A manager optimizes performance by looking backward at what has occurred and trying to improve results.

> **Leading and managing are the beginning and end of the performance development process. The middle portion is coaching.**

ASSESSING THE PERFORMER

True coaches look at each performer and coaching situation to ask the following questions:

- What is the desired end result?

- What performance is needed to reach that result?

- If the performer is not yet capable, what performance gap should be addressed?

- What causes and factors create this performance gap?

- What strategies, tactics, and interventions will narrow that gap?

- How will performance plans be managed and monitored?

- At the end of training, how will the performance plan be evaluated? How will the gap between actual and desired performance be measured?

- How can the program be periodically adjusted so that performance gaps continue to decrease?

⚘

Any domain shares this process. Coaches address performance gaps between actual and desired results, shrinking the functional reserve. You can't accomplish this without a great coach.

These assessment questions are part of a systematic process known as the Human Performance Improvement (HPI) model.[10] Developed by the Association for Talent Development (ATD), HPI is a systematic process that focuses first on results, not needs, wants, activities, or efforts. It is a combination of multiple disciplines: organizational development, analytics and evaluation, instructional systems design, management, behaviorism, and programmed instruction. HPI was designed to help the corporate and professional worlds improve organizational performance, but its lessons can be applied to any coaching situation.

HPI has a simple, circular model: identify goals; ascertain and quantify the gap between actual and desired performance; identify causes for the gap; develop and recommend specific solutions; evaluate the results. This process, designed to raise potential, shrink functional reserves, and adapt to new demands, continues ad infinitum. Since competition, conditions, and situations are always changing, performance gaps will always need to be addressed.

(6)

THE OCTANE HIGHPER
COACHING MODEL

As we know, improvement for a performer without a coach, instructor, or teacher is usually a very time consuming, frustrating, and expensive game of trial and error. Individuals and organizations can spend countless hours and dollars on unproductive activities and approaches. We discussed earlier how setting goals, modeling others, and engaging in basic training methods raises performers' potential, not their actual performance. The net result: if improvement occurs, that improvement is by sheer luck or at a high cost that cannot be sustained over time or when conditions change.

However, a high-performance coach can bring best practices to the table and identify the critical fundamentals that can be incessantly repeated. These coaches help design programs to push people beyond their current limits so they do not plateau. They manage competition and dynamic simulations to get the most out of their performers. This shrinks the functional reserve—the largest portion of the performance gap—and improves results.

The Octane HighPer Coaching model consists of five key elements: fundamentals, situational planning, simulation, reflection, and continuous improvement.

Like HPI, the Octane HighPer Coaching model is an ongoing process that emphasizes the art, science, and grit of high performance and allows for periods of feedback and review to fine-tune continuous enhancement of the program.

START WITH SIMULATION

We are first going to give special attention to the third element, simulation. This element is by far the most important aspect of coaching, but it is often the most neglected in domains where engagement doesn't put lives, property, or careers at stake. However, when results count—and you may only get one chance—simulation, regardless of domain, is always the most critical coaching component. It identifies gaps and evaluates performance in the most realistic way possible, guiding coaches and performers as they continuously achieve and maintain high performance.

Some believe that simulation is a more advanced stage of coaching that should only be introduced after a period of training, drills, and practice. However, we believe that conducting simulations is essential throughout the performance improvement program *including at the beginning, when followed by immediate reflection between the performer and coach.* (A more detailed description of the specific method, *reflective coaching,* will be described in detail in the next chapter.) Even if there is limited risk involved or plenty of time to prepare, simulation should happen immediately to ascertain performance gaps created by skill weaknesses and self-imposed limitations. Effective simulation shows the performer's exact level of operation.

Obviously, if the skill to be coached is learning to fly a plane, we are not going to recommend learning how to land the hard way (on a very hard runway). Computer programs and other exercises can simulate tasks without introducing undue risk. Likewise, new lawyers or law students would not conduct an actual closing argument in a murder trial when an actual client's life is on the line. They would practice in the comfort of a conference room at their law firm, with people playing the roles of judge, client, and opposing counsel. Business executives trying to land a multimillion-dollar client should not be learning on the job when such a deal could make or break the company's year; they should be simulating closing complex deals in a training environment until ready to go into the field.

However, in all cases, simulation should be conducted in a safe, yet real-istic, environment to establish a baseline of performance necessary to begin working on the individual skill components to improve over time.

Whole-Part-Whole

This technique is championed by USA Rugby, the national governing body for the sport of rugby union in the United States. The Whole-Part-Whole method involves some very basic instruction followed by immediate immersion into a simulated event. Mistakes and experimentation are to be expected and encouraged! After a period of time, the simulation is ended and performers can ask questions. Coaches give feedback about what they thought were the more challenging aspects of the simulation; this identifies fundamentals to work on and future situations to plan for. Coaches then work with the individuals on improving specific skills (e.g., passing, catching, alignment, etc.). After practicing and integrating key skills together, the simulation is run again to see how performance has improved and what gaps remain.

While this coaching method is based on sport, it is used in many high-performance settings where performers need to develop the ability to think and rapidly adapt to changing conditions.

Let's say business executives wanted to improve their ability to win multimillion-dollar deals. You could start by having them read sales books or attend training sessions. However, how would you know where they should start and what areas they need to improve? You need to start with the simulation. In this case, you offer the executives ten minutes of instruction and a basic description of a client conversation. Someone plays the client role (a demanding one), and the simulation begins. Most likely, the executives will not do exceptionally well. After fifteen minutes, the simulation would be paused and the executives and observing coach would discuss what happened. They both may agree on areas that need improvement: public speaking, handling price objections, and rebutting false claims by competitors. These are the fundamental skills and situations they would need to work on to address the performance gap. When the simulation is run again, the executives should do much better. They should gain confidence and evaluate where their performance gaps still exist.

This simulation-evaluation-improvement cycle defines the Whole-Part-Whole coaching method, which is the core philosophy of the Octane HighPer Coaching model. Improvement always starts with simulation, a recurring element throughout the performers' ever growing mastery of their domain.

The Opening Simulation: Scrimmage

The best coaching should always start with an introductory simulation, known as a scrimmage. Only afterward will the coach proceed to the other elements of the Octane HighPer Coaching model.

Scrimmage is defined as "a practice session or informal game between one or more teams." The word has its origins in the late Middle English word *skirmish*, which means a "confused struggle between players." That is why we chose scrimmage to describe the critical opening simulation and periodic evaluations designed to ascertain how individuals and teams perform in an informally structured event that mimics actual competition. The scrimmage is a type of simulation, but it has a specific purposes and limitations.

PURPOSES BEHIND TRAINING SCRIMMAGES

- Evaluate and rank talent

- Assess specific skills and abilities

- Judge performers' handling of pressure

- Observe decision-making capability

- Allow for innovation and creativity

- Introduce unknown situations and scenarios

- Test limits with fellow competitors and colleagues

LIMITATIONS

- Informal setting with modified rules and resolutions

- Controlled, reduced intensity and duration

- Unfamiliar and uncomfortable situations and positions

- Lower reliance on plans and standard procedures

- Reduced incentives and rewards for winning

- Identified weaknesses and strengths

As shown, many characteristics of the scrimmage differentiate it from other training methods (including full-scale dynamic simulations, which will be detailed in-depth later in this book). True dynamic simulation replicates the conditions of the actual competition so closely that it is almost impossible to tell the difference between the simulation and the real thing. The opening scrimmage's main goal is to determine the participant's present performance level in an event that has a more simplified structure and less formal rules than the real thing.

Think about the first day of tryouts for the women's US national soccer team. The players arriving in training camp have already established themselves as great college, professional league, or even World Cup players. However, hundreds of these prospects are now vying for one of the twenty-three slots on the roster. Coaches and trainers will conduct physicals, run some drills, and administer other skill-based tests. As soon as possible, though, coaches will split the prospects into teams to start a controlled scrimmage.

This is not like a true game simulation. The two scrimmaging teams have not gelled as a team yet. In fact, they are competing against "teammates" for roster spots! Coaches may periodically stop the scrimmage to give feedback and change the conditions to suit the evaluation process. Players hoping to make the team must demonstrate their abilities, show willingness to work as a team, make good decisions under pressure, and demonstrate how they react to unknown conditions and competitors.

After the opening scrimmage, coaches will have gathered a basic profile of each player's strengths and weaknesses. They will meet individually to offer feedback and get perspective on what each player needs to work on to generate a mutually agreed upon performance plan. Over the next few days and weeks, they begin more detailed testing and work to determine if physical or behavioral coaching can improve performance gaps. Coaches may run more scrimmages to determine if any of the players deserve to be a member of the final twenty-three-player team. In the end—as well as in the beginning—how each woman performs in a game situation will be the final arbiter as to who makes it and who doesn't.

Likewise, in a business or non-sports discipline, coaches can run an initial scrimmage to see how people with at least some form of familiarity with the task or skill perform in a controlled setting. For example, as a coach, you may be trying to help lawyers, doctors, or tech entrepreneurs develop new clients for their businesses. They are expert practitioners in their craft (e.g., law, medicine, writing code), but finding new sources of revenue is not an innate skill. It is a domain to be mastered. To kick off a training program, you would gather together these smart experts, offer some basic instruction, set expectations, and start running a scrimmage.

Now, let's be frank. These performers, especially the senior executives at the organization, are going to hate this approach. They will say these sorts of things:

"Wait a minute! You haven't taught us anything yet!"

"Let me watch a couple of other people first."

"I don't need to do this. I already know how."

"I'm an expert in X. This can't be as hard as that, so we don't need to go through all of this nonsense."

"How can we do this when we haven't completed the training?"

"No."

Remember, high performers have been used to being the best at what they do since they were young. They have been told they are special, and their lifetime of being selected, promoted, and applauded reinforces this perception. The last thing they want is to be put in a situation where they might look foolish or inept. However, metaphorically throwing them in the deep end of the pool is the best way to see how well they currently swim.

Coaches who lean more toward training to solve every performance issue may think this approach is overly harsh or risky. However, they should think through the realities of the scrimmage. First, the situation is safe. There is no risk of losing life, limb, or liberty. Second, the scrimmage allows us to see how people perform at their current level and identify any performance gaps. Third, and most importantly, many of the performers may *already be doing this task on a regular basis.* They are probably not doing it as well as they could, and that is exactly the point of starting a coach-managed performance enhancement plan.

In the earlier example, the same people who are resisting the opening scrimmage today are the very ones who go see a potential client tomorrow and ask for a big contract, discuss a crucial engagement, or deal with an important matter. They try to do their best without first training or watching other people. They are going to wing it. In essence, they are conducting scrimmages with real prospective clients! As hard as it is to believe, many performers would rather screw up a meeting with a client by themselves than screw a scrimmage up in front of their peers. Coaches who spend too much time teaching concepts and not enough time simulating real situations are doing their performers a disservice.

While an argument can be made for learning by "just going out there and doing it," winging it is an exceptionally risky and expensive alternative to controlled simulations. There's a reason that pilots and astronauts don't train that way. I think you can figure out why.

In short, the scrimmage is a controlled, limited simulation used to evaluate current skills and identify individual performance gaps. A properly conducted scrimmage has the following benefits—

SCRIMMAGE PAYOFFS

- Identifies specific traits and tendencies for each performer
- Individualizes performer plans, instead of working with generics that may be too remedial or advanced
- Uses realistic environments to better predict real results

- Provides constant feedback, reflection, and performance ownership

- Shows baseline performance measurements and demands continuous improvement

After the scrimmage is complete, it is important to debrief. Performers should be mentally exhausted from applying developed (and underdeveloped) skills in a new setting. After some reflective group feedback and individual meetings, performance gaps have been established and agreed upon. Then the coach will develop plans to improve performance.

Now it's time for the coach and the performer to get to work.

7

REFLECTIVE COACHING

"In my early professional years I was asking the question: How can I treat, or cure, or change this person? Now I would phrase the question in this way: How can I provide a relationship that this person may use for his own personal growth?"
—CARL ROGERS

"By three methods we may learn wisdom: First, by reflection, which is noblest; second, by imitation, which is easiest; and third, by experience, which is the bitterest."
—CONFUCIUS

"Without reflection, we go blindly on our way, creating more unintended consequences, and failing to achieve anything useful."
—MARGARET J. WHEATLEY

When you think back to all of the coaches in your life, you'll note wide variations in their styles and techniques. As we identified in the false coaching personas, some like pontificating, some like yelling, and others like to take you for a stroll down memory lane to reflect on their glory days. This may be somewhat effective for coaching children or people at their very first job, but it is the completely wrong way to coach adults and people with advanced proficiency. Imagine your favorite sports stars, talented neurosurgeons, or lawyers who argue before the US Supreme Court on a regular basis. Now imagine their reaction to being "coached" by someone yelling and carrying on about a supposedly subpar performance and how this superstar needs to listen to them if they ever want to be the best they can be. You could sell tickets to that show because it would certainly be entertaining.

When it comes to adults, especially those who are already in the upper levels of their domain, coaches must use a different approach. The most common traits associated with ineffective coaching have a similar theme: they are focused on the opinions, experiences, and preferences of the coach. The next steps and answers to improvement for high performers come from within the performers themselves. The coach's job is to ask the right questions, identify gaps, and gain mutual agreement about next steps. This is the essence of reflective coaching, the key to gaining the last few percentage points of excellence that take high performers from *good* to *great* to *elite*.

BAD COACHING CAN BE WORSE THAN NO COACHING AT ALL

Let's imagine that we had just finished a simulation, and it did not go well. Everyone was taken through a scrimmage to determine their initial skill levels and performance gaps. Everyone was drilled incessantly on fundamentals. Every performer was taught situational plans (what to do and when to do it). However, everyone just fell to pieces during the simulated event. Now the coach has to talk to the performers about what happened.

Think back to the false coaching personas we discussed before. How would each of them most likely handle this serious discussion?

Drill Instructor: "Well, it looks like no one is listening. I guess you slackers are going to sit here all night and practice until you get it right!"

Bean Counter: "I need to do some analysis on what happened and see the trend lines. Once I do, we will have a meeting about this."

Preacher: "You have got to want it more than they do! I know you are capable, and you have to dig deep into your heart and soul!"

Reminiscer: "Back in my day, we did it totally differently. You people have it easy compared to what we used to do."

Monday Morning Quarterback: "Oh my goodness! What were you thinking when you did that? What a horrible decision! Let me tell you what you should have done."

Backseat Driver: "I cannot believe this. That was terrible. I'm going to show you the right way to do this, so watch closely. Let's see if any of you can keep up with me."

I expect most readers were chuckling, shaking their heads, or reliving an unpleasant memory as they read these ineffective, yet common, attempts at coaching. As we mentioned before, there is a time and a place for each persona's unique characteristics, but each in isolation is not coaching.

We have talked about how coaching is defined as applying the art, science, and grit of repetitively helping others become better than they were yesterday.

Keep in mind that performance gaps get smaller and smaller as people improve, and it becomes harder and harder for performers to squeeze out those last percentages of excellence.

Now that you have thought about how the false coaches would handle a bad simulation, let's imagine how performers who are already pretty damn good at what they do would react to those comments.

Reaction to the Drill Instructor: "Who does he think we are? A bunch of kids? I work my butt off every day."

Reaction to the Bean Counter: "You have got to be kidding me. She is going to stick her nose in a spreadsheet to try and figure this out? You do that. I will be out here in the real world."

Reaction to the Preacher: "Hey, guess what? I don't need a lecture on commitment from you. When was the last time you tried this?"

Reaction to the Reminiscer: "That's great, but unless you have a time machine, that does me no good whatsoever."

Reaction to the Monday Morning Quarterback: "Oh, *now* he tells me. Thanks, but that's not real helpful. What do we do now?"

Reaction to the Backseat Driver: "Oh, here we go. Let's watch her try to impress us. I hope she doesn't pull anything."

❧

When working with high performers, bad coaching can be worse than no coaching at all because of negative effects on their attitude, demeanor, and commitment. Coaches who are regarded as peers can quickly become seen as rivals. If a superior, coaches can be looked upon as patronizing or authoritative, and the coach might well get them fired. Critiquing someone's current level of performance is always a challenge. Critiquing someone who already has more ability and potential than most people could ever dream to possess is much harder and must be handled delicately. Defensiveness, making excuses, and deflecting blame are all natural reactions. That's why it's incredibly important to establish high levels of trust and respect between the coach and the performer. High-performing adults cannot be treated like children, or they will start acting like them.

When it comes right down to it, coaching is a form of learning education that is designed to improve results in a specific domain. However, most coaches' learning theories and styles date from their youth. Coaches who have not been formally trained look back to the people who coached or taught them when they were developing a reference point on best practices. This is a rational and completely normal behavior.

However, there is a major problem with this reality. Teaching adults, especially high-performing ones, is not the same as teaching children or novices.

The word *pedagogy* refers to the principles and practices associated with the teaching and instruction of children. Some of its roots actually come from theories of animal-based learning, where tasks are regimented, specific, and reinforced through simple positive and negative rewards. This is absolutely not how to train adults, and certainly not how to work with high performers! Can you imagine a coach telling their high performers they would be treated like an insolent child or a stubborn ox to improve performance? Good luck with that.

In contrast, *adrogogy* refers to methods and theories related to adult learning and instruction. It emphasizes why and how things are taught (process and outcomes) instead of what (content and subject matter) is taught. Malcolm S. Knowles developed the theory about differences between teaching adults and children in the late 1960s. He wrote extensively about the main concepts that distinguish adult learning:

- Adults learn through experience, and mistakes are expected.

- Adults need to know *why* they are learning something.

- Adults learn best when there is a sense of urgency and applicability of the knowledge to solve short-term issues.

- Adults need to be involved with the planning and conducting of their own training as well as their own evaluation.

- Adults prefer problem solving and task solving versus content awareness and memorization.

- Teachers and coaches of adults should be collaborative, not authoritative.

- Learning should be self-directed and conducted in an emotionally safe environment.

- Adults want the freedom and autonomy to experiment and be creative.[1]

❧

The concepts involved in teaching adults are quite different from what many people normally associate with how we "get people to perform" or learn new things. We may have been willing to get yelled at on our high school swimming team or as a student in law school, but accomplished adults will not put up with that. Coaches who do not grasp this concept will fail almost all of the time because the coaching relationship *must* be one of partnership and collaboration.

While the coach must maintain control of the learning structure, pacing, environment, and progress expectations, it is the performer who actually owns the most important factor: the results. Coach and performer are *equals* with different roles to play. How they communicate in a partnership of equals is known as *reflective coaching* and it is a critical component of the coaching process when we want to facilitate continuous improvement.

Coaching should be a dialogue between partners of equal status. The performer does not sit and listen as the coach critiques, tells them what they should have done, and gives tips and tricks for next time. The coach should not feel less worthy due to not achieving what the performer can do. Both have their own expertise, so they meet as peers with different talents and a common purpose. If anything, the coach should do most of the listening, probing for details, and encouraging the performer, who should do most of the talking.

WHAT IS REFLECTIVE COACHING?

One of the benefits of conducting an opening scrimmage followed by subsequent training and drills on fundamentals, situational planning, and simulations is that performance gaps become readily apparent to everyone involved. If you have rational performers who genuinely want to improve and talented coaches who want to help them do so, there is a clear, smooth path to continuous improvement. That path is paved with the practice of *reflective coaching*.

Reflective coaching is a collaborative, purposeful, and results-oriented discussion. It is characterized by the coach asking the performer questions so that the performer and the coach can agree on desired results, confirm the actual results, identify reasons for deficiencies, and agree on next steps to enable continuous improvement.

Let's break the definition down into its components.

- First, the coach and performer are working together with a common process and end goal in mind. No matter whether this is coaching related to a particular drill, competition, event, or overall development, a specific objective is addressed.

- Second, the coach asks questions to lead the performer down a personal road to resolution. By asking questions instead of giving advice, the coach transfers ownership of the gaps and solutions to the performer.

- Third, four key points of reference are established:

Continued on next page . . .

- what was supposed to occur

- what actually occurred

- the reasons for the differences

- what should be done to do better next time

These components identify the performance gap, and the performer must concur on these points, or they will derive no benefit from the coach's directions for improvement.

We can find many examples of this method of coaching, instruction, and assistance in various disciplines and fields. The defining characteristic that makes them all comparable is the coach's use of questioning to lead performers to find the solution for themselves.

PROVEN EXAMPLES OF REFLECTIVE COACHING

Socratic questioning is used in many areas as a technique to analyze, probe, and explore problems and test perceptions as well as assumptions. It is most commonly associated with the study of the law, where professors challenge students' knowledge by continually asking questions that challenge students to clarify their positions. It is meant to be an exhaustive process of eliminating unfounded suppositions and exposing deficiencies in reasoning or knowledge. While movies and TV have characterized this method as the dramatic, gut-wrenching humiliation of students in front of their peers, this is not the true spirit of the method.

Some academics argue that Socrates himself developed the technique to reinforce his own belief that "I know that I know nothing." But the purpose of Socratic questioning in coaching is to identify gaps in performance and identify how to address them. The object is improvement—not just generating insight. The coach as the questioner must resist the urge to lecture, be systematic in approach, direct the coaching through their questions, and attempt to have the performer generate the solution through their answers.[2]

Client-centered (Rogerian) therapy was developed in the late 1940s by renowned psychologist Carl Rogers and continuously revised as it gained prominence in the field of psychology and counseling. It is still one of the most popular theories of counseling and therapy in use today. Initially, it was called *non-directive therapy* due to its belief that the answers to solving an issue lay within the client, not the therapist. The therapist directs the discovery through questioning.

Rogers stated, "A person cannot teach another person directly; a person can only facilitate another's learning," and "A person learns significantly only those things that are perceived as being involved in the maintenance of or enhancement of the structure of self."[3] This belief that the therapist (or, for our purposes, the coach) is a guide and partner in the process of improvement is a key feature of the theory. The safety, openness, and trust established in the relationship between coach and performer are critical to progress.

Rogers identified three core conditions that must be in place for positive change to occur. First, there must be *congruence* between coach and performer. Being genuine and transparent is critical if the performer is to open up and talk about experiences. Second, the coach must display *unconditional positive regard* for the performer. This shows that the coach is not being judgmental and values the performer's judgment and validity of perceptions regarding experiences. Third, the coach must demonstrate *empathy*. Performers must feel that the coach understands where they are coming from, their individual challenges, and the unique set of circumstances they face.[4] When performers feel they can safely share their views and feelings without judgment or penalty, they will own their problem as well as the solution to it.

US Army After Action Reports (AARs) are tactical tools used by the military to debrief participants after a project, training session, or event. Any leader or observer of performance can conduct an AAR. In fact, informal AARs are frequently conducted by junior officers and non-commissioned officers (most of whom are in their early twenties) due to their simplicity, structure, and near universal applicability.

Read the definition of the AAR from the US Army's "A Leader's Guide to After-Action Reviews":

> "An after-action review (AAR) is a professional discussion of an event, focused on performance standards, that enables soldiers to discover for themselves what happened, why it happened, and how to sustain strengths and improve on weaknesses. It is a tool leaders and units can use to get maximum benefit from every mission or task. It provides:
>
> **Candid insights** into specific soldier, leader, and unit strengths and weaknesses from various perspectives.
>
> **Feedback and insight** critical to battle-focused training.
>
> **Details often lacking** in evaluation reports alone.
>
> **Evaluation** is the basis for the commander's unit-training assessment. No commander, no matter how skilled, will see as much as the individual soldiers and leaders who actually conduct the training. Leaders can then better correct deficiencies and sustain strengths by carefully evaluating and comparing soldier, leader, and unit performance against the standard. The AAR is the keystone of the evaluation process."[5]

The AAR is a shared learning event, where emphasis is placed on what was supposed to happen and what actually happened. Through discussion and asking questions, all participants see issues from different points of view and take ownership of the solution. Disagreement is encouraged, because no two people will share the same experience. The objective is to learn and retain information that can be applied in the future to facilitate continuous improvement.

Any AAR has a very basic structure and utilizes open-ended questions to get at the core issues related to improving performance:

- What was supposed to happen?

- What actually happened?

- Why did that happen?

- How do we improve the results in the future?

COMMON PRINCIPLES OF REFLECTIVE COACHING

The previous examples have five common principles, which are listed here:

- Answers for high performance reside within the performer.

- The coach/therapist/mentor/instructor's job is to direct the performer through structured questions to find those answers.

- Coach and performer are collaborative partners with different roles to play.

- Identifying gaps between what is desired and what has been achieved is critical.

- Goal: Put in place tactics and strategies to continuously improve performance.

Creating tactics and strategies to continuously improve performance is the purpose of coaching, and reflective coaching is the method to get high performers to move from being very good to becoming great.

Socratic questioning is an example of how extensive examination can drill down to core issues and challenge comfort zones. Client-centered therapy teaches that the answers lie within the subject and a coach's job is to get them out in the open and agreed upon by both parties. AARs are an illustration of how a simple structure can be used to organize coaching into a systematic process that ties back to corrective measures.

THE WHYS AND HOWS OF REFLECTIVE COACHING

All of these approaches can be combined to create reflective coaching methodology that works well within any industry, domain, or field. The questions might vary greatly based on what the performer's role or activity might be, but the method remains the same. At the end of this book, you will find links to resources that will help you build your own reflective coaching tools. However, coaches know their performers, and they know what must be achieved for those performers to become great. They should start with a conversation, be genuinely curious, and let the performer talk. You will see some example conversations below.

> The tools, methods, and philosophies of reflective coaching hold
> the keys to improving performance in adults—especially those who
> want to be in the top tier of their domain.

These keys can be used in any industry, field, or discipline after a simulated or actual event. Upon reflection and agreement, the coach can then identify fundamentals that need to be worked on, adjust situational plans that need to be revised, and prepare a simulation to retest and validate any corrections at an individual, team, and organizational level. Once the reflection is complete, it is up to the coach to make sure that the performance enhancement plan is developed, followed, and reexamined—again, again, and again.

Applying Reflective Coaching in the Real World

Reflective coaching can happen in any performance-related field. I've included the following conversations that utilize its five principles to bring home reflective coaching's power.

Example 1: Business Post-Sales Call Setting

Coach: Let's take a few moments and debrief on your visit to that prospective client. I want to hear how you think it went and talk about next steps. Hopefully, this will make it easier the next time we meet with them.

Performer: OK, as long as it won't take too much time.

Coach: It won't take long at all. Tell me about the client visit. What did we hope to achieve?

Performer: We went in there to talk to them about our corporate services and retain them as a new client.

Coach: Was that the goal? Who established that?

Performer: Well, I assumed that was the goal.

Coach: Do you usually go into a first meeting and expect to come away with new business? How often does that happen?

Performer: Not often. Well, actually never.

Coach: Why do you think you took that attitude going into the meeting?

Performer: I guess this was a really big opportunity, and I really needed it.

Coach: What actually happened?

Performer: We did a great presentation, but their head of the department wasn't there. They were also really taken aback by our high costs.

Coach: Was she supposed to be there?

Performer: Well, this was a big meeting, so I assumed she would be.

Coach: Why was it a "big meeting"? Did they have anything at stake?

Performer: No, but we did.

Coach: OK. Tell me about the high costs issue. Why do you say they were taken aback?

Performer: They looked shocked when we showed our rates during the presentation. However, you would think they would understand why the rates are what they are after seeing the information we showed them in the presentation. All of our offices, experience, recruiting from the top schools—those cost money!

Coach: What did they say during your discovery and development phases that led you to believe they wanted to see about all of our offices and expenses?

Performer: Well, it's a standard presentation deck.

Coach: You said you wanted to close a deal. Why did we not achieve what we wanted?

Performer: I don't think we did a good job confirming attendees or finding out who the decision makers actually are. Also, we can get very defensive when discussing our fees, and I think it makes us look arrogant.

Coach: Let's back up a minute. Why were you going into a first meeting and expecting a quick decision that would have required all of their top people there?

Performer: We were told to get out there and generate new business. We worked hard on this one. It was our big shot.

Coach: You still haven't told me why the *client* would have thought it was an important meeting that would have required all their decision makers in the room. What would have changed that?

Performer: We didn't know much about what they were working on and what they sought in an outside partner such as us.

Coach: Why didn't we know that?

Performer: Frankly, we didn't ask. We were too worried about the presentation deck looking impressive.

Coach: Why do you care so much about the deck?

Performer: I don't like how cutthroat competition has become in this industry. I hate it. I just want to show what we do to them, have them be impressed at what we can offer, and get back to work.

Coach: Do you think the client can sense that you are just trying to get through this as fast as possible and get back to work?

Performer: Maybe.

Coach: How do we improve this type of visit in the future?

Performer: We need some additional training on how to handle price negotiations. I also think we need to practice more before we go into a meeting. Whenever price comes up, we freeze or immediately offer a discount.

Coach: Is that it? When is the next time you think we will have a meeting like this?

Performer: We don't get these too often. So, we may need to do something to keep sharp in between the big meetings.

Coach: Would you be willing to dedicate some time to simulating meetings like this on a regular basis? If so, I will set it up.

Performer: Sure. Let's do it.

Coach: Excellent. I will provide you with some fundamental exercises to work on. I also need you to study some of the plans we have with how we have dealt with price sensitive clients in the past. In two weeks, I will schedule a mock client visit to practice. I will be playing the client, so be ready!

Performer: Deal.

Example 2: Post-Training Simulation (War Game) Setting

Coach: Now that the war game is over, let's take some time to talk about what happened and get your feedback on how you think you did. I want to ask you a series of questions, identify any gaps in performance, and come to some common ground on areas for improvement. Hopefully, this will show us what we can work on together to improve our chances of winning when it's not an exercise. Sound good?

Performer: Sounds great.

Coach: Tell me about that war game and your team. What did your team hope to achieve?

Performer: We were going head-to-head against two other teams playing our competitors trying to win the business of a simulated client.

Coach: Was the defined goal of the exercise to win business?

Performer: I thought so.

Coach: Do most of your calls work that way? Do you often close new business with just one visit?

Performer: Not usually. Getting commitment to move forward with us exclusively is probably just as good.

Coach: What actually happened?

Performer: We lost badly. The judges rated us at the bottom, which I don't agree with at all. We were definitely the more prepared team and had a much better flow to our presentation.

Coach: What did the judges say about why they marked you so low?

Performer: We relied too heavily on information about our organization and telling them what we do. The other teams focused on client needs.

Coach: Why do you think the other teams decided to focus on the client needs and we didn't?

Performer: Probably because they didn't *have* very much information about the competitors they were pretending to be. They don't actually work there, so all they had was what was available on their website!

Coach: So, do you see that as an advantage or a disadvantage? Would you have done the same thing?

Performer: Probably. Also, it seemed to work.

Coach: That makes sense, and I understand where you are coming from. It is a challenging exercise! How would you and your team improve on your performance in the future?

Performer: We need to get better at researching the business issues of our clients, practice our public speaking, and have multiple options to present when we are in competitive situations. We also need to do more of this type of practice before we lose a client opportunity like this for real.

Coach: That can't be a new idea for you. Why didn't you do it that way the first time?

Performer: I think it's just easier talking about our own organization. I don't want to look silly in front of a client. I worry about them asking me a question about one of their business issues that I am not an expert on.

Coach: Would learning more about their industry and how to deflect direct challenges be helpful? What if we came up with a list of drills we could work on together as well as likely scenarios some of your peers have encountered? Would that help?

Performer: Maybe, if we practice them and see if they are realistic.

Coach: Understood. We want to make sure it feels natural for you. I will put together a plan, and we can get the team together for another go at this in a less public arena. Sound reasonable?

Performer: It does. Thanks!

Example 3: Sports Setting

Coach: OK, take a knee and relax for a bit. With the game still fresh in our heads, I wanted to walk through how it went compared to how we prepared. I want to ask some questions to get your point of view of how you felt out there and what you saw. Afterward, we can start thinking about practice structure for next week. OK?

Performer: OK, coach.

Coach: I think we can both agree that was an interesting game. What was supposed to happen?

Performer: We were supposed to win the game. We were supposed to crush them here at home.

Coach: Any reason you were so confident?

Performer: The team has really started coming together. We had a great week of practice, and I felt really good.

Coach: What actually happened?

Performer: We lost in the last two minutes of the game. It is very frustrating. I'm really angry with myself and some of my teammates.

Coach: Angry at the result or how we played?

Performer: Both, of course. But how we played really aggravates me. We are better than that. I am better than that.

Coach: Let's just talk about your point of view for now. You can open up and tell me what affected you personally. You said you felt good. What changed?

Performer: When things started going badly in the last part of the game, I started trying to take it all on myself. I was pushing hard since no one else seemed to be doing so.

Coach: I noticed that. Why did that happen?

Performer: We were not prepared for losing one of our key players, dealing with their defensive scheme, or running out of steam in the last few minutes. I kept trying to push my teammates, but they kept missing key plays, dropping balls, and committing penalties.

Coach: You mentioned that you were really tired. Were they?

Performer: I am in pretty damn good shape, so they had to be, right?

Coach: Do you tend to make more mistakes when you are tired? Does rushing when you are already tired make it harder for you personally?

Performer: It does, and I see where you are going with this . . .

Coach: You tell me. What do you think happened?

Performer: I started rushing the plays, everyone was gasping for air, and our play deteriorated. That is on me.

Coach: Hey, I get it. You are a leader. I can see myself doing the same thing. So, how do we improve on our performance in the future?

Performer: We need to be in better shape so we don't let fatigue beat us. We also need to spend more time watching film and preparing for how we deal with having to change our game plan when the situation changes. I also need to work on my own coolness under pressure.

Coach: We all have those days. Let me get with our conditioning coach for some things to work on that will help. We will also work on more situations at practice where we are pressed for time, but we will insist on no mistakes. On Wednesday, we will run against our scout defense squad to practice it in a realistic way. Sound good?

Performer: It does. Thanks Coach. Sorry about today.

Coach: Don't give it a second thought. You will get better. You always do.

You will notice that the conversations seem very natural and may vary based on the situation or activity. There isn't a script. However, all utilize the five principles of reflective coaching. The answers reside within the performer, and it is the coach's job to use questions to find those answers. The performer will only open up to the coach when there's established trust and respect between partners. Once performance gaps between what is desired and what is achieved are identified, the coach and performer mutually agree to an improvement plan.

REFLECTIVE COACHING STRUCTURE

Reflective coaching uses a combination of questions, collaborative discovery, and systematic approaches to formulate action plans. Keep in mind that reflective coaching, discussed in this Chapter, should follow a general structure meant to generate dialogue between partners. Let's revisit those important steps:

- Reach agreement on reason, approach, and payoff (why the coach and the performer are having this discussion)

- Discuss what was supposed to have happened (goal)

- Discuss what actually happened (actual result)

- Reach agreement upon performance gaps (the difference between goal and actual)

- Reach agreement on why the performance gap occurred

- Agree on how improved performance can be achieved next time (corrective action)

- Determine action items for coach and performer (program for improvement)

- Plan for reassessment (measurement of performance gap after corrective action)

This structure is not meant to be a script or rigid in its application. It is meant to guide a conversation that will feel natural and genuine. If a conversation sounds canned, the performer may perceive a lack of empathy or authentic concern. However, with a familiar structure and approach each time there is a coaching conversation, performers become used to the process. They anticipate the coaching discussion and become better at sharing and receiving feedback.

HIGH-PERFORMANCE COACHING NEVER STOPS

Coaching should occur in the moment and as close to the time of the performance (real time) as possible to ensure that the event, project, or competition is still fresh in the coaches' and performers' minds. Some "coaches" schedule discussion sessions on their calendar for a certain time every week—especially if coaching is not their full-time job. For example, ineffective sales managers would "coach" their account executives every Friday from 1:00 to 3:00 p.m. instead of right before or right after a key sales call. Ineffective flight instructors would have monthly reviews instead of immediate post–flight simulator briefings. Ineffective litigation partners coaching young associates on their trial performance would coach at their regular, biweekly catch-up meeting instead of having that meeting standing right outside on the courthouse steps.

Many coaches will ask, "When is the best time to coach, and how much time should I spend doing it?" The answer is pretty straightforward. **If you are in charge of other's development—making them better at what they do—then the majority of your time should be spent actually coaching.** It may be five minutes here and twenty minutes there, but coaching should be under way constantly. Every moment can be a coaching moment.

In an actual event or competition, time cannot stop for coaching. But if there's a break in the action, coaching should occur immediately. If it is a training or practice activity, coaches should stop performers periodically to ask what they are trying to accomplish, what they are actually doing, and so on.

Remember that coaching is not just pointing out deficiencies and giving advice. It is about agreeing upon deficiencies identified by the performer and having them come up with the solution. The coach owns the structure, style, and ensuing performance enhancement plan. The performer owns the execution of the plan and the expected improvement if they follow it.

It would be very logical to think of a coach who uses reflective coaching as an advisor, mentor, or even therapist. All of those people make use of questioning, mutual respect, collaboration, and a results-based structure to identify gaps in performance. The difference is that, as long as continued high performance is expected, coaching can never stop. You may eventually stop seeing a therapist or learn all you can from a mentor.

> **It does not matter whether you are an individual performer, leader, or CEO. If you are competing at a high level and your environment and challengers are keeping you from realizing continuous improvement, you will always need coaching. Coaching never, ever stops.**

A.J. Hawk is an exceptionally gifted and intelligent athlete who served as the captain of the defense for a Super Bowl champion team. However, he is very coachable. He knows that he always has room for improvement, situations are always changing, and he needs coaches who will treat him with respect while being very candid. Here's what the NFL football great had to say in our interview.

Q: What about coaches at this level? Top performers in all disciplines could say, "I don't need a coach. They're not as good as I am and never were." So, why use coaches when you are all in the top 0.1 percent already?

A: I think everybody can get coached, no matter what your job is. I love how, as you get older in the NFL, your relationship with the coaches can change and grow. It's more of a back and forth relationship and good positive conversations than there are negative ones.

You always know though who your coach is. You know that he's the boss. You have to respect that. Now, the coach who loses that is screwed. They're going to lose the team. If you have someone that you just feel is not a great coach, you don't have a lot of respect. You feel almost like it's us against them, players against that coach, and that's just not a good thing.

When a coach feels like he wants to do whatever it takes to make you the best player possible and to make the team the best team possible, you have something mighty special. When that happens, you'll bounce all kind of ideas off of each other.

But, when you mess up, you have to admit to it. The coach is going to let you know in front of everybody that you messed up, and you can respect that as a player when a coach does coach you.

I think everybody, whether they admit it or not, wants to be coached. You want to have somebody there that's going to be able to either affirm that what you're doing is right or let you know when something is wrong. It may be tough to handle at the moment, but we all know when we do something wrong, whether you want to admit it or not. You have to have that coach there to kind of guide you in the right way and let you know when you get off track.

If someone is just surrounded by yes men, it's terrible. It's the worst thing that could ever happen. You have to have people that can check you and get you back on track when you do or say something wrong, whatever it may be.

Some people may wonder why someone in the top 1 percent of performers in an elite organization such as the NFL needs continual coaching. Shouldn't he know all he needs to know? Hawk understands that he never will. He continues challenging himself, but he needs others to challenge him as well. His teammates will push him, competitors will push him, and coaches will push him. This is why he will be a champion in anything he does, even after his football career is over.

If a Super Bowl champion linebacker for one of the most storied franchises in sports appreciates the value of continuous, reflective coaching, shouldn't you?

8

FUNDAMENTALS AND SITUATIONAL PLANNING

FUNDAMENTALS. CONSTANTLY.

Police officers go to the shooting range. NBA basketball players shoot free throws. World-renowned cellists practice musical scales. Navy SEALs rehearse entering unfamiliar rooms. Business executives practice disaster and crisis communications. These professionals continue to engage in the rigor and repetition of practicing the basic components of their skills. They are already the best in the world at what they do, but they still continue to go through the exercises that they started with when they were novices.

This might not surprise you. You might even say, "Of course they do! If they didn't, they would get rusty! Use it or lose it!" So, why is it in some fields we stop practicing fundamentals after we master a domain at a certain level?

Performers who cease practicing fundamentals are common in fields that do not have terminal consequences for failure. It is rare to see accountants practice debit/credit reconciliation before engaging in a multimillion-dollar business analysis. It is uncommon to see CEOs practice negotiation techniques before going out to sign a big deal. You would be hard-pressed to find practicing lawyers or doctors going through some of the rudimentary exercises they worked on in school in between big cases or patients. This is because doing so is optional and accepted as such. It is not because they shouldn't be constantly working on the fundamentals of their craft.

Would you want an armed police officer who had not been to the gun range in ten years in charge of rescuing hostages in tight quarters? Would you give the final scoring opportunity in a sports match to the player who didn't make time to practice shots? Would you want the airline pilot flying your family's plane to be one who thinks practicing how to handle high-wind landings is a waste of time?

**When risks and consequences of failure are extremely high,
how we train and prepare is not up for debate.**

Performers in any domain who want to improve abilities and retain their gains must practice fundamentals: This is the grit of high performance that must be completed by the performer. There is no shortcut or magic pill. This is not the time to get creative (art) or fine-tune (science). The mind-numbing, repetitive, and tedious activities associated with fundamentals are not enriching or particularly stimulating. They are, however, necessary and non-negotiable. This is why a coach can be a critical part of making sure they are completed: Performers need to have accountability to someone else.

Trumpet master Wynton Marsalis and legendary cellist Yo-Yo Ma often speak about the importance of practice for everyone, including themselves. Marsalis has been performing since he was eight years old, and Ma has been playing for more than fifty. Each still practices scales, basic pieces, and simple arrangements. In their work, *Tackling the Monster,* they outline twelve key elements of practice:

1. Seek out private instruction.
2. Write out a daily schedule for practicing all fundamentals of the instrument.
3. Set goals to chart development.
4. Concentrate when practicing.

5. Relax and practice slowly, then play faster and faster.

6. Spend more time practicing pieces you cannot play.

7. Always invest yourself; play everything with a maximum of expression and you will have fun.

8. When mistakes are made, don't be too hard on yourself.

9. Don't show off when you play.

10. Think for yourself.

11. Be optimistic; you do not want pessimism in your music.

12. Look for musical connections in other things.[1]

Marsalis and Ma are trying to help people become better musicians with these recommendations. However, can you think of any field where this advice would not be helpful? If these performers—the absolute best in the world—still have such rigorous routines involving practicing fundamentals, why don't you?

Performers skip fundamentals for many reasons. First, they can find fundamentals boring. Despite what Marsalis and Ma might say, fundamentals can be as exciting as watching paint dry. Second, high achievers may feel that fundamentals are actually something only for beginners. Once they move past a certain level, they think there is no need to go back. Third, they may think that performing in live settings is all the practice they need. Performers can come up with many more reasons—they all are excuses. The fact is, people who are the absolute best at what they do work on fundamentals. Period.

Novices and Experts

We must note, however, that fundamentals, drills, and routine practice are different for novices and experts. Yo-Yo Ma is not going through a simple G major scale and its seven notes at sixty beats per minute (even though he would probably sound *amazing* at it). That was what he did when he was about four years old. Now, due to his skill level, his scales are exceptionally complex. Though they are still rudimentary drills and activities, scales are meant to reinforce skill at his present level of achievement. This is the same for any domain. Accountants, lawyers, pilots, swimmers, or salespeople all need to be working on fundamentals that are challenging and appropriate for their current level of performance.

Deliberate Practice

Fundamentals can be employed simply for the maintenance of present skill levels. But pushing through to the next level requires a more advanced set of fundamentals known as *deliberate practice,* which we addressed in chapter 3. However, once a performer reaches a new standard of performance, the fundamentals and their corresponding difficulty must advance in congruence with that new standard if the performer hopes to retain, or progress, from that level.

Try this experiment. Go to the driving range and hit a hundred golf balls a day for a year. Apply Marsalis and Ma's principles to your practice routine. On day 366, take three months off. You can play regular golf two days a week, but you are not allowed to go to the driving range. After three months of playing golf only (averaging thirty-six drives a week versus seven hundred), return to the driving range to see if you are as good at driving a golf ball as you were three months ago.

Do we *really* need to go through this fifteen-month experiment to know how it will turn out? Most of us who have ever hacked our way through a golf course know exactly what will happen. Your performance will slip. It won't be bad, but it won't be as good as it once was in that particular part of our game. Maybe we can cover for it in other aspects of the game. We could make excuses. Or we could work on our fundamentals.

Think about your domain of expertise. What aspects you are trying to improve? What's your attitude about practicing fundamentals? You may not care about golf and you may not be flying fighter planes at Mach 2. However, whether the domain is sport, performance arts, business, military, or scrap-booking, performers who want to become masters need to work on their fundamentals. Constantly.

COACHING TIPS TO REMEMBER

- Fundamentals are the primary and underlying skills that provide the ability to perform a task or understand an idea. Fundamentals are specific to the level of skill and expertise.

- Drills and practice are a method to reinforce fundamentals. They promote the acquisition of specific skills or knowledge through repetitive practice.

- Drills are for the reinforcement and retention of previously learned skills. Practice, especially deliberate practice, is performed in a progressive manner to improve skills.

- As performance improves, the drills and activities to maintain that level must get more advanced. To continue to improve, deliberate practice must be employed.

- Coaches should build drills that are specific to the task and typical environment in which the performer would perform. Flawless, meticulous performance is the goal.

- Drills are a type of "warm-up activity" that prepares performers to compete or engage in deliberate practice.

- Coaches should employ deliberate practice that allows performers to learn and stretch their abilities. Improvement, not perfection, is the goal.

Continued on next page . . .

- Steps to properly build a drill:

  ◦ Identify the specific skill related to actual performance.

  ◦ Break the skill into basic, component tasks.

  ◦ Combine a few of the tasks into a series of logically ordered activities, but not so many as to be mentally exhausting.

  ◦ Have a defined starting and end point and expectations of time and speed to completion.

  ◦ Perform multiple repetitions that get progressively more challenging by using time, speed, or other predictable variables with periodic breaks for recovery.

  ◦ Create multiple drills to cover all tasks (in small groups of two or three at a time, if needed) and repeat incessantly!

SITUATIONAL PLANNING

Another element of great coaching is *situational planning*. Because it is historic in nature, it is actually one of the simpler elements to handle. Situational planning is compiling a list of all the probable scenarios that could occur based on a set of conditions. By looking back at what have been the most common challenges, we can then determine how best to handle them in the future. We have the benefit of hindsight, retrospection, and wisdom on our side.

In sports, coaches have playbooks and play cards for assistance on game day. It is not an alphabetical listing of every play. Plays are grouped by situations and conditions. It is the difference between what coaches *could do* and what they *should do* in any circumstance.

In the NFL, coaches have made a science out of how much information they can cram onto two sides of a laminated sheet. Those sheets guide their decisions. There are formulas about how to go for a one-point versus a two-point conversion after a touchdown. There are specific plays to run on third down with eight yards to go versus third down with two yards to get a new set of downs. Defensive calls and schemes vary greatly based on the week's opponents. That laminated sheet is not meant to be static. It might change every week based on the conditions, opponents, and players available—even if the basic principles stay the same.[2]

A.J. Hawk, a student of the game, played for the NFL's Green Bay Packers and Cincinnati Bengals. After a stellar college career at Ohio State University, where he was twice named an All-American player and won the Lombardi Award for best college linebacker his senior year, Hawk was the fifth overall pick in the 2006 NFL draft.

Hawk is a soft-spoken man with a big heart and a soft spot for his wife, three children, and little, yappy dogs. Make no mistake: Hawk is an imposing figure on the field, an athlete who combines power, speed, and extreme intelligence with an uncanny ability to almost predict what will happen next on the field. He also has an incredible work ethic and curious mind, which drives him to improve each year, each game, and each individual practice. One of the big tools he uses to improve—with the help of his coaches and fellow teammates—is situational planning. We interviewed Hawk to get his insight on why situational planning is an essential part of high performance.[3]

Q: Think about how you look at the game, how offensive schemes look, what quarterbacks are doing, the different types of offensive schemes people are running now versus ten years ago. How do you prepare for that?

A: When you're younger, you hear old guys talk about it all the time, how "You've got to watch film. You need to watch film." Coaches will nail it into your head. A lot of times, young guys go in there and they turn film on. They're watching it, but they really aren't. It's like reading a book, and all of a sudden you get through ten pages and have no idea what you've just read. That's what you do when you're younger, and that is definitely what happened to me.

I'm always trying to find a way to get something out of what I'm watching. You can't just put on a game film and just sit there. I would always have to have a point. I think, "I'm going to watch this next fifteen or twenty minutes. I'm going to watch their first drive, first possession of every game in their last six games. I will see if there's any techniques I can get out of that or see what kind of plays they like to come back to."

Also, as I get older, I've started to pay attention a lot more to whoever the offensive coordinator was on the team, because a lot of the coaches in the NFL move around. They bounce around from team to team. Whoever was calling the plays on offense, I always wanted to know if it's something that they're going to come back to. Their playbook is kind of set. They are going to mix and match little things here and there over time. But they have a general scheme that they kind of run, and they take it to whatever team they're at. You can look to know—what does this guy run, what do they like to do in certain situations, or just the play calls.

Q: Do you get to the point where you recognize a situation? Let's say it is third and six. You see a certain lineup, it's a certain time of the game, and you're sitting there on defense going, "They're probably going to run one of two or three things." Does it get down to that kind of level of confidence?

A: You can definitely kind of narrow down stuff like that. We go over that all week, and coaches break down things to show what their tendencies are. At the same time, you've got to not get locked up in thinking this is all that they can do. These are the only two plays that they've ever run here. The second you do that is when they throw a trick play at you or something they haven't shown before.

But, you know, there's a good probability. After the first one or two steps of the running back, how the center or the guards are coming out to block you or what others are doing, that is when you can kind of let it click in and think, "Oh, this is it. This is the play that we knew was coming."

Q: You had mentioned preparing and using film. I think I had heard that you guys actually use things like iPads and Surface tablets now that they can actually give you a three-year history of what the other team has been running as part of game practice. Is that accurate?

A: Yeah, about four years ago, they started putting all of our playbooks and our game plays on our iPads instead of giving you a huge binder.

✢

In a typical NFL game, the offense runs about sixty-five plays. A team might have 300 plays on the books, but the game plan and changing conditions throughout the contest act as a limiter. One of the biggest variables is the other team, who is desperately trying to win. Situational planning allows coaches and players to anticipate the most likely scenarios and prepare all week for the game. They minimize prep time on extremely unlikely situations, practice for those most likely to arise, and develop contingencies for unexpected scenarios.

There's no need to obsess over all the things that could happen because those possibilities are infinite. Narrowing to possible options allows performers advanced practice handling those typical, recurring situations, which improves their performance. This approach for developing high performers and coaching is also very common among other disciplines, such as aviation, military operations, firefighting, police work, and so on (our friends in the terminal consequences business).

Pilots have procedures for engine failure. SEAL teams know how to enter a room in the dark (and what to do if they encounter a brick wall where a door was supposed to be). Firefighters choose to handle a building fire depending on its construction and contents (whether wooden or steel-supported structure, or if it contains explosive chemicals). These are known situations. These performers understand how to handle them. Therefore, the skills required can be anticipated, practiced, and rehearsed, which allows coaches to determine which fundamentals need to be developed based on the expected situations.

Outside of these disciplines, situational planning does not occur as often as it should. Many performers, coaches, and organizations do not plan for anything other than crisis situations. They know what to do if an IT system crashes or a major press outlet covers their organization in a bad light. One of the reasons they know what to do in these situations is based on damage control; these kinds of situations could damage the organization irreparably. In essence, crisis situations are terminal consequences. Thus, responses and procedures for handling critical situations are planned, prepared, and executable in a moment's notice.

What about things we encounter on a regular basis? For example, let's say you're a senior executive at a company in a very competitive industry with exceptionally demanding clients. Do you have situational plans in place for these situations?

- Competitors cut their rates by 20 percent.

- Your biggest client asks for a 20 percent discount (just because).

- Your largest client merges with a company that doesn't use you.

- Your main contact with your client retires.

- You are in a head-to-head competition with your biggest competitor.

- You are in a head-to-head competition with a smaller, unknown competitor (and you are losing).

- A supplier country no longer allows import/export due to geopolitical conditions.

- The company's two top performers left for the competition.

These are not wild fantasies. These scenarios occur every single day in most businesses. And they have probably already happened in the past. *Therefore, there is no reason not to plan and prepare.* You have the historical view: what worked in the past, what didn't, and how contingencies could be improved for the future (situations that probably *will* happen again).

If you are a high performer who frequently uses the line, "I know what I am doing. I have been doing this for twenty years!" but you don't have situational planning in place, you are gambling. You are counting on the fact that you will be able to instantly recognize a situation as it occurs, have the perfect solution in mind, and perform perfectly without prior practice. This outcome is nothing more than wishful thinking. Even if truly outstanding performers could make this seat-of-the-pants response work, how would the rest of your team react? What about support personnel and systems? Will everyone you depend upon be ready in a crisis?

Granted, every situation is not mission-critical. We're not suggesting you create a cumbersome blueprint for any and everything that could possibly happen. However, the situational planning *method* has been proven to help performers consistently do their best by narrowing options and scenarios they can—and must—plan for, practice, and rehearse.

In any scenario, coaches need to determine the situations, best response methods, and instruction needed so *everyone* knows exactly what to do. Review the following example based on the scenario introduced earlier, a common situation with a significant impact on an organization's strategy and response, to see the simplicity (and extreme importance) of planning.

SITUATIONAL PLANNING SCENARIO: COMPETITOR CUTS RATES BY 20 PERCENT

1. Conduct market research on competitor to investigate their financial situation, changes in leadership, or offerings.
2. Conduct a call with vice president of sales to discuss options.
3. Review the financial projections for this quarter with CFO and determine the potential impact of a price adjustment.
4. Work with marketing to determine talking points for sales reps; conduct sales training.
5. Talk with product champions about potential bundling offers, with emphasis on exclusive services company offers.
6. Communicate policy: No sales representatives are authorized to match discounts without VP of sales approval.

Many people reading this have encountered this scenario, but few have planned for it. If an official plan exists, has it been communicated to all performers? If not, and individuals or departments have their own ways of dealing with this type of price challenge, how many dozens of possible outcomes might occur? How, then, would you prepare and train for those dozens of possible outcomes when the same scenario arises in the future? You would accomplish nothing but constant training!

The situational planning scenario we discussed is based on many organizational factors that can vary greatly. How has the company responded to price challenges in the past? Is its product or service the lower- or higher-priced option? Is the challenging competitor on solid or shaky financial ground? Any situational planning should be unique to the individual and organization, taking into account resources, abilities, and backgrounds. However, individualization only goes so far—imagine the chaos and potential for disaster if everyone handled that price challenge in an independent way!

High-performance coaches document, research, analyze, and prepare for common situations that will affect their performers' results. Coaches plan for these situations, put responses in place, and teach performers how to adjust. We know that limiting options allows performers to focus on the most likely solutions, work on the needed fundamentals, and simulate situations so they can prepare for the real thing.

SIMULATION AND WAR GAMES

"The only Japanese tactic that was not foreseen in war games prior to World War II was the use of kamikazes."
—ADMIRAL CHESTER W. NIMITZ

"We have nightmares because our brain is running simulations to put us in jeopardy to see what we'll do or to acclimatize us to that idea that something bad could happen. It's just how human beings are wired because the entire time we were evolving we had to jump quick or the leopard would get us or whatever it was. It's Darwinian."
—JAMES CAMERON

It's impossible to overstate the usefulness and efficacy of simulation as a coaching and performance development tool. Anyone who expects to be fully prepared for real-world challenges simply cannot avoid simulations, models, war games, and other dynamic training methods.

We view simulation and its related applications as the most important element of coaching for great performance. When the consequences matter, all great performers run simulations. Because simulations are often awkward, uncomfortable, mentally exhausting, and physically taxing, many performers avoid them at all costs (especially those who lose). Whether or not the consequences of losing are important enough that you'll use simulations to permanently change training is an individual decision. Domains such as

sports and military use simulations and war games, and more business organizations would be well served to follow their lead. Adopting simulations
encourages best performance by practicing and preparing for the real thing.
Why not use it?

Athletes practice, prepare, and participate in simulated, realistic events
to understand how they and others will react in competition. Boxers use
sparring partners with similar physical and performance characteristics of
their upcoming opponent. Teams have players from their own organization
run through rivals' playbooks while blasting recorded crowd noise to more
accurately replicate expected conditions. Coaches may even change the
rules, the players, and playing conditions to pressure test their plans and
performers' strategies.

Pilots and astronauts log thousands of hours in simulators. They rehearse
fundamental tasks in familiar situations as well as what could go wrong. Firefighters stationed at airports practice putting out plane fires (there's a burned
out airplane fuselage at every airport, just beyond the runway), and SWAT
teams simulate hostage rescues in environments where "bad guys" and "good
guys" are difficult to recognize. US Marines spend time in the Helo Dunker to
practice the art of underwater egress (also known as getting the hell out of a
helicopter after you've crashed in the water).[1]

Political candidates use immersive simulations to prepare for important events that could determine the success or failure of their entire careers.
Presidential candidates in the United States have used simulation for debate
preparation since television became the primary broadcast medium.[2] In 2000,
candidate Al Gore demanded that debate simulations exactly mimic actual
event specifications, down to exactly positioned podiums and adjusted the air
conditioning. Candidate Mitt Romney (2012) faced off against his own staff-
ers, who played the opposing candidate and future president, Barack Obama,
to the point where flashes of anger crept into their tone and demeanor. President George W. Bush participated in more than ten mock debates before

facing the more articulate Gore and candidly stated, "The interesting thing about presidential debates is that I don't think you can ever win them, but you darn sure can lose them."

Feeling brave and a little cocky? You are welcome to tell any of the instructors, coaches, or leaders in these examples, "I do not have time for this. It's silly. I am a professional. I will figure it out once I get there."

Simulations allow performers to test the models created during situational planning and identify possibilities not previously exposed and considered. Tactics and strategies, as well as performers' abilities to employ them, can be "pressure tested" during simulations. What use are highly trained people who fold under stress or disregard situational plans once things start falling apart? As former heavyweight boxing champion Mike Tyson once so eloquently stated, "Everybody has a plan until they get punched in the mouth."

Simulations also show coaches which fundamentals need improvement. Perhaps performers have been through training but emerged with only a superficial knowledge that doesn't survive distraction or disruption. For example, it is much more difficult for a basketball player to shoot free throws when 10,000 college students are screaming and waving banners at her. Shooting straight is a much harder activity when a soldier is freezing and hasn't slept in thirty-six hours. A lawyer trying to win a major, new client is sure to be thrown for a loop when unexpected client demands and a competitor waiting outside in the lobby create pressure.

In all of these circumstances, simulations show which fundamentals are weak and which situational plans are insufficient to handle real-life challenges. This is the only safe, risk-free, learning-based environment to test how good performers really are. Performers can certainly figure it out "on the job" but in these examples, that means losing the game, putting individuals and others at risk, or losing a client worth millions of dollars. Given those circumstances, do we *really* think we should allow our performers to simply figure it out?

As we've said, most people do not like simulations. They produce a grade, threaten social status, expose flaws in thinking, and shine a big, bright spotlight on weaknesses. That is all 100 percent true of simulations, and that is exactly the point in doing them. Like the opening scrimmage (a simplified form of simulation), coaches must use safe practice environments to analyze performance, review plans, and reinforce fundamentals. Wisdom gained and the history of actual performances is incorporated into learning, but simulations let performers practice what has been learned before taking the field again.

If you were a high performer in *any* domain, we would go so far as to say that not simulating key activities—situations that might make (or break) your year (or career)—is malpractice. If the coach and performer are avoiding simulation because they "would rather not know," the problem is attitudinal. If the process of running dynamic simulations is "too time consuming," the problem is prioritization. Do organizations lack the expertise to run them? The problem, then, is with resources.

If this sounds like your organization, team, or personal point of view, performance issues are not likely the result of insufficient training or other external factors. Poor performance is most likely related to cultural issues. The organization, its leaders, managers, and performers are avoiding discomfort and hard decisions. They may have created (or inherited) a culture that does not believe challenging people to test their abilities and reveal areas they need to improve is important. If so, the culture *must* change. There are far too many examples of how and why simulations improve performance to ignore.

However, there is an upper limit to how realistic single-performer simulations can be. For one thing, even in well-designed simulations based on previous circumstances and most-likely scenarios, the rules tend to be fixed. Another item: Simulations can become stale once scenarios are mastered. What if we add another complication? What if another individual or team was trying to outperform you *during* the simulation? Adding an unknown competitor to the simulation with you offers an infinite number of new challenges and possibilities.

WAR GAMES, A SPECIAL TYPE OF DYNAMIC SIMULATION

Today's US armed forces are generally acknowledged as the most capable and effective military organization in the world. While technology and state-of-the-art weaponry are part of the reason, the most important factor is the persistent application of realistic, demanding, and recurring training at every level, from the individual to the largest task force. The most effective training is conducted under duress against a capable and determined adversary. The military branches have all established competitive units (Red Teams) whose mission is to simulate adversarial actions. This is intense, no-holds-barred work, epitomizing the high value of training under duress against a skilled adversary in a realistic environment.

Visiting the US Army's training center at Fort Irwin to watch coordinated infantry and armored cavalry operations is a real eye-opener, as is observing at the US Air Force's Red Flag training facility at Nellis Air Force Base. These high-performance simulations provide tremendous value in training under duress while using realistic simulations and adversarial Red Teams.

So just how is the process of "playing under pressure" applied in the military? Training under duress starts simply, by developing individual capability through emphasis on fundamental skills and teaching performers the art of "situational awareness" of their environment. Once a pre-determined level of individual expertise is attained, the next step is to train as a *team*. This develops camaraderie and trust and teaches the importance of effective communication and coordination of effort. Because the military believes in the enduring principle "if you can't measure it, you can't manage it," carefully designed performance metrics are built into every phase of the training process. Only when teams have achieved and demonstrated mastery of both the theory and practice of their assignments are they deemed ready for the hardest part of their training—a *field* test under pressure, against a skilled and determined adversary, the Red Team.

These dynamic simulations using adversarial variables are known as war games.

Using a Game to Solve a Problem

Imagine a dreary, overcast day in the Pacific Ocean, one hundred miles southeast of Okinawa, Japan. Winds have been strong for the past forty-eight hours, and waves have built significantly overnight. Despite the rough seas, the nuclear aircraft carrier USS *Ronald Reagan* is rendezvousing with a navy cargo ship to top off aviation fuel, ammunition, and other stores needed for her impending deployment to the North Arabian Sea. It's a very tricky operation, especially with the seas this high. The carrier is approaching from astern at twenty knots, while the cargo ship maintains a steady course and speed of fourteen knots. The goal is for *Reagan* to arrive at a position just 140 feet alongside while reducing her speed to match that of the cargo ship. It's then a matter of precise control and maneuvering of the 100,000-ton carrier to maintain this position within twenty feet for the next four hours. The most experienced bridge crews are executing this maneuver and captains of both ships carefully monitor every move. Except for the conning officer's concise orders, there is total silence on the bridge as *Reagan* approaches her position. All realize that, with these large ships so close together, even the slightest error could lead to a disastrous collision. Focus and concentration on the bridge and on the decks below is intense.

Once in position, *Reagan*'s captain orders steel cables to be passed from the carrier to the cargo ship. These cables will support a set of powered winches that transfer pallets of ammunition and other stores back and forth, passing over the large waves generated by the water channeled between the ships. In addition, three twelve-inch reinforced rubber hoses pump aviation fuel to the carrier's storage tanks. It's a carefully planned and choreographed operation. Skill, vigilance, and discipline are required from each of the more than 1,000 members of the carrier's crew.

After four grueling hours alongside the cargo ship, the carrier has received 1,000 tons of ammunition, a million gallons of aviation fuel, and enough food and supplies to last for forty days at sea. The crew heaves a great sigh of relief as the ships break away—the cargo ship heading off for more supplies, *Reagan* and her seventy-five aircraft to potential combat. Depending on the flying tempo, this operation will be repeated about every ten days during the carrier's seven-month deployment. It's a demanding life, but the job always gets done because *Reagan*'s officers and sailors are high performers! How, though, did they ever learn to perform this complicated maneuver? Why not just go to the nearest port to pick up supplies? And how did anyone figure out this was important to do?

Transferring stores between navy ships at sea (a process called *underway replenishment*) has been the standard method of logistical support for carriers and other ships since World War II. Its inception was the direct result of insights gained through a series of war games conducted before the war at the Naval War College in Newport, Rhode Island. The Pacific's expanse and lack of US support bases west of Hawaii presented a complex and formidable logistical challenge for the navy: how to keep ships so far from friendly territory supplied. The solution was to design and build a new class of supply vessels that followed the warships as they moved westward, always at the right place at the right time. This revolutionary concept, a veritable "aha moment" for the navy, still serves as the standard operating procedure today.

War games addressed other difficult challenges. How and where could cargo ships be restocked so that the supply chain always remained intact? How often would ships require underway replenishment to remain combat ready? How many, and what types of ships and airplanes were needed to conduct a successful naval campaign? What role would Pacific allies play in the action? Would the United States invade Japanese home islands or could we blockade supply routes and "starve" their military into submission? And, of course, there was a long list of "what ifs" dealing with unknown Japanese actions and the inevitable fog of war.

Answers to these and other questions required fresh ideas, great involvement and debate among operators, and a much broader view of the future nature of naval warfare. The Newport war games provided the forum to test these questions and served as the catalyst for change that would lead to victory in the Pacific.

So what were the key elements that contributed to the war game's success? Certainly the list includes keen foresight, visionary thinking, team building, inclusiveness, and a compelling need to reduce uncertainty. These same elements can and should be applied by businesses today when contemplating new strategic plans or significant market moves. We will describe how leveraging the power of war games can be used by businesses in just this way in later chapters.

History of War Gaming

As the navy learned in World War II: the more complex the challenges, the more beneficial the war games.

The use of war games began well before World War II. In fact, if chess can be considered a form of war game, the roots of war games can be traced back to the sixth century in India. It's not hard to understand why the military was one of the first adopters of this practice. War games reduce uncertainty and bring clarity to complex problems. They allow the military to test theories without experiencing the horrors of warfare. With nearly continuous fighting among the Europeans in the nineteenth century, it's no surprise that the first recorded use of war games/simulations began in Prussia in 1811 with the emergence of a board game called *Kriegspiel* (War Game). The game became quite popular among Prussian staff and regiments as a tool for developing new battlefield strategies and tactics. More significantly, it highlighted the value of strategic thinking and inclusiveness in the planning process. Much credit has been given to the game as a key factor in the Prussian victory in the Franco-Prussian War and earned Chief of Staff Helmuth von Moltke the moniker of "the father of military war games."

Prussian success stirred interest among the militaries of numerous countries, including the United States. In 1889, the newly established Naval War College incorporated gaming into its curriculum, specifically to gain advantage over the British navy (still considered a potential adversary). The Germans used war games to develop the infamous "blitzkrieg" strategy of rapid and overwhelming maneuver warfare, which had great success in World War II. The "left hook" maneuver General "Stormin' Norman" Schwarzkopf used in the first Gulf War was essentially the same strategy and was gamed extensively before US tanks and troops set off over Iraqi deserts.

Before execution, virtually every modern major military operation is subjected to a form of war gaming. But the military has learned that war games do not always produce a positive outcome. Certain principles must be followed to realize a reasonable chance of success. Use of *factual* information, not assumptions or organizational bias, is the most important. Active Red Team participation is key. This independent, adversarial group finds and exploits weaknesses in strategies, challenging assumptions and "thinking like the enemy." Simply stated, strategists and decision makers look to Red Teamers to provide the essential elements of competition and performance under pressure that make war games effective.

From time to time, military planners and politicians are criticized for being too preoccupied with past military strategies, or "fighting the last war." They develop systems, plans, and tactics based on what they have seen before, and this entrenched thinking can have dire consequences. War gaming helps to prevent such thinking. This phenomenon exists in other fields, such as business or the public service sector. Executives and planners develop long range, three- to five-year strategic models based on their aspirations, goals, and objectives, but these plans may have little connection to reality. Whether the plans hold up over time (and whether they were ever valid in the first place) can be pressure tested using war gaming.

Applying War Games in Business and the Public Sector

While the military is recognized as the earliest adopter of war gaming, other federal and local government organizations have recognized their value. During the Cold War, the first non-military organization to leverage war games as a method to reduce uncertainty and provide policymakers with better analysis was the intelligence community. Since that time, the practice has matured significantly, overcoming many of the inherent challenges (i.e., institutional bias and various government agencies' differing political agendas). The successful operation to locate and target Osama bin Laden was the result of broad collaboration within the intelligence community, who used war games to analyze potential outcomes and address a plethora of "what ifs." The Department of Homeland Security has used war games as a collaboration tool between federal, state, and local governmental agencies, helping to overcome many of the multi-jurisdictional issues faced when conducting anti-terrorism campaigns. In areas where terror attacks are an ongoing threat, US police departments have integrated a form of war games into preparations for high-profile crowd events. Since New York City is one of the highest risk targets, the New York Police Department (NYPD) was one of the first to institute a comprehensive series of games to educate, inform, and pressure test senior decision makers and first responders prior to major events around the city. NYC Police Commissioner Ray Kelly is a particularly strong proponent of the gaming process and described the games as "the only time that we really stretched our imaginations."[3]

It's clear that, within the public sector, war games have improved decision making, enhanced collaboration, and built more cohesive teams. The diversity of government applications has also highlighted how war games can be adapted to a broad range of users and applications.

In contrast to the military and public sectors, use of war games in the business sector is a relatively recent initiative. Driven primarily by accelerating globalization and the dramatic impact of technology on knowledge proliferation, competition, information security, and social interaction, boardrooms are searching for leverage tools and new developments to address the huge degree of complexity and increased ambiguity and uncertainty the business sector is experiencing. More and more business leaders recognize the need to overcome these challenges and deliver better ideas to the market faster than their competitors.

Benchmarking, case studies, balanced scorecards, client relationship management (CRM) software, and the like all have their place, but they lack the ability to leverage knowledge gained by employees who work "on the edge" (closest to the needs and trends of customers). Moreover, these tools do not question strategic assumptions, overcome organizational inertia, or challenge groupthink that often constrains initiative and undermines competitive advantage. In contrast, business war games with associated Red Teams are designed to do just this and have proven their worth for an increasing number of businesses.

Leveraging the Power of the Game

When did you last challenge your organization with a "what if" question? To whom did you pose the question? Were those people the most knowledgeable about your customers and the market involved in the ensuing discussion?

Were managers quick to respond with good answers? Asking tough "what if" questions and developing solid answers and solutions is one of the primary benefits of war games.

Wouldn't we all like to know how our current business strategy would stand up to future challenges? How does rapidly advancing technology affect business? How will changes in demographics and social interaction affect the customer base? Is our operation susceptible to security breaches, and if so, how should we prepare? War games can be the best crystal ball to address tomorrow's issues. They provide a proven method of pressure testing an existing strategy to catch a glimpse of the future.

War games have the potential to improve organizational performance. We've seen that, in both government and private sectors, the games' value is best suited to situations where a significant amount of complexity and uncertainty exist.

Examples of these types of business situations in which war games might have a positive impact include leadership turnover, rapidly changing market conditions, unexpected regulatory restrictions that cause significant internal discontinuities, or new processes and technologies that dramatically alter competitive environments. It's important to keep in mind that, rather than prove an existing idea or concept, the ultimate goal of the games is for participants to learn and gain new perspectives. As Chinese general and strategist Sun Tzu once said, "To know your enemy, you must become your enemy."

Another important use of gaming is to overcome *organizational inertia.* Every organization has assumptions: how business should be run, how to portray itself, how it should be managed, how it should interface with the market, how it should deal with competitors, etc. In today's fast-paced business world, where innovation and agility are increasingly important, strict adherence to long-standing assumptions can often lead to groupthink and organizational blind spots that impede improvement and progress. War games have proven to be successful in identifying these blind spots and providing ways to overcome them.

Two of the least appreciated (but nonetheless very important) benefits of gaming are team building and improved situational awareness. The game provides an opportunity to tap the knowledge and insight about markets and competitors from those who have the greatest interaction with them. These edge workers include sales and marketing people, business development managers, product or service managers, systems engineers, and anyone else who deals with customers or competitors on a frequent basis.

Having these edge workers participate in war games alongside senior managers and staff sends a strong signal of inclusiveness and respect, two conditions that are essential to team building and camaraderie. In addition, insights and information that were well known on the edge but never considered in the boardroom or conference rooms will be gained.

WAR GAME BENEFITS

- Provides an enduring learning experience through storytelling and story-*living*

- Enlightens and strengthens the decision-making process, especially in complex decisions fraught with uncertainty

- Helps overcome organizational inertia, blind spots, and groupthink

- Highlights important "what if" problems and generates potential solutions

- Tests new strategies and ideas under pressure

- Provides a glimpse of the future

- Enhances teamwork and promotes inclusiveness

- Improves situational awareness of markets and competitors

With these benefits in mind, consider how war games can address leadership change, sudden losses in market share (taxis vs. ride share services), new market-disrupting technologies (Blackberry vs. iPhone), new marketing or selling processes (brick and mortar stores vs. online shopping), or the sudden implementation of market-altering government regulations (Congress passing Dodd-Frank financial reforms). These are just a few of the many situations in which war games can improve business.

While war games have proven benefits, success requires a finite commitment of assets, most importantly time and energy. The leaders, middle managers, and edge workers who represent your organization and the market and competitors involved are key parts of the process. Creativity and out-of-the-box thinking should be encouraged and leadership open to innovative ideas and alternative solutions.

FIVE QUESTIONS FOR
POTENTIAL WAR GAMERS

Q: How can war games improve my business?

A: Enhancing creativity, discovering new ideas, challenging assumptions, overcoming organizational inertia, bolstering teamwork, and promoting inclusiveness are among the key advantages you can expect through gaming. War games provide a unique and innovative way for leaders to tap the knowledge and imagination of a larger, more diverse group of people, thereby gaining valuable insights. But war games come with a finite cost of time, energy, and brainpower that must be understood and accepted by the sponsor and the participants. Setting the stage and selling the idea are important prerequisites in making a war game successful. With innovative leaders, imaginative players, and a relatively small amount of administrative support, it's highly likely to reap a positive ROI from war games!

Q: What kind of war game is needed?

A: We've seen this is a tool best employed as part of the decision-making process. War games can be applied to strategic decisions ("where should we go?") and tactical decisions ("how do we get there?"). *Strategic* decisions usually follow significant organizational events, such as leadership change, major disruptions in the market (technology or competition), or unexpected discontinuities in operations (regulations, security breaches). *Tactical* decisions support strategies and address such things like roll out plans, asset allocations, execution timelines, and expected competitor responses. War games can be successfully used in more common, day-to-day tactical situations to reduce uncertainty and pressure test potential outcomes. The good news is that war games can develop better boardroom strategies and conference room tactics. In either case, keep in mind that the greater the uncertainty, the more valuable the game.

Q: Who should participate in war games?

A: As with most things in business, success or failure depends on the quality of the people involved. Players should include leaders and managers involved in the decision being tested, edge workers, respected strategic thinkers, rising stars, and a few outside consultants who know the market well. "Yes" men or women prone to telling superiors what they want to hear should be scrupulously avoided. Focus instead on including participants who demonstrate motivation, experience, commitment, and passion.

The typical war game involves about fifteen to twenty people, including administrative personnel (although more or less can be used depending on the objectives and complexity of the game). Participants are assigned to two "opposing" teams: the Blue Team, which represents your business, and the Red Team, which portrays the market, competition, and inevitable "Black Swans" (those rare

Continued on next page . . .

but potentially game-changing "what ifs" that dramatically alter the competitive equation). The Blue Team is comprised of leaders and managers within the organization who were involved in the decisions for which the war game was designed. Their task: explain and defend their decisions against the Red Team's challenges, alternatives, and "what-ifs." The Red Team is typically made up of edge workers, successful business development teams, and sales and marketing people who are most familiar with the market and the competition. They are the best challenge to the Blue Team's plans and decisions. Outside consultants are often added to the Red Team to provide an independent market perspective and potential competitor response. Rising stars and strategic thinkers can be either Blue or Red but we've found that, generally, the Red Team provides the best learning experience for these "up and comers."

Q: When—and where—should war games be conducted?

A: War games are best suited to coincide with decision formulation, vetting, and debate. These may occur in the boardroom at the corporate level, in conference rooms at lower management levels, or at periodic off-site conferences or retreats. Periodic off-site events, especially when a limited number of senior leaders and managers are present, are particularly good venues. War games provide a unique and interesting "twist" to these events and can serve as a catalyst for discussion and debate at the end of the day.

Wherever the war game is played, audience size is important . . . too big an audience makes the game difficult to manage, too few limits creativity and "out of the box" thinking.

Duration depends on two factors: sponsor objectives and degree of uncertainty. If the sponsor's objectives are to generate new ideas, challenge existing assumptions, or pressure test an impending strategic or tactical decision, the war game would normally last longer. Greater uncertainty requires more analysis and debate. On the other hand, if the primary objective is to send a message to the organization about creativity, teamwork, and inclusiveness, the game could be shorter. Most objectives can be met within a full day. The feedback from players, observers, and sponsors will determine the frequency and venue for follow-on war games.

Q: What expectations should war game participants have?

A: The greatest expectation should be the unpredictability of the results . . . and it's that unpredictability that makes war games enjoyable and effective. We've seen that gaming can be used to analyze and pressure test complex decisions, discover new ideas, send a message on the value of creativity, and strengthen teamwork and inclusiveness. The mere fact that a game is being played signals organizational creativity. You can expect participating edge workers, rising stars, and strategic thinkers to be particularly supportive and eager to carry forward the message of teamwork and innovation.

Not all participants and observers, however, will be positive supporters. Some might perceive the activity as a threat to individuals who already have a vested interest in its outcome. Face it—challenging long-standing assumptions and organizational bureaucracy stirs up a lot of emotion. It's important that the sponsor understands the risks and takes the necessary steps to maintain a positive learning experience.

AFTER THE SIMULATION: MORE REFLECTION

At the beginning of the Octane HighPer Coaching model, we always start with a simulation, and reflection always happens immediately afterward. The best time for performers and coaches to drill into the details is while the memory of the arena is still fresh. Keep in mind that reflective coaching should follow a general structure meant to generate dialogue between partners:

- Reach agreement on reason, approach, and payoff (why the coach and the performer are having this discussion)

- Discuss what was supposed to have happened (goal)

- Discuss what actually happened (result)

- Reach agreement upon performance gaps (the difference between goal and actual)

- Reach agreement on why the performance gap occurred

- Agree on how improved performance can be achieved next time (corrective action)

- Determine action items for coach and performer (program for improvement)

- Plan for reassessment (measurement of performance gap after corrective action)

And then, the cycle begins once again. This reflection on the simulation results in identification of fundamentals that need work, situations that need planning, and future simulations to run. All of this will lead to the performer's continuous improvement, the model's final element.

As stated from the very beginning of this book, if you want to learn how to develop the very best performers, look to the world of the elite teams operating under terminal consequences and emulate their methods and philosophy. Failure is too costly an option, and this mindset leads to specific approaches proven to develop performers and teams that are extremely effective in predicting success in dynamic, fluid situations. Their continual improvement is built on a primary foundation based upon simulation and war games.

Simulations and war games show true levels of performance, strengths, and weaknesses. They reveal where the team and individual have operational gaps, situations that have not been fully analyzed, and fundamentals that need work and refinement. Most importantly, individuals, teams, and organizations can practice and prepare for the worst in a realistic, yet safe, environment.

Coaches don't have to use simulations. Eventually, they discover how good people actually are when they come back from a key meeting, event, or challenge. However, coaches must decide how much they are willing to risk. Is making people feel slightly uncomfortable and challenged worse than losing a big deal, a key client, or an opportunity that comes along once every few years?

Exceptional organizations and their coaches know there is only one answer: Run simulations as much as you can.

STORYTELLING AND SULLY SULLENBERGER

With plenty of sunshine and a mild breeze out of the northeast, January 15, 2009, dawned a cold but pleasant winter day in New York City. US Airways captain "Sully" Sullenberger was on his last day of a four-day flying trip and was assigned to an A320 passenger jet, Flight 1549, from New York's LaGuardia Airport to Charlotte, North Carolina, a short flight pilots generally considered a "piece of cake." Sullenberger and his copilot Jeff Skiles boarded the jet about forty-five minutes prior to scheduled takeoff and began a series of preflight checklist items while the passengers boarded the plane. He decided that Skiles would perform the takeoff as part of his ongoing captain's training.

At 3:25 p.m., the jet lifted off and began climbing to the north over the Bronx. Just before reaching an altitude of 3,000 feet, the jet hit a flock of geese, which caused a "flameout" (a complete loss of thrust) on both engines. Sullenberger immediately took control of the jet and radioed to the air controller that he had lost both engines and was returning to the airport. He quickly realized, however, that he had neither the altitude nor the airspeed to get back to LaGuardia—or any other airport. His only alternative was to put the plane down on the nearest flat surface . . . the Hudson River. But landing a passenger jet with 155 people onboard in the Hudson River in January? Impossible!

Sullenberger deftly guided the powerless jet over the George Washington Bridge and impacted the water near a group of workboats and ferries, which he knew could help in the rescue effort. Although he had never practiced such a maneuver in flight training (or even in a simulator), Sullenberger performed a perfect "ditching" maneuver; the aircraft remained upright and intact as it skidded across the water and came to a stop. He and his crew then proceeded to safely evacuate every passenger and crewmember.

Sullenberger was the last to leave the barely floating jet. The total flight time for US Airways Flight 1549 was six minutes.

⚜

As you read this story, what were you thinking? From a passenger's perspective, you might have thought about how you would have reacted to the sudden emotions of fear and helplessness that must have been pervasive in the cabin. Perhaps you thought about whether you could have quickly found the emergency exits or whether you could have found and inflated your life preserver. Or perhaps you thought about how you would have helped the passenger next to you if he or she were in a state of panic? I bet you learned that paying attention to the flight attendant's safety instructions before takeoff was a lot more important than you'd previously thought.

The story is also a great learning tool for pilots, flight attendants, and anyone concerned with best outcomes. As the pilot, what would you have done in this situation? Would you have tried to return to the airport instead of ditching? How far could your airplane glide from 3,000 feet at 250 knots if you had to execute a 180-degree turn to line up on the runway? What is the proper landing attitude for a ditching? What would you and your flight attendants do after the landing? These are all questions that were widely discussed in pilot lounges and aircraft training facilities around the world, and we are all safer as a result of the lessons learned.

The main point of the Flight 1549 narrative is learning the power of storytelling. While there are many methods of learning, storytelling is nearly always the most effective because it evokes an emotional and psychological reaction to real-life experiences. The ability to imagine yourself in the story transforms you from a mere reader or viewer to an "active" participant, thereby greatly enhancing the learning experience.

Dynamic simulations, including war games, are a step up from the storytelling experience because they involve individuals who are not just hearing or reading a story but are actual players in the narrative. These "story-livers" have the most powerful and enduring learning experience of all.

CONTINUOUS IMPROVEMENT

If we had a working, dependable time machine, we could host one hell of a race. Think back to all of the Olympic gold medal winners since 1896 in the premier speed event: the 100-meter sprint. We could pick the most advanced stadium and track in the world to host it (it would need to be a really wide track). We would pack the stands with screaming fans from all over the world. And it would be the most anticlimactic race in the world. We already know who the winner would be. In fact, many of the gold medalists from yesteryear should consider themselves to be very lucky to attend because they wouldn't even have qualified for today's high school state track meet.

The current world record holder for fifteen- or sixteen-year-olds would have beaten Jesse Owens, the 1936 Olympic gold medalist. Carl Lewis's gold medal performance in the 1984 games would have put him in seventh place, behind Usain Bolt, in the 2012 final (and narrowly in front of Jamaican runner Asafa Powell, who suffered a groin injury mid-race). In the most extreme example, the fastest man in the world in 1896 could have had a *twenty meter head start* and still lost to Bolt.

We have already talked about the prowess and superhuman ability of the current world record holder, Usain Bolt. However, depending on when you are reading this, he may have been (or will be) surpassed by yet another set of fleet feet. *That is the nature of performance. As long as there are competitors, there will be new champions.* In fact, it is safe to say that we can never call someone "the best that ever was." It is more accurate to call current champions "the best of their time."

That rules applies to all of us and in all domains. Whether your arena is sport, combat, flight, technology, business, law, or music, resting on your past achievements and experience only guarantees that, in the future, you will have a great view of your competitors' backs as they run ahead. That is why the last component of effective coaching for high performance is *continuous improvement*. Each day, you are either moving ahead or falling behind. If it matters, it must be measured. If it is measured, it must improve.

Continuous improvement can be defined in many ways, but for our purposes we will use the following definition:

Continuous Improvement is the ongoing, never-ending process of incrementally enhancing a performer's skills, abilities, achievement, and results through the highly disciplined use of cumulative gains, which serve as the new foundation for further development.

Once you see it written on paper, it makes a great deal of sense why continuous improvement is so important to both coach and performer. It also might look very similar to other things you have read about improvement (including in this book's previous chapters).

We have already talked about the incremental gains experienced by British cycling teams, Turkish weightlifters, and Jamaican sprinters. Sports are a simple way to express improvement concepts because the variables are controlled and definitions of winning are relatively straightforward: If you want to win a race, go faster.

However, throughout this book we have discussed how that simplistic attitude is a fallacy. Desire, experience, ability, and hard work will only take you so far because they only create *eligibility* to compete at the highest level. *Once you reach the top tiers of a domain, everyone around you is one of the best.* Only those who continue to improve every aspect of their performance will reach and maintain elite status.

Continuous improvement is what made it possible for the space program to progress in just ten years from launching a 3,000-pound Mercury capsule into a single Earth orbit to sending three men on a trip to the moon (and back). Continuous improvement allows medical professionals to go from using crude instruments more suited to a carpenter's workshop to robotic, laser surgery in just a few decades. It is what allowed a time-sharing network of computers called ARPANET to evolve into the ubiquitous Internet that impacts so many of our aspects of modern daily life.

One common theme that you may have noticed from the earlier examples is that they represent constant forward motion. That does not mean that mistakes, disappointments, and frustrations didn't happen along the way. However, seeing things in new ways, perfecting the craft, and pushing beyond current knowledge and ability, has propelled scientists forward. Achievement does not move backward. The latest achievement becomes the new minimum standard. Thus, we move on.

The Japanese term *kaizen* describes this process, and it has been adopted into multiple fields and industries. Kaizen is a loose translation of the words "change" and "good" and has become synonymous all over the world with the concept of improvement. It can mean incremental or breakthrough changes in performance, but the idea is to constantly collect the incremental gains necessary in every aspect of an enterprise—as opposed to massive reinventions that could prove too costly or risky.

In fact, the concept of kaizen was developed and introduced in Japan by American business executives and trainers after World War II to help rebuild the devastated Japanese manufacturing base. This approach sought small-gain improvements and was influenced by the realities of the US business demands to support the war effort back home—where major investments in time, resources, and radical innovation were not possible. There was a war on!

Ironically, these exported practices were behind the remarkable ascension of the Japanese industrial model throughout the post–war period. The Toyota

Motor Company was one of the biggest proponents of the kaizen philosophy, stating in their management principles, "We improve our business operations continuously, always driving for innovation and evolution."

Too often, performers search for a magic pill or shortcut to success. They want to find an easier or faster way to the top. Some think that they can move from novice to expert with a couple of brilliant training sessions. Some believe success in one area will automatically translate to another. Others are so concerned about looking foolish that while they become proficient at each new level, they become obsessed with the aspect of high performance that deals with art (seeing things in new ways) and do nothing but contemplate what could be at the expense of forward movement. Their quest for perfection has become the enemy of "good enough to keep moving."

While there are breakthroughs and prodigies to distract us from the concept of incremental improvement, they are exceptionally rare. Whether a person is learning to play the piano, swimming the backstroke, practicing law, performing heart surgery, or selling a product or service into the market, there are a progressive number of steps and achievements they must attain before moving on.

The next time you think this might not apply to your domain, try to picture getting on an airline flight with your family and overhearing the pilot say, "No, I have never flown a 757 before. But I have been flying Cessna prop planes for years! How different could it be?"

Do you get on that plane?

THE COACH'S ROLE IN CONTINUOUS IMPROVEMENT

But let's get back to the coach. Continuous improvement is the primary metric that should influence a coach's approaches and plans for improving high performer's progress. Goals are helpful, of course, but they only address wants and needs. Behaviors and activity are important to monitor, but they are merely a means to an end. Remember—coaching is the art, science, and grit of repetitively helping others become better than they were yesterday. If, despite hard work, talent, and experience, a performer is not improving, there is a strong argument to be made that it is not their fault. *It is the coach's fault.*

Continuous improvement is not a stage or point in a pipeline. It is the core of the entire coaching process; everything revolves around it. An opening scrimmage followed by immediate reflection establishes an original baseline for a skill or ability. Work on fundamental skill development and the ability to apply those skills in situational plans prepares performers for the next simulation or actual event. Further reflection after simulations and events allows the performer and coach to agree upon fundamentals, situational plans, and future simulations—the next steps in addressing current performance gaps.

However, it is continuous improvement that allows us to verify if all of this is actually working.

If an elite performer is improving, the fundamentals should become more challenging; situations should be getting more complex, and simulations and real-life contests getting harder. If performers are not improving, it means coaches are only reinforcing their current level of performance. And we know from earlier discussions that reinforcing current performance is a recipe for being left behind in any competitive environment.

THE DENSE CORE OF CONTINUOUS IMPROVEMENT

Imagine the Octane HighPer Coaching model as a spinning system with continuous improvement as its core. At first, the core is small and doesn't have a great deal of "gravity" to support extremely the advanced concepts of reflection, fundamentals, situational planning, simulations, and war games. At an early stage of performance development, the coach must manage the process to make sure that the level of difficulty is not above the ability of the system to support.

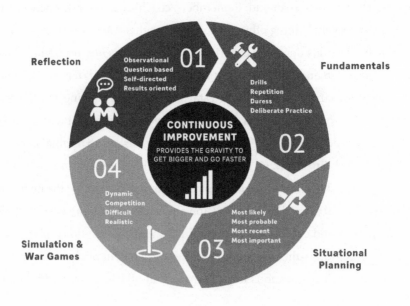

For example, if you were to take novice piano players and have them start working on Mozart's *Piano Sonata No. 18 in D major*, the center wouldn't hold. They have not progressed enough to build to such a level of performance, and thus, no amount of coaching or desire could help them attain it. The argument "if they can play this, they can play anything" may be ambitious and idealistic, but it has no basis in fact or research as effective. The efforts of both coach and performer would go spinning off into space and accomplish nothing.

However, if coaches were able to test those piano players to see their current level of ability, they could prescribe scales and drills to work on. They would have the pianists play sections of music in keys and styles common to many sonatas. They would make sure players engage in continual and deliberate practice to master their current level and push to the next. At this point, with demonstrated improvement, the coach can move to a more advanced level of development. The center has more gravity, and the pianists can move to a higher "orbit."

Think about a business example. Let's say you take new employees with great education, ambition, and promise and put them straight into advanced negotiation skills training during their first week on the job. Keep in mind, they are also trying to learn how to log in to their computer, discover the best place to get coffee, and navigate office politics. Saddle them with advanced negotiation training without the proper progression of fundamentals, situational planning, and simulations, and they will certainly fail. Their potential will never be realized because you have tried to make them leap across too far of a performance gap.

This concept also applies to accomplished professionals who are learning a new skill outside their domain of expertise. Picture an exceptionally talented lawyer, accountant, or investment banker with fifteen years experience working on complex deals and matters. However, the market is changing due to client demands and competitive threats, so these professionals no longer spend their careers in their offices churning out work product. They have to start selling. Businesses often make a major mistake in addressing this new demand by placing executives in a few hours of training, showing them the tips and tricks of complex business development and sales, and then putting a big "certified" stamp on their forehead. The leadership of the organization may think, "These are smart people. They are the best in the world at what they do. How hard could a little sales training be?" Ask twenty-year sales veterans what they think of this approach and the idea that all their skills and knowledge can be mastered after a few hours of watching someone present PowerPoint slides.

Like the pianist, business performers must be coached to their present level on the specific skill they are trying to develop. Their mastery of other skills is irrelevant. While there might be some traits to help them master others (communication, reasoning, mathematical forecasting, etc.), they have to start at a basic level with the new skill and progress toward proficiency and excellence. At an early stage of learning, the density of their continuous improvement core is weak. The center will not hold with the rate of intensity, speed, and difficulty of the subject matter applied to the process.

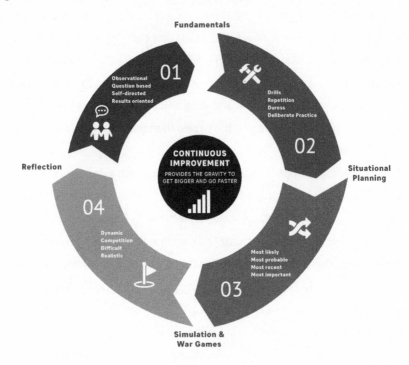

As performers develop, so does their ability to handle more advanced methods of development. This is represented by the larger motion arrows in the diagram above. However, keep in mind that some variables never change. We cannot create more hours in the day, perform beyond our mental and physical capacity as human beings, or truly concentrate on unlimited areas at one time. When it comes to newer employees, organizations may be tempted to ignore these challenges of time, capacity, and concentration, and it is understandable why they might do so. The new employee's primary job for the first few days or weeks might be to go through training. There is a demand to get them up to speed as quickly as possible, so they can begin having an impact. The employees themselves may demand to move faster by dispensing with all of the formalities and getting to the work at hand. It is a coach's job to manage the process of continuous improvement and make sure the intensity, speed, and difficulty of a performer's development is appropriate.

However, for more experienced professionals with other responsibilities, the intensity, speed, and difficulty must increase greatly. Their expectations are higher and potential impact is larger, yet they have less time in which to develop new skills while still maintaining, or improving, existing ones.

For example, such an established professional might only have a few hours a week hours to work on new fundamentals, plans, and simulations. This may be limited for a number of reasons (client demands, schedule, priorities, fatigue, to name a few), *so more must be gotten out of those few hours.* The coach's expertise must rise when dealing with more accomplished and time-constrained performers. If it doesn't, performers who do not suffer fools will surely let the coach know what they think.

Thus, the same rules of progression on the components of coaching apply to the coach as well. Remember, coaching is also a skill! It follows the same rules of continuous improvement as the performers served. A busy coach, with perhaps multiple performers to support, must create powerful drills, map the most impactful situations, and create realistic simulations that have the most impact in the shortest amount of time. This means they also must build systems and templates that best serve their individual performers and not waste time re-creating the wheel for everyone.

The coaches' role requires them to make sure that the performer is using time wisely and not engaging in efforts that are too advanced to maintain progressive improvement or are so simple that performers begin to regress. This is what makes the role of the coach so difficult and so important. Good coaches must come up with plans based on the individual performer and the specific leader, *and* those plans must be refined to fit the individual's exact stage of development at any particular moment. Once again, we are reminded of the need and importance of a true partnership between coach and performer at all times.

THE IMPORTANCE OF GOALS AND MEASUREMENT

There is one last thing for the coach to consider in continuous improvement: how to measure it. Obviously, every leader, performer, team, or organization wants to win. Winning—however we define it in any unique setting—is the goal and manifestation of the art, science, and grit of high performance that the high-performance coach has been applying over the course of training. In business, a win might look one way; in sports, another. However, no one can compete every day because mental, emotional, or physical fatigue naturally occur during high-intensity training and development.

Therefore, a high-performance coach must and will find other ways to monitor progression and improvement. Coaches have an unlimited number of metrics they can use to measure improvement. They bear full responsibility in finding and employing the most appropriate ones for the coaching program that are most directly related to the desired performance result. A good high-performance coach will always share some metrics and expectations with the performers, but good coaching does not overburden performers with so many details that they cannot maintain focus on their task: performing.

For example, if running coaches want to have a sprinter come out of the blocks at a lower angle, they should say, "Come out of the blocks at a lower angle and try to stay low for the first few strides." It does no good to say, "The ideal angle is 44 degrees coming out of the blocks, and you are at 60 degrees. Bring it down 16 degrees." There is no way for the performer to process this kind of fine-tuned adjustment, so it does nothing more than occupy much-needed mental space. The good coaches fine-tune and deal with the details. They share the concepts in the performer's language, not their own.

It is very common to see this kind of overuse of detail and analysis in business. Especially at large companies and firms, departments full of people charged with efficiency and productivity experts who live for running reports and creating spreadsheets. It may be vital to the future of the company to make sure these metrics are measured and managed. However, they have their limitations in business performance coaching. A great coach will take metrics from other sources, such as their own evaluations, and turn them into simple adjustments that can be communicated to the performer.

For example, if you were to say to someone responsible for generating more sales that they needed to increase their successful closing percentage from 21.3 percent to 22.4 percent, how would this help? How would they make that adjustment? What is its practical application? It is the coach's job to translate data and say, "We need to do a better job closing business once we get a proposal in front of the client. From what you said, it sounds like making sure we are talking to the real decision maker from the start is the issue. Do you agree? Let's work on that."

Another example might be that the head of a department or practice might be asked to raise their financial realization rates from 87 percent to 88 percent, which represents millions in additional cash flow to the organization. This might be true, but what is the performer as the head of a department to do with that information? Once again, it is the duty of the coach to ask, "Why do you think our typical clients are not paying full price on our invoices? What could we do to improve that? Do you agree that we should perhaps get our invoices to them sooner and with more detail? Let's try that."

However, measurement is only relevant when it is attached to a goal, and it has to be the right goal. This might seem like common sense, but it is surprising how many organizations track statistics and activity for tracking's sake. For example, a business might track (and reward) employees for how many appointments they have with potential clients in a month. However, if the goal is to generate new business, having one hundred appointments a month and no sales is an indicator of *poor* performance.

Coaches need to understand the performers' state of mind as they set goals and help them set the proper ones with the highest chance of driving success. This is the difference between *goal orientation* and *goal setting*.

Goal orientation refers to the performer's predisposition to goal setting and their general approach to achievement. According to research, most people default to one goal orientation or the other: performance or mastery. A performance goal is simply about achieving a result, whereas the mastery goal is about reaching a level where those results can be reproduced at will. There has been much debate over the years over which types of goals are most effective, producing lasting effects on acquisition of skills, abilities, and knowledge. Performance and mastery are two separate constructs with their own strengths and weaknesses.

Performance goals are aspirations to demonstrate competence or ability to others. Recognition of achievement is key and may come from coaches, peers, teachers, competitors, clients, and anyone else who may extrinsically motivate the performer. Their performance defines their level of achievement, and passing the test is the end game. This type of goal can also have two sides: performance approach and performance avoidance.

When individuals follow the *performance approach* orientation, they want and strive to be high performers for the potential rewards offered. They crave feedback, recognition, and praise. In fact, they may do whatever it takes to "win," including taking shortcuts or finding the minimum way to complete a challenge. An example of this would be a student who is focused on achieving a certain GPA rather than mastering a subject. As long as the grade is excellent, it doesn't matter how it was achieved.

Performers who have a *performance avoidance* orientation shun any situation that may *disprove* their competence in a domain or activity. This may be because their skills are undeveloped, declining, or no longer effective. However, it also may be that they are high achievers in one domain, and they are accustomed to being held in high regard. Think of the brilliant business executives, doctors, or lawyers who are asked to use new technology or approaches and dismiss them as being unnecessary or irrelevant to the way they work. They may be right, but they may also be highly accomplished professionals who are used to being regarded as experts their whole life. They are avoiding performance in an area that may label them as novices or make them look stupid.

MASTERY GOALS

Mastery goals are aspirations that have a learning orientation. They are identified by the "desire to develop the self by acquiring new skills, mastering new situations, and improving one's competence" and are not necessarily concerned with comparisons or outside approval.[1] This is the traditional "student" approach, where seeking knowledge is the objective. Setting mastery goals is highly correlated with intrinsic motivation and long-term success in a domain. It is learning for the sake of learning without promise of reward.

Mastery goals are set by performers who wish to become the absolute best they can be in a particular field or domain. They immerse themselves in learning and constantly seek new challenges to test ability. This is very common in people with advanced degrees or many years of experience in a specific field. The goal is not to pass a test; the goal is to be a virtuoso.

However, this orientation can have its downside. Performers who have a mastery orientation may feel that everything they do has to be perfect when they should be simply seeking proficiency. For example, business executives, doctors, or lawyers who have a deep rooted love for the profession and its mastery might try to apply that standard to everything. If they play a musical instrument, they have to be the best before they will perform in front of people. The end result is that they never end up performing because they are permanently engaged in seeking mastery, despite the fact that they do not have the time to devote to becoming a great musician. Perhaps they should learn a few chords and a couple of songs instead! This may seem like an innocent problem, but this can have detrimental effects when these people must learn something that relates to a major change in their profession. If they can't master it, they will resist it.

The coach's job is to notice a performer's tendency toward goal orientation and address it directly. However, an individual's goal orientation can vary based on the situation. "State versus trait" is something a good coach has to consider. *State* refers to the task or situation at hand for the performer. *Trait* refers to the predominant way a performer's goal orientation preferences are typically applied.[2]

Research has shown that individuals can have different goal orientations depending on whether they are in an academic or work domain. When it comes to their professions, those in fields with a highly formalized academic process are likely very learning-goal oriented. Mastery of the subject is necessary, and it is highly stimulating for the performers who chose to pursue it. Think of doctors who go to medical school, pilots attending flight school, or accountants enrolled in business school. While there are performance components to their educations, mastery of the subject matter is the paramount goal. No patient or passenger wants to have a surgeon or pilot who crammed for each test and then forgot the material the next day! In all likelihood, this is a performer trait that influences their tendencies toward progressive achievement.

If you ask those same professionals to do something new—like learn how to run a clinic, generate new clients, or practice public speaking—they may switch to a performance-goal orientation. When they need to learn a new skill, they hire a coach, and they perform. That is their current state, so the goal becomes getting to a level of proficiency that allows them to get back to what they enjoy. Pass the test and move on.

Research also shows that performers in unfamiliar situations with few reference points revert to their natural goal orientation—also known as their trait.[3] Whether mastery or performance goals, that is where they will find comfort. We've seen this before with performers who revert to their art, science, and grit tendencies.

Thus, good coaches are always watching for two things: a performer's natural tendencies and stage of development. The coach uses performance as a method of measurement and a way to push performers beyond what they thought possible. However, if it is important to future success, what coaches truly want their performers to develop is *mastery*.

ACHIEVING MASTERY USING GOAL SETTING

Achieving mastery is a challenging undertaking for high-performace coaches. They make sure the performer is using *performance-based goals* to keep moving forward through managed competition, simulation, and training under duress. However, they are also making sure that the performer is using *mastery goals* for key skills and abilities through an emphasis on fundamentals, deliberate practice, and situational planning. First-rate coaches cannot allow the performer to superficially learn a new aspect of a domain, "check the box," and move on. They will also discourage performers from being so consumed with learning every last detail of a domain that they will never go out into the real world to perform because they never feel they are ready. No one said being a coach is easy!

If you are reading this book, you are probably a high performer and/or coaching high performers. You are used to being around people with a strong need for achievement and successful track record. Keep in mind two last points.

First, how people act when they are presented with performance goals is very illuminating as to how they really feel. If performers avoid or seek performance goals that are so high their chance of achieving them becomes an excuse in itself, the real problem may be a high fear of failure. The best coaches make great efforts to develop self-efficacy in that specific area of expertise. As confidence improves, so will the effort and willingness to engage in more difficult tasks. It also encourages a learning-goal orientation, which leads to what every good elite coach wants: mastery.

Second, performers who have high ability need to use metacognitive awareness (also known as "thinking about thinking"). This relates back to the concept of reflective coaching, where the performer is pressed to recount what happened, compare it to desired outcomes, and come up with solutions for improvement. Metacognition is directly related to skill retention and application in future events—thus, it is critical for those who will be performing in more challenging, unpredictable scenarios.

In the end, if the performer is not improving despite possessing the right abilities, experience, and resources, there is very likely a coaching problem. Continuous improvement is *the* core for coaches and performers. It is where both parties need to focus, although they have different roles. The performer must balance art, science, and grit and be receptive to coaching. The coach must evaluate simulated and actual events to identify performance gaps to customize programs and plans that address those gaps.

The core of continuous improvement must grow stronger to allow for more advanced development of skills and abilities. Otherwise, all the efforts of everyone involved are simply activities with high opportunity costs that become less and less effective with the passage of time. Performers deserve better than that. It is up to their coaches to make it happen.

Coaches also need to help performers manage the types of goals they set to make sure that results become permanent and can be the foundation of the next level of achievement. While some people may debate which goals should be set, research has shown that the efficacy of goal setting as a performance enhancement strategy is not up for debate. Analysis of more than five hundred studies on goal setting has shown a direct correlation on improved performance in all populations and activities with improved results of as much as 16 percent from simply using goal setting![4] This is a great example of how using better strategies to tap into a performer's functional reserve leads to improved results without the need for retooling or major investment of time and resources. Goals must be specific, difficult, measurable, and achievable.

Highly ambitious performers focus on outcomes. Winning, scoring points, and putting trophies on the mantel (real and figuratively) are what matter in the end. The challenge is that anyone can set a goal to become the best in the world at what they do. It is how you will get there that is the difference. That is why it is important to know the difference between outcome, performance, and process goals.

This approach has been studied in sports, an excellent environment for goal theory. Unlike many other domains, sports have consistent rules, relatively little politics, and (in ideal circumstances) are a true meritocracy. *Outcome goals* deal with the end result, such as being the best in your field, winning a gold medal in sprinting, or closing $1,000,000 in annual new business. *Performance goals* deal with the milestones along the way, such as winning awards and competitive situations, breaking a specific time on the track, or closing $100,000 of deals during March. *Process goals* are concerned with tasks and steps, such as reading competitive intelligence every day to know more about industry trends, getting up at 5:30 a.m. every day to run at the track for ninety minutes, or committing to make thirty phone calls a day to set appointments with qualified prospects. Of these types of goals, most people tend to focus on outcome goals: what they want to achieve. The elite have these ambitions and dreams as well, but they concentrate more on how they will get there (process goals).

One of the reasons that process goals are so effective is that, for the most part, they are completely controlled by the performer. They can adjust them at will and show direct ties to progress, which encourages a further commitment to the goal. With the proper use of process goals guided by a coach, the performance goals and outcome goals will be achieved. An outcome goal is the destination; a performance goal is how to make sure you are on track, but the process goal designates how to get there in a realistic, methodical manner. The integration of the efficacy of goals as a performance tool, goal orientation, goal setting is known as the Competitive Goal-Setting (CGS) model.[5]

The CGS addresses another aspect that coaches should consider: Is the person they are helping to improve *performance, success,* or *failure* oriented? Performance-oriented individuals tend to prioritize process, performance, and outcome goals (in that order). They tend to be positive and patient in their development but may spend endless hours working on their craft—to the point where they don't notice they may not be doing as well as they think they are. Failure-oriented performers may set high outcome goals but avoid performance goals that lead to competition. They also may have poor process goals because they take on easily achievable tasks to check things off the "to do" list. They also tend to see things as out of their control and have a generally pessimistic view of their potential. Success-oriented performers also emphasize outcome, performance, and process goals (in that order), but they are extremely competitive and seek social reinforcement of their achievements. They have extremely high confidence in their ability, but this can lead them to impulsive behavior or under preparedness. They are used to winning and just want the next chance to get on the field to show what they can do.

All of these orientations provide challenges for the coach. For failure-oriented performers, you must build up their confidence and make them stretch themselves. If performers are success oriented, focus them on process and doing the work required to reach mastery. For performance-oriented individuals, encourage their use of process goals while making sure they do not become someone who insists on incessantly pushing a boulder uphill when it is not contributing toward performance and outcome goals.

One last thing for the coach to keep in mind: Mastery of all skills and tasks is not always necessary. Do world-class sprinters need to perfect their shoe-tying skills? Technically, it's part of preparing to run. But the fastest people in the world just need a basic level of proficiency in shoe tying; perfecting this skill would waste valuable effort. Focusing on mastering everything related to a domain can lead to failure, and can be a symptom of performance avoidance. A performer spending too much time on things that don't matter might be trying to stall for time or completely sidestep an upcoming demonstration of ability.

High performers use process goals to achieve performance goals that lead to outcome goals. This is the way to win, and the coach's job is to help them do so.

REVIEW OF THE OCTANE HIGHPER COACHING MODEL AND PHILOSOPHY

We all remember our bad coaches and our great coaches for the same reason: They impact on our performance and leave lasting memories. Ineffective, mediocre, or nonexistent coaches have no impact and leave no memories. Even though bad coaches can be detrimental, at least having a bad coach shows what *not* to do! People who want to perform at a high level need impactful coaches. We would argue that having mediocre coaches is the same as having no coach at all. An unexceptional coach wastes time, offers no perspective, and lends no guidance. Thus, one way or another, individuals, teams, and organizations need to cultivate great coaches, improve bad ones, and eliminate coaches who just go through the motions.

Holding a whistle and being the person in charge does not make you a coach. You may be leading, managing, yelling, documenting, or telling stories from yesteryear, but that does not mean coaching is taking place. Remember our definition of coaching:

Coaching is the art, science, and grit of repetitively helping others become better than they were yesterday.

If your performers are not getting better at what they do (even if they are already very good at some things), there is a problem that might include coaching.

This assumes that the performer has the ability, education, experience, attitude, and a high degree of coachability. If all of these factors are in place, the coach can use a systematic way to determine the causes of performance gaps. This is part of their detective and analyst role; coaches diagnose root causes, whether mental, physical, or external, that, despite the coaches' efforts otherwise, cause persistent performance gaps.

One of the coaches' primary analytical tools is the Octane HighPer Coaching Model, which is built on the whole-part-whole philosophy of evaluating actual or simulated performance and then breaking the needed skills and abilities into their component parts before periodic retesting and reevaluation.

The scrimmage starts the process (whole). After reflection, the coach and performer identify performance gaps. The coach then recommends fundamentals to work on, situational practice (parts), and a process for retesting and reflection (whole).

At every stage of the model, and as part of an ongoing relationship, coaches engage in reflective coaching to elicit solutions and courses of action from the performer. It is a simple series of questions that should not be used as a canned script but as a guide for discussions that become a familiar part of the coaching relationship. Keep in mind that coaching occurs all of the time. It is not an activity meant to happen during a specific time or day of the week. Coaching is constant, whether a two-minute chat or conversations spanning days of training events. Eventually, this way of interacting with performers becomes embedded in the coach's day-to-day parlance.

However, none of this matters unless both performer and coach are highly focused on continuous improvement. It is the core around which all of the HighPer Coaching activities orbit. If it matters, it must be measured. If it is measured, it must improve. The growing density and gravity of continuous improvement allows the coach to prescribe more difficult challenges and situations. Performers must move to the next level and respect the need for balancing art, science, and grit as they continue to progress.

In working with top performers and coaches over the past three decades, we are periodically asked a pointed question from even the most dedicated individuals: "When are we done?"

Since competitors, peers, and changing conditions constantly influence who's on the winner's podium, we always answer by saying, "Only when *you* are done competing. Until then, keep going."

HIGH-PERFORMANCE TEAMS, TRIBES, AND COMMUNITIES

"Teamwork is the ability to work together toward a common vision. The ability to direct individual accomplishments toward organizational objectives. It is the fuel that allows common people to attain uncommon results."
—ANDREW CARNEGIE

"Finding good players is easy. Getting them to play as a team is another story."
—CASEY STENGEL

We have spent a great deal of time focused on individual performers and the coaches who help them. We've shown some examples about how teams come together to help improve individual performance through managed competition and impactful coaching. While high-performance individuals may be the output that coaches seek, keep in mind that, in almost all cases, people depend on high-performing teams to unleash potential.

You will be hard pressed to find a single exception to this statement in ANY domain.

You may be an Olympic sprinter (a solo event), but you also have a training partner, and you may work with a coach who also manages three or four other athletes. You may have come from a university track team; perhaps you hope to win a spot on Team USA and represent your country. Though your entire career may boil down to less than ten seconds on a track, that brief time is the culmination of years and years of team involvement and participation.

This same notion applies to members of a sales team, a group of software coders, or a collection of lawyers at a firm. If you are truly an independent, free agent with a dedicated coach and singular purpose, teams might not matter to you. However, that is a rare instance. Almost all of us belong to a tribe or a community, and we crave these connections to give achievements meaning. Human beings are social animals that need individual fulfillment in addition to the pleasure of communal contribution.

To be the best at what they do, individuals, teams, and organizations are often codependent. Individual excellence creates great potential for the organization; on the other hand, organizational and team dysfunction limits potential. Thus, whether individuals and coaches are members of a company, law firm, sports team, or orchestra, their ability to be the best will depend on those around them. Members of teams collaborate, challenge, and compete with each other. They push each other beyond self-imposed limits, which raises the team's performance and showcases individual members. Individual performance is maximized by preparing, planning, competing, and performing on a team. Why, then, do people insist on going it alone, when research and practical experience show the importance of teamwork in reaching potential?

In a landmark article published in *Harvard Business Review*, McKinsey & Company partners Jon Katzenbach and Douglas Smith argue that teams can be the most important performance unit inside companies and other organizations. They define teams in the following way:

> "A team is a small number of people with complementary skills who are committed to a common purpose, set of performance goals and approach for which they hold themselves mutually accountable."[1]

The authors take great care to distinguish teams from working groups, which are mere collections of similar people working on a common task within a traditional vertical hierarchy. Teams differ from working groups in that they are a collection of people with different skill sets who work together in a largely self-managed style.

There is another major difference: Groups may produce a fine work product, but high-performing teams deliver great work AND develop great performers.

An ideal team consists of three to nine people. Such a small group rarely requires outside management and monitoring. Leadership roles are shared, team members depend on each other, and there is pressure to perform. The primary motivation—don't let your teammates down or hold the team back.

Does this sound familiar? Every single high performer in domains with terminal consequences develops mastery. Navy SEALs and sports stars train as a team. Corporations with breakthrough success and lasting market dominance utilize team training in aspects such as product development, key accounts, and software coding. These teams become tribes and communities, safe (and competitive) environments in which performers can thrive.

Human beings naturally seek out others like themselves. As social animals, we have an affinity for others and need to feel connected to them. Sometimes, these preferences are rational; sometimes, personal connections are irrational or even random. If you are a fan of a particular sports team, seeing that familiar jersey invokes an instant sense of connection to the stranger wearing it. Likewise, a rival team's jersey provokes an instant disdain.

During filming of *Planet of the Apes* (1968), this desire to form tribes and communities was surprisingly illustrated. The iconic movie is set in a futuristic world, where man has become enslaved and apes are the dominant species. Three types of apes form the new society: chimpanzees, gorillas, and orangutans. Live actors played these apes, and the make-up artistry involved to transform dozens and dozens of cast members into apes each day was simply amazing. Once these actors were in costume, something curious happened. Every day at mealtime, the actors playing chimpanzees ate exclusively with other "chimpanzees." The same curious behavior was repeated with gorillas and orangutans. Almost no mixing between groups occurred after the first few days of filming. The actors naturally bonded with their fellow "apes" even though their identities were no more defined than the costume and makeup they were wearing.[2]

The same type of behavior is found on football teams. Defensive players tend to associate with others who play defense. Linemen associate with linemen and not lanky wide receivers. The kickers are off by themselves doing whatever kickers do. All are on the same team, but each finds a tribe.

This sorting behavior occurs among the pilots on board an aircraft carrier. Fighter jocks make fun of bomber pilots. Helicopter pilots bind together instead of hanging out with the fixed wing aviators. And, the C2-A COD pilots who just visit the ship periodically for key supply deliveries? They may stay a night or two, but let's just say it is best they head back to the other COD pilots as soon as possible. Their tribe is back on shore, and these pilots are in "unfriendly" territory while at sea.

Innovative corporations, where speed to market and momentum are critical, promote these tribes and communities. Software and social media giants use specific design teams that are attached to individual features to churn out new ideas; each team takes great pride in working on the next big thing, even when doing so requires extreme overtime. Automobile manufacturers employ teams that specialize in various aspects of new car design . . . and the workers that then build these new cars form teams . . . and then those workers responsible for producing a specific PART of the vehicle form teams.

In all of these examples, individuals on the same team share a common goal. Whether they are filming a movie, winning a championship, conducting flight operations, or building a great company, their ultimate success is measured as a group. However, individuals perform better as subsets of the greater organization. These tribes and communities are self-governed, setting their own standards of performance, expectations, and work ethic. In addition to the team, specific coaches who specialize in the details and typical challenges and characteristics support performers in their role. These organizational communities have a sense of pride in what they do, which fosters healthy internal and external competition between groups. When managed properly, these high-performance teams accomplish exceptional things as an organization.

On the other hand, it is not hard to see how tribes could become detrimental. We do not have to think too hard to picture examples of how "those people over there aren't like us" can have negative or even tragic consequences. In corporations, rivalries between sales, finance, or marketing are natural. In business, clannishness can quickly turn into a dysfunctional culture of finger pointing and blaming. Sales complains that marketing doesn't provide enough leads; finance complains that sales discounts prices too much (and plays golf while they do the hard work); marketing never gets the budget they want, and sales blows the opportunities they are given. In professional service firms, practice groups may segregate themselves. At hospitals, doctors and nurses form tribes governed by their experiences and points of view. When subgroups cause rifts between practice areas, departments, and divisions, that dysfunction can lead to losses in profits, opportunities, and even lives (depending on the case and discipline). These are warning signs that teams and tribes are becoming toxic to the organization's overall mission. In addition, such dysfunction may limit individual development; with no hope of progressing, employees develop a hunker-down mentality to preserve the status quo.

Performers need training, coaching, and leadership to succeed, and they need teams. Weaken any one part of that equation and the results are unacceptable. That is why the elite in any domain don't go it alone. They get better as a member of a team. And it's a leader's role to make sure teams become the ultimate performance tool.

WORKING THE MOST DANGEROUS
4½ ACRES ON EARTH

The "business end" of a navy aircraft carrier is the most dangerous 4½ acres on earth. Made of HY 80/100-grade alloy steel and covered with a hard, non-skid coating, this is the flight deck, home to more than seventy-five combat aircraft capable of inflicting devastating damage to an enemy.

Four powerful steam and electromagnetic catapults are built into the deck, each one capable of accelerating a 60,000-pound jet fighter from zero to 160 mph in 2.5 seconds. Stretched across the aft part of the deck are four large steel cables ("arresting wires") that bring these jets to a jolting stop within 150 feet of touchdown. Four huge elevators, each capable of lifting two fully loaded fighters, transfer aircraft between the flight deck and the hangar deck, where major maintenance work is done.

Also on deck: four ammunition elevators that bring bombs, bullets, rockets, torpedoes, and other ammunition to be loaded on aircraft from the ordnance magazines far below decks. Numerous high-speed fueling stations quickly deliver thousands of gallons of jet fuel to thirsty aircraft. Fire on any sea-based platform is the most dangerous hazard, so dozens of high-pressure nozzles able to dispense fire-retardant foam with the push of a button, are located on deck. However, this complex machinery and advanced technology is not what makes these 4½ acres work. It's the people!

Flight operations on an aircraft carrier are a carefully managed execution of precise teamwork. The operational tempo is astounding. At the height of combat, two hundred or more daily aircraft sorties may be conducted, with about twenty-five aircraft launched and recovered every 105 minutes. After landing, each of the twenty-five has to be repositioned, refueled, re-armed, and resupplied within a thirty-minute period. There's no time to spare; each of the 250 or so people working on the flight deck must be at the exact right place, at the right time, with the right equipment to make it work. And the crew must do their work among turning jet engines, helicopter blades, and propellers!

To safely and effectively pull this off, each person on the flight deck is assigned to a team, and each team is identified by its jersey color:

- Yellow: flight directors

- Red: ordnance handlers and crash responders

- Purple: fueling operators

- White: medical personnel and safety observers

- Green: equipment technicians

- Blue: aircraft movers

- Brown: plane captains

A quick look around reveals who's responsible for what and allows crews to coordinate their efforts accordingly.

Each team member puts in hours of required study and practice, followed by more hours of apprenticeship with an experienced flight deck operator. Dozens of drills test the mettle of each team, certifying their readiness to work well internally and with other flight deck teams wearing different jerseys. Storytelling also plays an important role in this teaching and learning process, when recounting the deadly deck fires on the USS *Forrestal* and USS *Enterprise* or accounts of aircraft crashes during landing.

To first time observers, flight deck operations look like total chaos. In reality, what they're seeing is an extraordinary display of efficiency and effectiveness made possible by high-performing teamwork and self-discipline.

Let's go deeper into life on an aircraft carrier's flight deck. Imagine a fueling operator (purple shirt) who we'll call Aviation Boatswain's Mate (Fuel), 3rd Class, Williams. Williams is highly proficient; he had great training and coaching to get him right where he is. Williams might be the absolute best at what he does on his particular fueling team. However, *all of his colleagues must be highly proficient.* All purple shirts must reach a certain level of competency or none of them can do their job.

Each purple shirt team must be highly proficient. When Williams's specific team leaves the deck, one that's just as good must take its place; otherwise, flight operations can't continue without readjustment. Don't forget the blue shirt team! They move the aircraft around. Are planes in the proper, safe position for refueling? Is each blue-shirted individual competent? If not, the purple shirts can't do their job and Williams, the best purple shirt in the fleet, can only relay frustrations to his superiors.

REVIEW OF HIGH-PERFORMANCE TEAMS, TRIBES, AND COMMUNITIES

It is the natural state of things for people to form connections and rely on each other. It is completely artificial to make them work by themselves to better themselves or their condition. This is a fact that is hardwired into our DNA since the time we have been chasing mammoths for our next meal. The creation of cubicles and corner offices does not change this fact.

Teams are the ultimate performance tool. If you were to take nothing else from this book, using teams to develop high-performance individuals and amplify their results is the most important lesson. The simple act of placing individuals into three-person "performance pods" where they can collaborate, encourage, and compete with other will dramatically improve each of the individual skills in which they are being trained. Three-person teams are ideal for self-management and progress on basic tasks and activities. An individual or two-person team can convince themselves to take a break or fight the system, but a three-person team always has someone keeping the team honest. Larger teams need guidance and logistical support, so they require more effort and management. Larger teams can handle more complex solutions as well as develop more performers at the same time. There are uses for both.

All well-defined teams have advantages for their members, but they do have to be monitored by leaders, coaches, and managers. A team can evolve into a tribe or community that is opposed to the overall strategic direction of an organization, and their collective power generates momentum that requires great force to stop. This is a testament to the power of great teams: They can work for you or against you. Exceptional organizations know that they must harness this power to continue to compete.

It is often said that people are an organization's most important asset. The individual performer is who makes things happen and achieves greatness through their personal effort. However, teams may be an organization's most UNIQUE asset. The blend of people, skills, situations, infrastructure, support, methodologies, and organizational strategy is a combination of variables that can never be truly duplicated. Even if a star performer leaves an organization or team, they will have completely different currents to navigate. They may be a star at their new home, but it will not be instantaneous or in the same way as before. Thus, the organization should take great care to build, leverage, and cultivate teams. Performers can leave, competitors can change, and approaches can be copied at a moment's notice. It is an organization's collection of high-performing teams that are their true differentiating factor.

As we defined earlier, teams are collections of performers with complementary skills, common purposes, goals, and approaches that hold each other accountable. They help each other be the best they can be. They depend on each other to be an expert in what they do, which allows them to be an expert at what they themselves do. They also push each other to keep up through managed competition with each other.

There is a great pride and camaraderie in a well-run team. The incentive does not need to be in the form of monetary rewards or prizes. A high-performance team wins for the joy of winning and not letting each other down. It creates exceptional performers along the way.

Do not make your performers go it alone. The team is the ULTIMATE performance tool.

HIGH-PERFORMANCE CULTURE
STARTS AT THE TOP

Performers perform; coaches coach; leaders lead. Simple. But this concept is hard for organizations to master. While each role has an understanding of (and an opinion on) how best to perform, coach, and lead, separation between these responsibilities maximizes results. We have talked extensively about performers and coaches, but what does it mean to be a leader?

Business guru Peter Drucker once said, "Management is doing things right. Leadership is doing the right things." A leader's role is to see that the overall organization cultivates talent, provides its members access to resources needed, ensures proper coordination of all organizational aspects, and plans for the future—all while staying out of their performers' and coaches' ways. Except in the case of direct reports, leaders are not in the coaching business and need to stay *way* out of the individual performance business. They may have expertise, experience, and insight into these areas, but coaching is not part of a leader's role. They provide vision, direction, and an environment that demands teams whose efforts are in congruence with the organization's goals.

As discussed earlier, the HPI model is a systematic process focused on results instead of needs, wants, activities, or efforts. Once leaders determine an organization's vision, direction, and goals, they can quantify the gap between actual and desired performance. They then try to find the causes for that gap, thus providing critical information for the coach to develop and recommend specific performance improvements and solutions at the individual level.

Leaders of organizations perform on a much grander scale, one where improving performance is no longer about a single team or person.

Leadership success is about *all* of the teams improving and creating exponentially greater results through collective efforts. Steering superstar performers, their coaches, and their teams so that the strengths of the parts is a net positive for the whole is a complex, intensive process. If an organization is built on truly great performers, this will be a bit of managed chaos. This is why being a leader is such an arduous task.

Leaders must work with coaches to address the high-performance change continuum, using a step-by-step process that can be implemented at the individual, team, and organizational levels.

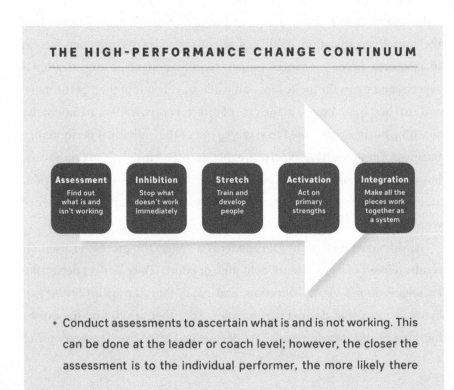

THE HIGH-PERFORMANCE CHANGE CONTINUUM

Assessment	Inhibition	Stretch	Activation	Integration
Find out what is and isn't working	Stop what doesn't work immediately	Train and develop people	Act on primary strengths	Make all the pieces work together as a system

- Conduct assessments to ascertain what is and is not working. This can be done at the leader or coach level; however, the closer the assessment is to the individual performer, the more likely there will be individual improvement. In all likelihood, assessments are administered at individual, team, and organizational levels and addressed in distinctive ways.

- Stop whatever isn't working immediately. Any identified dysfunction at any performance level must be inhibited. Though it might be tempting to slowly ease out of bad behavior or practices, think about it this way: Would an astronaut or pilot handle mission problems in that manner? Probably not.

- Stretch your people to new performance levels and higher standards. Team and individual coaches will handle this by providing practice on fundamentals, planning, and exposing people to uncomfortable simulations. Through reflection, participants learn what works and then repeat it. However, don't neglect the organization's coaches—they may need development and opportunities to improving their skills and abilities as well.

- Act on primary strengths. Activate the areas where the organization is already strong and compensate for those inhibited activities to build on the increasing capabilities of your individuals and teams.

- Integrate these pieces into one system. Just as a coach puts individuals together to form a winning team, a leader forms a winning organization. If substandard progress still exists, reassess and readdress.

Properly coached individuals and properly led teams have more confidence, improved capability, and wins. They will be able to handle ever more complex situations, more aggressive competitors, and more challenging conditions. They will do more because it is asked of them. And, eventually, they will thank you for it.

THE WAY TO WIN

"What is success? I think it is a mixture of having a flair for the thing that you are doing; knowing that it is not enough, that you have got to have hard work; and a certain sense of purpose."

—MARGARET THATCHER

Once people learn what high performers do to reach the top and stay there, the next logical question is "What do I do now?" Performers may look inward and attempt to honestly assess their preferences, attitudes, and accomplishments. Coaches might take a retrospective look at their methods, plans, and approaches. However, since performance is measured in the arena, external feedback is an important tool in discovering whether performers and coaches are on the right path. This combination of internal and external feedback leads to *metacognition* (the ability to think about thinking), which allows the best to actually do their best.

There is no magic here. People are as different as their circumstances, advantages, and challenges. What is consistent is the path. There is a way to perform. There is a way to coach. There is a way to win.

Imagine for a moment that you have decided to scale Mount Everest. There are numerous reasons someone might want to take on this feat (and many why others wouldn't) but there are not many ways to actually do it. Most climbers take one of two routes: the Southeast Ridge from Nepal or the North Col route from Tibet. Also, tackling Everest requires the completion of many, many previous ascents and challenging climbs, but even that experience is no guarantee. Hundreds of the most experienced climbers in the world have failed to reach Everest's summit. Finally, get out your credit card; an expedition to the top of the world will cost as much as $100,000—for travel, support, training, gear, and someone to come rescue your oxygen-depleted self should you get in trouble.

The consequences of failure are high, so how do climbers succeed? They constantly look for new advantages in climbing, protective gear, training methods, and mental preparation. They perfect techniques: how to conserve oxygen and energy, traversing a crevasse, and navigating the infamous Hillary Step (a forty-foot, almost vertical wall of ice). Years are spent learning to become a great climber, taking on harder and harder ascents, before the final two months of training and acclimatization required once they set foot on the great mountain.

Climbers also use experienced Sherpa guides to help them get there, and this expense represents the bulk of money paid for an ascent. What do these Sherpas provide that is worth tens of thousands of dollars? Three quarters of the way up Everest, one of the more unforgiving mountains in the world (some argue that K2 is a harder climb), the value you place on an experienced guide who can say, "Don't step there, or you will fall" is incredible.

Guides and Sherpas assess their climbers' abilities, prepare them to accomplish the ascent, and then coach them through the most effective way to reach the summit. For example, if you ascend via the south side, base camp (at 17,600 feet) is a forty-mile walk away. Past base camp, there are three more camps, each with its own challenges (for example, specific times to arrive and depart to avoid dangers such as avalanches, extreme cold, and total darkness).

No one goes up Mount Everest alone. Climbers are part of a team. In addition to Sherpa guides, those team members, who are experiencing equal levels of misery, provide encouragement to take just one more step and not turn back.

Does any of this sound familiar? Climbers are another example of performers who must master the proper balance of art, science, and grit. They depend on coaches to help them achieve goals. They rely on teams to push them farther than they'd go as individuals. The activity has binary (and, in climbing, perhaps terminal) consequences.

The next time you need to find a way up your own personal mountain, keep Mount Everest in mind.

NEXT STEPS

In the following pages, you will find tools, guides, and plans to help you on your way. Performers: You need to realize why some move from *very good* to *great* to *elite,* and why these high performers all have a coach. Coaches, you need to coach well. If you lead an organization, insist on continuous improvement from your performers, emphasizing that teams and coaches will lead them there. Everyone has a role, and everyone shares responsibility for success.

All of us can accomplish amazing things. In all aspects of life, we are so much more capable than we think. Look at children taking their initial steps, riding a bike for the first time, or performing at a first piano recital to behold the wonder of moving from mere exploration to awe-inspiring accomplishment. Most children always want to do more and holding them back is sometimes difficult. That fearless push is an attitude we should never lose.

With all of the pressures of adulthood, we sometimes settle for *good enough,* even though we know we could do more if only we knew the path to get there. Luckily, the elite have shown us the way, and we can emulate their approach.

Art, science, grit, coaching, teams, and leadership are the ingredients to cultivating excellence.

Now let's get to work.

APPENDIX A

NOW WHAT? HOW DO YOU
GET STARTED?

If you have read through this entire book and taken heed of its message, you realize that the process of improvement never stops. While we commend you for getting started by reaching this page, it only signifies the beginning of a circuitous journey forward. Intentions and aspirations are different from actions and results. We know that sometimes the end of a book also means the end of thinking about the topic and moving on to the next problem to tackle. Do not lose your momentum. The time to take action is now.

First, read the interviews that follow. They were conducted with top performers and leaders from a variety of fields that verify how art, science, and grit are important to individual performance. They reinforce the importance of coaching for even the most elite performers. And they talk about how teams are the ultimate performance development tools. You will learn how to get the best out of people from those who lead astronauts, military officers, special operators, and protective services personnel under the most extreme conditions.

Second, visit our website at www.artsciencegrit.com to access tools, templates, and practical examples that show you how to take what you have learned in this book and apply it to your business. You will find a variety of exercises and best practices tailored to different industries and situations to help develop performance at the individual, team, and organizational level.

This toolbox is complimentary, and we welcome your feedback as to how to continuously add to it.

Third, we strongly encourage you to pull out a piece of paper or your favorite electronic device to begin mapping out what you plan to commit to your organization, team, and personal improvement plan. To help you get started, we have listed three ideas related to the major sections of this book that you can try immediately. Some may be easy, and some may be hard. That is why we have also included a list of "circuit breakers" that signal when it is time to raise your hand and ask for help.

We stand ready to help you on this journey. Whether we like it or not, it is a journey that has already begun. So, let's get to work.

APPENDIX B

During the course of researching the concepts of this book, we realized that concepts and theory are helpful, but performers always struggle with application and execution. They want to see how others have used the principles outlined in this book, even if those performers were not even aware they were doing so at the time.

In the following pages, you will read the transcripts of interviews that we conducted over eighteen months with a variety of elite performers in different fields. We wanted to hear why they consistently performed well at every level over a period of decades. Their success also was equally consistent when they switched roles, jobs, or even entire careers! We were curious why some performers become elite, and others—while very good—never seem to quite unleash their full potential.

The overall themes that emerged as we heard from these performers were quite consistent. First, the ability to balance art, science, and grit is essential to consistent, ever-increasing performance in constantly changing environments. Second, the need for coaches and being coachable *increases* as you become more skilled and compete at higher levels. Third, *how you train* is much more important than the subject matter of the training. Many people are exposed to the same content and resources, but most cannot apply them in a way that puts them among the very top in their domain.

Finally, a somewhat surprising common statement from all the elite performers we interviewed was that they would have never achieved their level of success without being part of a team. No great performer goes it alone.

Teams are not simply support members to handle the administrative tasks and act as a concierge to a performance diva. Our interviewees all stressed that teams of equals with diverse styles, skills, and abilities that challenged, competed, and collaborated with them were the reason they are where they are today.

Thus, our conversations started with us trying to learn about what makes an individual exceptional. But we ended up hearing more about all the other people who helped them achieve success. If you take nothing else from this book and the subjects herein, we hope that will be the one gem you share with others as well as apply to your own passion.

In this section you will learn from the following exceptional performers, coaches and leaders:

Captain Chris Cassidy, USN. Captain Cassidy is a Navy SEAL, two-time astronaut and current Chief of the Astronaut Office at NASA. He graduated from the US Naval Academy and also has a master's degree from MIT. He served active combat tours in Afghanistan, where he was awarded the Bronze Star. He spent over six months living in outer space including thirty-one hours and fourteen minutes of spacewalk time.

General Michael Hagee, USMC (Ret.). General Hagee served as the 33rd Commandant of the United States Marine Corps from 2003–2006 and graduated from the US Naval Academy. He is also a graduate of the Naval War College and recipient of the Bronze Star as well as the Defense Distinguished Service Medal.

Cathy Lanier. Chief Lanier was the first female chief of the Metropolitan Police Department of Washington, DC. She moved up through the ranks of the department, starting as a foot patrolwoman in 1990. She progressively held command positions including Major, Narcotics Branch/Gang Unit and in the Office of Homeland Security and Counter-Terrorism. She currently serves as the Chief Security Officer for the National Football League.

A.J. Hawk (interviewed in chapter 8). Hawk was the 5th overall pick of the

NFL draft as a linebacker from Ohio State University and went on to win a Super Bowl with the Green Bay Packers. After also playing for the Cincinnati Bengals and Atlanta Falcons, he retired from football with 644 tackles, 20 sacks, and being named as a Pro Bowl alternative three times.

INTERVIEW WITH CAPTAIN CHRIS CASSIDY

Q: Could you tell us a little bit about your background, some key influential moments when you were growing up that had an impact on you, and about your military career as well as your current role?

A: I grew up in Maine, southern Maine, small town, not a whole lot of . . . in fact, no military influence to speak of in my upbringing. My dad did a short stint in the Marine Corps Reserves around the Vietnam time frame, but it was just a short tour. It wasn't until I was in high school trying to figure out where to go to college that I remember seeing this really cool picture of a Naval Academy with nice buildings and sharp-looking people in uniform. I thought that looked pretty cool, and then I read that it was free. You just owed time in the US Navy, so that sounded perfect for me.

I went through the application process, and this was before the Internet, when it was hard to find information. I was digging around, asking people, trying to get the best gauge I could—and I read you had to apply to your congressman or senator for a nomination. So I did that and had the interview. I didn't know it at the time, but it was a new congressional staff. They had never done the process before, and the woman told me, "Okay, great job, Mr. Cassidy, you did fine. We'll take it from here. We send all your paperwork to the Naval Academy, and you'll hear back later." So naive me—seventeen years old at the time, thought, *This is great, that's it.* But, I never sent anything directly to the Naval Academy.

Looking back, it was kind of a knucklehead move, but I just took the staffer at their word. So, in March or April of my senior year, everybody's getting acceptance or rejection letters from all the colleges, but I hadn't heard anything. I called the Naval Academy admissions office and said, "I'm wondering about the status of my application." I hear the lady reply, "What's your name? What's your social security number? We've got nothing on you." That's when I realized, *Oh crap, what am I going to do now?* Well, it just so happened that my buddy's dad was taking a trip down to Washington during our spring break at school. I jumped in their car with my friend and his dad and drove from Maine to Annapolis and went to the admissions office.

I'll never forget that when I got to the front desk, they told me to go back and speak to the guidance officer. It was this Marine Corps officer. Even then, as a kid, I realized that, as I'm talking to him, he was looking me deep in the eyes, trying to figure out, *Is this guy worth it for me to go a step beyond and help him out?* I explained my situation, and he said, "Okay, Cassidy, I understand. I'll get back to you." So, I went back to school, and he called me up the next Monday or Tuesday and said, "Hey, Cassidy, I have good news for you. I can get you into the Navy Academy Prep school, but you've got to tell me right now, on the phone, if you're in or not." And I said, "Oh, yeah. I'm in, all in."

I was excited, yet a little bit disappointed in myself for not knowing all the background and everything. Still, I went to the Naval Academy Prep School. It was one of the greatest things I ever did, because you mature greatly between eighteen and nineteen years old. You learn all the same military stuff that you're going to learn as a plebe at the Naval Academy. In fact, you take the same classes. I was a decent student but not a rockstar academic guy. I was a good athlete in small Maine, but I got there and found out that this was a place where a lot of the recruited athletes go. I realized that this was a whole different athletic environment. It was also a whole different academic environment. I just matured so much. That one year really set me up for success because when I got to my plebe year it was a piece of cake. Class academics were a review. The military was a review. I had a bunch of friends already. I just really enjoyed plebe year. It was easy.

The rest of my time at the Naval Academy was fine too. I had some leadership roles my senior year as a top commander and got motivated to apply for the SEAL team from some of the mentor SEAL officers and the other mentors who were there. That's what got me going down towards the SEAL team career. After graduation, I spent a year or so at BUDS and then four years driving underwater vehicles called SDVs in Norfolk, Virginia. Then I went to graduate school in Boston at MIT and then out to San Diego for some SEAL Team 3. That's when September 11th happened. I was a SEAL platoon commander around that time. When I came home from that deployment, I moved back to Virginia and was executive officer and operations officer at Special Boat Team 20 and then SEAL Team 10. After that, I got selected for NASA. So I spent ten years in the SEAL teams before coming to NASA, and I've been here for twelve years.

As an astronaut, I went on one space shuttle mission for sixteen days and then one mission on a Russian Soyuz to the International Space Station for 166 days.

Q: You were a Navy SEAL for ten years. The SEALS have gotten a lot of attention in the last years for various reasons, mostly in a positive way, but I think most people kind of associate it with just being really tough. Being able to take the cold, a little bit of misery, and being in tough situations. Can you speak about the science of being part of these teams?

A: Well, I don't think there's a science in the traditional sense. The nice thing about BUDS (which is the entry-level SEAL training Basic Underwater Demolition/SEAL school) is that it's sort of like the baseline for all people who enter the community, much like nuclear power school is for anybody that's going in submarines. There's a common bond instantly once you get to your team. Everybody knows you made it through it, and there's always—in every community, particularly the SEAL teams—the joking around that "my class was harder than yours and my hell week was colder than yours and blah, blah, blah." But the bottom line is, there is a mutual respect that you made it through and you didn't quit.

Even though it is elite, not all people are equal. Everyone's got strengths and weaknesses that they bring to the team. That's what makes teams wonderful. In some instances, a different team member, or a pair of team members, or a group of team members will pick up the slack. That sounds negative, but it just means that they get a bigger share of something that they're stronger at, and then when it swings around, then somebody else maybe steps in.

It's really a well-running team when the people—without coordination and without really speaking—know when to go in and out of figuratively pulling harder on the rope. It is also about the moving fluidly between leadership and followership, so that the team is firing on all cylinders at all times. That's what the best teams that I've been a part of function like. I don't think it's a science. It's really just art that comes with a group of people training, practicing their craft, preparing for their mission, and then ultimately executing it.

Q: So, would it be fair to say that, to execute that level of art, there has to be a baseline of technique and fundamentals and skills in place? Like, how people enter a room, how they operate a boat, and how they deal with a certain situation—those things are so rigid that they allow you to be more artistic in changing situations. Would that be fair?

A: Yeah. I think that's fair, but you bring up the boat thing. Some guys are more "motorheads" than others, for instance. If I happen to be the guy driving the boat, and the motor conks out when there's big waves coming, it's knowing that person is the motorhead; knowing that he should come right away to fix it. I'm not going to feel one bit that my feelings got hurt because I move aside and that guy gets it running again. I think what you said is accurate.

Q: How do you make a transition from SEAL to astronaut? I would have loved to know the moment where you went home and said, "You know, I think I'm going to do this instead." It seems like a completely different domain. How did you know you would succeed, and how did you actually succeed at it?

A: I didn't always want to be an astronaut. I was in the SEAL teams when I met a guy named Bill Shepherd, who was the first SEAL—the only other one, actually—to become an astronaut. After meeting him, I realized the navy commands that he had were similar to mine. He was SEAL team, special boat team, and had a graduate degree from MIT. I thought to myself, "Well, if he was successful and was a competitive applicant, then what the heck do I have to lose? I might as well apply." So, that's what motivated me to apply. Then I got excited about it and started thinking, *Oh, wow, that's just a pretty cool mission; maybe it might be real for me. Maybe I have a fighting chance to get selected.*

I told my wife at the time that that's what I was going to do, and she was excited for me. However, both of us were realistic that statistically it was not super likely. The process is long. I had my interview, which was a week here in Houston, and then I went away on a six-month deployment. I got a phone call right at the end of that deployment while I was home for a weekend. NASA asked, "Would you like to come work with us at NASA?" I remember high-fiving my kids and hugging my wife. We were all super excited, but the transition was interesting.

The technical stuff was okay for me. What was challenging was my experience in the quiet, professional existence of being a SEAL—at that time, not every book on the shelves at Barnes & Noble was written by an ex-SEAL. It was not like that. It wasn't something I spoke about. But, as an astronaut, it's part of our job to be a public figure and talk about what we do. The fact that I was a SEAL was common knowledge to the folks that I would be speaking with at schools and communities and so on. So, it was challenging for me to get comfortable with talking about all that, talking about myself, and it took a little while. The operational stuff was a relatively smooth transition. Doing space-walk training, preparing for missions and simulators, talking on the radio, thinking with situational awareness was all that stuff that I was doing in the SEAL teams. It was just a different mission, so that part wasn't so hard.

Q: One of the things that we talk about in the book is the concept of functional reserve, which we define as the difference between what you think you're capable of and what you can actually do. For example, the first time that you ever had to go through a challenging thing at BUDs or the Naval Academy, when you have people chasing you; or you're chasing other people; or people are demanding things of you that are much more than you can perform, and then that becomes the norm for you. How do you tap into that? Is there a way that you tap into that reserve to try to get the most of what you possibly can do?

A: For me, it's the fear of letting my teammates down. If I'm doing a workout by myself that calls for doing a set of ten pull-ups a night, and I'm tired, I've already done a couple sets, and that last rep is hard to get, it's easy to stop at nine and not try. But if you're sitting there and you've got all your teammates on the pull-up bar and everybody's knocking them out, it's easy to push through because you don't want to let the people down. That's a simple example, but if you take it to combat or in the cockpit of a spacecraft, and you're tired, you're having to focus hard and concentrate in those uncomfortable, somewhat stressful environments, it's not wanting to let people who are counting on you down. That's what it is for me. When I'm in those situations, I just keep on going and it's not until the stress is removed or the situation is secure when the feeling of "wow, that just happened" kind of comes over you.

Q: How do you inspire people who are already the best to do better? With your exposure with SEALs and astronauts, you have seen people who have already passed a lot of tests along the way, but, still at some point, you're asking them to be better because the mission changes or the challenges get harder or the competition improves. How do you inspire the top 1 percent to keep working as hard as they used to?

A: Well, I personally think that it depends on the people you're working with. For instance, the motivators, way of talking, competitive jiving, and verbal teasing in the SEAL teams would not work at NASA. You could tell a SEAL, "Hey dude, if that's all you can do, then I'll go get your mother. She'll work harder than you're working right now" or something like that. I'm being a little wise guy here, but SEALs are motivated by the team thing, and it was good, competitive, good-natured ribbing with people you already count on.

That same level of humor would fall very flat and probably end me right in the Human Resources office here at NASA. So, it's a little bit different tactic here in that it's more of an inclusive way of talking, and it's probably an older, more mature crowd. The average astronaut is in their forties, whereas the average SEALs that I was working with and leading were in their young twenties. It's a different type of crowd, but I have not found there to be a cookie-cutter approach. Those leaders that I've seen try to use one recipe for all scenarios end up not being successful.

Q: As Chief of the Astronaut Office at NASA, your current role, what are your responsibilities?

A: I decide who the crewmembers are for particular missions. That's not every day, but since we assign crews about every three to four months, it's an ongoing process. With the space station, we're constantly launching people and people are returning. Therefore, in the front side of that process they need to be assigned to begin the two-year training cycle to do the mission. My day-to-day job is much like a commanding officer of a navy unit: daily leadership. We're changing some of our organizational structure at the moment right now, and leading through change has been a challenge as well. We have instructor astronauts. I used to be one. However, the coaching role is more distributed amongst this cadre of senior astronauts that teach, mentor, and guide the other astronauts.

Q: Whether we're talking SEALs or we're talking astronauts, training must be pretty heavy in simulation as well as situational planning and emphasis on the fundamentals, correct?

A: Yeah, absolutely. Situational awareness is one of the most critical functions. Somebody can be highly talented and highly skilled, but if they can't prioritize and make decisions about what's important, what's urgent, and decide from the important stuff whether it's real, they can't execute efficiently and therefore, they flounder a bit. So, having dialed-in situational awareness is really, really important. We're going through an astronaut selection period right now. That's what I was doing all day today—interviewing prospective astronauts, and it's a challenge to measure that.

Q: I would think one of the more challenging things about being a SEAL or an astronaut is you that you can go through this training, know all about science and aeronautics, be as tough as nails, but you still can't predict every scenario. So, how have you personally applied the art of high performance when you're forced to see things from a new perspective, or adapt and innovate to a challenge or a threat that you haven't seen before?

A: That's a great question because—I don't really know. I don't know how what I've done is different than others. I think there have certainly been folks I've tried to emulate who I thought were fantastic SEAL operators, who I thought were awesome astronauts. On the astronaut side, one in particular was Joe Tanner, an older astronaut. He was a real experienced guy when I got here as a new guy, and I just watched everything he did. He was so smooth in the airplane. He was so smooth in the simulators. He was so smooth in the neutral buoyancy lab, which is where we practiced our spacewalk training. He was really well respected. Whatever he said, people listened. When he opened his mouth and had a comment, it was always right on, and it brought the team along in a manner that was really impressive. I've always strived to be like Joe Tanner, and whenever I'm doing something I actually think to myself, *What would Joe do in this situation?* In the SEAL teams, it was the same kind of thing. I guess it's emulating the people who I thought did it well.

Q: When we talk about art, science, and grit of high performance, we've been studying sports, aviation, space flight—anything where there's what we would call "terminal consequences." If something goes wrong, they go really, really wrong. So, how can we apply how people prepare in these fields to everybody? Art is being able to see things in new ways, science is perfecting your craft to the nth degree, and grit is doing the deliberate practice over and over again in more challenging ways. It makes people better in any domain they're in. Would you have anything to comment upon that—or any way that you've seen or reason to make you define it differently?

A: I like how you bring in the art and the science of it—because it's really elements of both at certain times. That's why I think it's so hard to quantify. You can't really test it. You can't put it on a piece of paper and have a candidate circle A, B, or C and have a bubble sheet pop up that says that somebody specific is going to be the one that's going to go from *good* to *great* and then on to the top in their craft.

Q: You kind of hit the lottery on multiple things. You've been selected into the Naval Academy, very hard to do. You then were selected to the SEAL teams, the astronaut program, and then as chief of the astronaut office. All these things are almost one-in-a-million shots, and over and over and over again, you keep getting selected. Space walks, running ground force assault teams and boats are all very different things, so it can't be just doing the same thing over and over again for twenty years. What do you think the secret is? What is the common thread to all of these things that you think has allowed you to be in this position?

A: I think it's the ability to listen. Nobody wants to be around people who are always transmitting. That's what I learned very early in my career. Watching people who just think they know it right from the get-go and are quick to tell you that they know it, get nowhere fast. For instance, when I was a SEAL platoon commander in Afghanistan, I thought of it as if I was swimming with sharks. The sharks were the other SEALs in the platoon, and all I really did was point the sharks in the right direction and keep them in the lane lines every now and then. The platoons just knew what to do.

When you go through an astronaut selection, there are about twenty people in an interview week, and we interview generally for six weeks. That's about 100–120 people who interview, and I remember thinking, *Holy cow! In my one week alone, the other nineteen people were all awesome, and that's just one week out of five other weeks. Gosh, I really have a pretty low chance of getting picked.* And I thought, *Well, all I can do is just be myself in this process, and we'll see what happens.* Now that I am on the other side of it, selecting people, I really see that. I see the people who are genuine and are being themselves and are not trying to impress you or tell you what they think you want to hear. Those are the people that I want to be around and want to operate with in the future.

I really think that it's the ability to listen, take on the lessons that the other talented people around you have to offer, be one's self, and have a decent head on your shoulders. You need to be capable of processing data as it comes in and making solid decisions. Sometimes those decisions seem to be made quickly with limited information, and sometimes those decisions need to be made collectively. If you have time, you can discuss it, and you can do it in a manner in which everybody feels like they have a say. But you have to get smarter over a career in knowing the difference between those situations and how to walk that line.

After becoming chief of the astronaut office, I remember thinking to myself, *Wow, I'm kind of humbled here because there are other folks who have been here for longer and are more experienced than I am.* I realize now that my job is not to be the most experienced astronaut. It's just to make decisions that give us the best crews that we can put forward on the missions. The key to success certainly starts with listening to people who can give you all the skills—and by that I mean mentors.

Q: You have a unique opportunity to train with the Russians as part of the Soyuz team and spend a lot of time with them. Do they have a different approach or is it *completely* different? How do they go about doing the things that we prepare for?

A: Yes. It's actually quite different. It's cultural, and it was very interesting for me because a Soyuz is a small spacecraft with a crew of three. So, I had two other Russians in my cockpit with me. One of them was Pavel Vinogradov, who turned sixty years old while we were in space. So, he spent his youth in the Soviet Union. The other guy was a thirty-four-year-old cosmonaut named Sasha Alexander Misurkin, and he did not grow up in the Soviet Union. His upbringing was as a Russian, and it was very interesting for me to watch the difference in their reactions to the same situation, social setting, or operational environment. Both of them are my dear friends and I respect them tremendously, but it was eye opening to see just how differently they would view things.

The older guys are much more authoritative because that's what they grew up with, and the younger cosmonauts are more willing to be inclusive and hear everybody's thoughts. I really enjoyed working with both those guys. They'll be my friends for life, but the cultural differences are definitely noticed in the operational and social settings.

INTERVIEW WITH FORMER DC CHIEF OF POLICE CATHY LANIER

Q: Chief Lanier, thank you very much for joining us. One of the things I thought would be great just to get things started is to get some context. Tell us a little bit about your background, your key influential moments in your life, your career, and also the new role that you're in.

A: So far . . . influential moments. They're not really moments per se. There was a parent, grandparent, mother, or grandmother who always pushed me to work harder and strive harder. So it was not really about influential moments. It's been more people who have inspired me—people who are extremely successful who have inspired me. They have attributes that you look at, and you think, *wow, you know, I wish I could learn how to be like that person.* Or, people who have pushed you to do things you wouldn't normally do yourself. So, for me—that has been the key. It's not been singular moments, but mostly it's been people, and then, it's particular times. You know—opportunities. Like the time I made the decision to leave policing and move into the private sector. Those were influential times. There was a lot going on in policing and a lot that I had tried to change in policing. But it just felt like at the time that I made the decision to move out of policing, it was time for me to do something else.

Q: You mentioned people being involved. Is it you wanting to model people that you admire or people who proactively reach out to you that help you along?

A: I think a combination of both. That's a great question. I would look around me and see who the people were who did a job well, or the people I looked up to. And then I would try and latch on to those people. And in many cases, those people who are very similar were looking across an organization and saying, "Hey, you know, here are some people who are trying really hard and have some potential." And they latch on to you. So it's combination of both. I've never reached out to a person who I thought would be a great role model and said, "Hey, you know, I'm interested in learning what you do" and had them say no. I've also had some leaders reach out to me and say, "I think you have more potential than you think you have. Let me help you." So it's been a combination of both for me.

Q: Excellent. And so, in your last role, there were 6,000 officers, give or take here or there, who were with the metropolitan police department. Can you talk to us a little bit about how they're trained—from the time that they're recruits and throughout their career? Because I would imagine in policing, it is a constant training environment, both with fundamentals or new situations that they have to be ready for.

A: Unfortunately for policing—and this is one of the things that I've been frustrated about my whole career (a total of twenty-seven years)—is that police forces are a government entity. So, like many government entities, it is very difficult to change training and policy rapidly; it's difficult to change a government organization as quickly as change is happening in society. And as the chief, what I would try to do is keep pace with change outside of the organization. So, I would tell you today, that no matter how good a chief is, or no matter how good a government is, you will never have a police department that is training commensurate with the speed of change in society, and that's a problem. So, training a recruit historically has always been very militaristic. It is: "Know your policy, know your orders, know the written law." But it has not yet evolved to a point where it's flexible. Importantly, training has to be scenario-based, so you have to throw everyday scenarios into it. You can teach people the law all day long. You can teach mere policy all day long. But until they learn how to apply it and not memorize the content, but know how to apply that in a kind of a soft social scenario, you're going fail, and that's unfortunately where our policing is failing right now.

Q: I'd imagine that every situation you walk into is potentially a brand new one, because the people are different and the situation's different.

A: Yes. You can't just have new police officers memorize things and then expect them to apply it correctly. It's got to be very situational.

I mean, think about the military. They give you rules of engagement and they say, "Here are the times that you can engage and here are times that you can't." And then you're in Afghanistan today, you're in Iran tomorrow, you're in a different part of the world—Russia—the next day. And the rules of engagement are not static. They're different. They're different with the society and the people you deal with. They're different with the scenarios that you deal with. You can't revise policies every five to seven years and think they're going to keep pace with the environment that your operators have to engage in every single day.

Q: Now, do you think they're aware, like even some of your more, let's say mid-level to senior-level people in a department, or any organization . . .

A: Oh, of course. I mean, street cops—street cops get that. They understand. They know that the policy says X and that the policies get revised every ten years; they get it. They understand what the policy says and that they have to improvise, adjust, and overcome. They get that if they do something that's outside of policy, they're going to get in trouble. They do what they have to do to survive, but it's just understanding the dynamics that the bureaucracy will never keep pace with the change that we see in society when it comes to professions like military, law enforcement, firefighting, you know, those public and life safety professions.

Q: It sounds like that they kind of crave training. They want more training.

A: Absolutely.

Q: We will run into some places like senior professional type things—lawyers, doctors, businesspeople—where they say, "Oh, I've already covered that before. I've got this. I've been doing this for twenty years." But it sounds like it's just the opposite of yours.

A: Well, it's because the worst thing that could happen to them is they can get sued. The worst thing that happened to us is we could die.

Q: That's correct.

A: You crave training because it keeps you alive.

Q: So that's a great response because the whole premise of this book is that you deal with terminal consequences. Things go very well or they go very wrong. The plane is up in the air; the plane is not up in the air. You know . . . firefighters put out the fire with no problems, or there's a big problem. How do you apply that to other fields? I mean, you're moving into the private sector. You've encountered other people in other professions. How would you think is the best way to communicate that this way to prepare applies in all these other domains?

A: You have to really look in your organization and find the people who kind of have it in their DNA, you know? It's in their DNA; it's what they want to do. They want to be the best. They want to make sure things don't fail. You find those people, and then you let them lead; and they will lead. Hopefully, you have enough of them. If there are not enough of them, then you have to—and it's not personal—you have to go get enough of them. There are people out there who understand that terminal consequences

are a part of what we all do. And even in the private sector, that's important
to understand. Finding the people who understand that our job is not just
a job; that it has significant consequences. You have to be passionate about
what you do. So you seek those people in your organization who share that
understanding and you let them lead. You find the people who don't share
that understanding, and you replace them with people who do. Because
that's just how important it is—no matter what your profession.

Q: You mentioned earlier that you had people that kind of tapped you on the shoulder and said, "I think you can do more." I think that's a common thing that we see.
How do we use things like coaches, mentors, whatever you want to call them, to
get people to tap into what we call the functional reserve? So there's a difference
between what you're doing now and what you're actually capable of. The simple
example we sometimes use is, "You're running a 5K with one of your friends and
all of a sudden, in the last hundred yards, you see them creeping up to pass you and
you instantly become faster." That's tapping into your functional reserve. So how
do you tap into people's functional reserves? Is it through giving them more challenges, higher expectations? Is it competition with each other? Is there anything
that you'd like to share on that?

A: I mean, it's kind of different for everybody. It's funny how different people are. There is a baseline of performers. You recognize that there is talent
in your organization and you try and get to know them. That's why it's so
important to get to know people. You can recognize what motivates people.
For some people, it is competition. For some people, it is just recognition.
And for others it is, "Give me the hardest things you got and let me show
you that I can do it." For them, it is a constant challenge. If they don't have a
challenge, they'll leave. They'll go somewhere else where there is challenge.
So it is individual to every single employee. You can't just say, "I'm going to
lead this way, because I think my employees need a challenge." It's different
for every employee, and if you don't know your employees and leave your

office and talk to people, you won't know them. So if you're talking about command or an executive level, you have to know what inspires them so that they will be able to run their team.

Q: So a big part of *Cultivating Excellence* is coaching. The way we look at it, is it's really about art, science, and grit and helping, one-on-one, people get better at what they do every day. Managing is more inspecting and auditing. Leadership is more about direction setting. But coaching is actually the interaction between performer and coach. Have you found that coaching is an essential part of developing people?

A: I would have to say that there's a really important role for auditing and assessing what's going on in terms of management. Find out what their potential is. And then you try and get them to drive their own performance. But you have to coach it. I think that coaching is the key, but it's essential that you still have some auditing function. Because you can't coach a winning team if you don't have some audit function in terms of knowing how good you are. There are always opportunities to improve. And if you don't audit as part of your coaching, you're going to miss that.

Q: So one of the big things that we put as part of our kind of coaching fundamentals is an insistence on fundamentals, and situational planning—but also the use of simulation. You know, whether you're going to modify, or tack rooms, or how you turn this corner. We reflect upon it, and then we do it again, you know, over and over again. Do you see that as a realistic model of how you develop people over time?

A: I do, because you can run a scenario today and everybody performs flawlessly with their role. Then tomorrow, if you run the same scenario, their answers can be completely different and their role is completely different because the environment has changed. You have to continually challenge people's ability to be flexible. You can't just say, "Study for the test. Come in here and run this exercise." You can't just give the standard answers or have a checklist. The checklist changes every day.

Q: That's what we would refer to as the art of high performance. How you see things from a new perspective.

A: Yes, I agree. I think you do have different perspectives every single day, because every single day there are subtle changes in your environment, and if you miss them, and you keep following the same script, you're going to fail.

Q: So, to wrap things up a little bit, you're moving into this new role. You had this great, great career and are very widely respected for things that you did. Now you have to move into a totally new domain with different types of customers, or clients, or employees. You're now working in cities all over the country with variables that just increased quite a bit. But what variables didn't change? I mean, what are the principles that you're going to bring with you to help develop people, still accomplish the mission, and be able to deal with situations that you may have never heard of, even thought of, but that might become normal maybe even a year from now?

A: I'm kind of back to my answer earlier about finding what's in people's DNA and then feeding the drive. I mean, for me, what's in my DNA is—and what I crave—is a challenge. And also, working with people to fix, or find solutions to a challenge. After twenty-seven years of policing and ten years as the chief, I wasn't sure I had a sufficient challenge anymore. And now I have this exciting new challenge, and it's feeding my drive. So I have a whole new group of people that I can tap into to accomplish a new mission. That's exciting to me.

Admiral Cross: Chief, I've really enjoyed hearing your remarks—really, really good stuff. The other interviewees that we've spoken to have talked a lot about team building. What is the core part of building teams, your philosophy on it, and some of the techniques that you used? How do you see team building, and what are your key characteristics or key principles of building a team?

A: To me, one of the most essential components is for everybody on the team to feel comfortable. So regardless of what your skill level is or what you bring to the table, everybody who's part of the team has to feel, "I look forward to something." I've never worked in an environment where somebody on the team had nothing to add. You know, maybe the only thing someone has to add to the team is that they've got a really good spirit and are just happy to be there. They might not add much to the work product, but they do bring the right environment. So, for me, it's making sure every single person brings more of what they have—and that inspires the other people on the team.

INTERVIEW WITH GENERAL MICHAEL HAGEE, US MARINE CORPS

Q: General, could you tell us a little about your background—the key moments when you were growing up that were influential to you, your career progression, and some of the achievements that you had along the way?

A: I actually grew up in Texas. I grew up on a small family ranch. My dad was a US Navy chief during World War II and was very proud of being in the navy. He always thought jokingly that the navy went to hell in a hand-cart when soldiers no longer could wear their uniforms ashore. If someone said anything bad about a ship to a sailor, those were fighting words, and he thought a good sailor would stand up and fight for his ship. He was very sorry to see that culture change. He was wrong in some respects. But, the bottom line is he loved the navy.

He served in the Atlantic in the first part of World War II on old four-stack destroyers, and then he changed to aviation and served in the Pacific on PBMs and PBYs during the second part of the war. I grew up hearing those stories and shared his love for the navy. That's what motivated me to join the service. I tried to get into the Naval Academy out of high school. I was unsuccessful in that, so I went to the University of Texas for a year. I was in an ROTC there, and I was lucky enough to be selected to go to the Naval Academy the following year. I had all intentions of going into the navy, but after four years of the Naval Academy, and seeing the marines that were sent there, to be quite honest, I wanted to be more like them than I did the sailors that were sent there.

So, I selected the Marine Corps. On selection night, I actually called my dad. I had not told him about this before. I called him and said, "Dad, I selected the Marine Corps." There was silence on the other end of the line. He said, "The Marine Corps? Marines only do two things." He said, "They guard gates, and they harass sailors." I let him know that we no longer guarded gates, but we still continue to harass sailors.

So, I went in the Marine Corps. I was lucky to immediately go to postgraduate school. Then I did the normal thing by becoming an infantry officer. I served in Vietnam and had a wide variety of tours throughout the Marine Corps. To me, the most enjoyable tours were when I was serving with marines, in command of marines. I was lucky enough to command at all levels.

I actually served later in my career at the Naval Academy three times and survived—which most people say doesn't happen, but it did.

The last time I served at the Naval Academy I was a colonel, and after a year and a half, I was selected for general officer. During that last posting, the Naval Academy had a significant cheating incident in electrical engineering. At the time, it was nationwide and, unfortunately, very well known. The admiral who was there was really a great guy. I thought he was destined to become chief of naval operations one day. Of course, the scandal ended his career. That is an example of why I would disagree with a famous quote from Aristotle, "Choice, not chance determines your destiny." Maybe. There's an awful lot of chance, I think, in it, and this particular admiral had bad luck there. He made some bad choices, but he had bad luck.

At any rate, the Board of Governors of the Naval Academy said, "We need to send someone there to fix it." Whatever that meant [chuckles].

The head of the Board of Governors told the Secretary of the Navy that not only do you need to send someone over to fix it; you need to send a marine. And for whatever reason, I was selected. I went to the Naval Academy to "fix" what was wrong.

I think they thought that a marine would come down there and install discipline. And, in fact, what I've found was that discipline was not what was really needed. They really needed a character development program. So, I completely changed the direction they thought it was going to go, and I briefed the Board of Governors about four or five months later. I told them that I didn't want to become the discipline officer or the conduct officer. We needed to set up a full-blown character development program across the curriculum, and that's what we did. I'm really proud to say that that program is still being carried on.

I then served as general officer at several locations, and then finally was fortunate enough to be selected as commandant of the US Marine Corps. I was commandant from January of 2003 to almost January of 2007. The big event during that time was when we crossed the line of departure for Iraq in March of 2003. So the war in Iraq and Afghanistan consumed most of my time.

Interestingly, before I became commandant, I was commanding general in the First Marine Expeditionary Force, and of course, that's the unit that went up on the right-hand side when we went to Baghdad. Over a year before I became commandant, we all worked on that particular plan of going into Iraq. To put that together and get everyone on the same page—especially with a large staff—required a little different type of leadership.

Q: Going back to that issue at the Naval Academy where the first thing people thought of fixing was discipline, and you came back and recommended character development: Could cheating be defined as achieving No. 1 status or succeeding or getting straight As—at any cost? Does breaking the rules or taking shortcuts become acceptable? Is that part of the character development you were brought in to address?

A: I don't think so. First off—everyone cheats, everyone lies. And anyone who says he hasn't cheated or lied, in my opinion (and the literature is quite clear on this) is lying. Your grandmother bakes a fruitcake for Christmas, and it's a terrible fruitcake. Do you tell her it's a terrible fruitcake? No, you don't. You tell her it's a good fruitcake. And so you're lying. Now, there are degrees, I get that, but, I think it's much more complicated than most people think. For example, a student might say, "I'm going to become a surface warfare officer. I really want to be a surface warfare officer. I love it. I know the electrical engineering has nothing to do with becoming a surface warfare officer. And this stuff is really hard, and ... okay, I want to become a surface warfare officer." So, they cheat.

Is that wrong? Yes. Is that a rationalization? Yes. A classmate is failing and you know he could be a really superior officer. But, he's failing his electromagnetic wave theory class, which you know has no bearing on anything, If you took the test on Monday, and he takes the same test on Friday and comes to you and says, "You know, I'm going to fail out of this school unless I pass this test. Can you help me?" Do you help him? Classmate loyalty says you do.

All services preach that you take care of your individuals. So, who are you more loyal to—your classmate or to the Naval Academy? There are right and wrong answers to that, but they're not simple right and wrong answers and that's what was not being addressed. Interestingly enough, research shows that the most important part of your character, your ethical development, occurs after you leave home. Assuming you have a good home environment, your parents give you right and left boundaries. Then you go off to school, and there are no right and left boundaries. You have to reestablish them, and people struggle with that. The literature is really quite clear on that, and the Naval Academy, as with the other academies, was not doing a very good job helping students set boundaries.

Q: So, it sounds like there is an art to this. There's not just a formula you apply, or come and apply the right level of volume with things or just be tough.

A: Oh yes. You're dealing with human beings. You're dealing with different human beings with different motivations, backgrounds, and experiences. Leading is absolutely an art.

Q: In the US Marine Corps or Navy, there's always been a pretty rigorous selection process. These people have been weeded out by having gone through recruitment screenings and boot camp; they've passed tests, achieved rank, advanced schools, and more selections. However, there's still a subset of those people that become truly great, and this applies to marines, sailors, artists, musicians, sports figures—whatever it might be. So, what is it that holds people back from being one of the top in their profession versus just very good?

A: That's an interesting question. I honestly do not know. I think a lot of guys and gals work very, very hard and are not always successful. Some of that is they might just not have the ability, and some of it is they're applying the wrong efforts. But what I have noticed more often than not is that it's not a lack of working. It's what your priorities are.

What quite often gets in the way of becoming what some writers call a Level 5 Leader (of which there are very, very, very few, in my opinion) is that they're thinking more about themselves than they are about the organization, the people with whom they're working, or the mission. To me, individuals who become extremely successful are those leaders that do care about more than themselves. Unfortunately, you don't hear about those leaders, because they are not focused on promoting themselves. They are focused on the organization and the mission that that particular organization has.

Q: Have you seen the movie *Sully* yet?

A: Yes, I did, just last week. I thought that was a really powerful movie, and you can see the struggles that Captain Sullenberger went through. He did not want to be famous, and I think he was a good pilot. He may be a great pilot, but it wasn't because he was particularly skillful as a pilot. He thought about what he was doing, what the mission was, who was the last guy off of the aircraft, and who was the last guy in the boat. He was concerned about his mission and other people, and he did that throughout his life. Now, I know there's an artistic license used by the director, but I think that movie pretty much captured Sullenberger. He was always working on his skills—not to be great in and of himself, but to be in service of other individuals and the mission. I have seen some very, very talented leaders who have gotten in trouble because of ego. And, I come back to this thought that some of the best leaders around are never heard of because they're too focused on their organization and the mission to be concerned about whether they're getting any accolades or not.

Q: I want to talk about the role of coaching. So, leadership sometimes is guiding direction, defining what policy is, what to do, what not to do, and setting priorities. There are many definitions for it. When I'm using the term coaching, I'm talking about individual relationships between a leader and a performer to make them better. What have you seen working with the Marine Corps and other examples of how coaching improves individual performance?

A: Coaching is absolutely critical. But I think coaching is actually more than that. The top individuals and top leaders need to be focused on building a team. You're trying to help everyone on that team realize his or her full potential. Now, there are some individuals that have more potential than others. You're probably going to . . . I don't want to say help them more . . . but in some ways you will, because you say, "Whoa, this guy is really quite good, and he's got what it takes. Not only can he help the team and us accomplish the mission, but he could go on and become a chief of naval operations, commandant, chairman, a great musician, or whatever." So, it's about building that team and helping each one of those individuals realize their full potential. That, to me, is proper coaching.

I remember once when I was a company commander and we had another company commander who was unbelievable. The battalion commander called each one of the company commanders in to get our fitness report. When it was my turn, I came in, he handed me my fitness report, and I read it. It was very complimentary. I looked up, and the battalion commander asked, "You're surprised, aren't you?" I said, "Yes, sir, I am." He agreed with me and said, "Let me tell you something. Your fellow company commander may be the best natural leader I have ever seen, but you have the best company. So, whatever you're doing, keep doing it."

Building that team and having that team ready to perform is not about you. I come back to that same thing. It's not about you. It's about the individuals around you, your team, and your mission. That's what, in my opinion, makes what I would call great leaders. I sort of have a little adverse reaction to *elite* because I don't want to be considered elite. I really want to be part of the team, and that is probably one of the most difficult things in a larger organization.

When you make admiral or general, all of a sudden you are automatically the funniest, the handsomest, the smartest, the whatever-est in the organization. When you have that, and you have individuals looking at you that way, you are not going to get the best performance out of that organization. They're going to wait for you. One of the most difficult tasks that I had, as I was fortunate enough to move up the chain of command, was to build that team wherever you were. In larger organizations, it took more time to build a team where individuals felt very comfortable saying, "Hey, General, I think this is wrong. I think this is the right way, and you need to consider this." Everyone knew who was in charge, but you want a team functioning to where everyone truly checks their egos at the door. They're in there trying to accomplish a mission.

I remember as we put together the role plans for the movement of the marines into Iraq in 2003. We were probably about six months into the planning. We'd come to what I thought was a pretty good plan on how it was going to move, and we were having final discussions. We were just about to slap the table on this thing, and a young captain said, "Hey, sir, I think there's a better way to do it." Silence. There was silence in the room. I said, "Great. What do you have?" And he went through it, and you know what? That became the ultimate plan that we executed because it was a better plan. Unless you build that kind of team, you're not going to get the individuals coming out saying, "Hey, sir, I think there's a better way to do it."

Q: That's an enormous amount of discipline to be able to do that, and it is a true artistic way to do it. There's a lot of organizational inertia at that point and momentum that would make you want to stay on that track, but you changed it obviously because the consequences are so high. It does sound like that there is a strong relationship between the team members and the leadership team to be able to do so, right?

A: Oh, it absolutely is. It is focused on one thing: the successful accomplishment of the mission. When you have a real team working, and I've been fortunate enough a couple of times to be a part of such teams, no one cares whose recommendation is followed. If you don't like one individual's recommendation, you can comment on it, and no one takes umbrage with that fact. They don't see themselves as being attacked. They see everyone trying to come up with the best solution. I can tell you, that does not happen by chance. One has to continually work on that, and all it takes is one person, especially in very senior groups saying, "That's the dumbest thing that I ever heard." If they do, you can forget about individuals volunteering their opinion after that.

Q: One of the things we have seen that helps performance in some of the research we've done, whether it's somebody fighting for a spot as a top cellist in an orchestra, racing in a swimming pool, or trying to make a unit in the Corps, is managed competition. How do you get members of a team to compete against each other to try to enhance their own performance, but still be able to perform on the team after the decisions have been made? What are your feelings on the importance of managed competition to get people to do their best?

A: If you are in an orchestra, what are you trying to accomplish? Yo-Yo Ma talks about this, and he is the top cellist in the world. People ask him, "When you are playing, what are you thinking about?" He replies, "I'm thinking about how can I get this beautiful music that this composer has made and make the audience understand what the composer was trying to say." If you are in an orchestra, the director and everyone else in that orchestra is trying to do the same thing. I saw John Williams when he came and conducted the Marine Corps Band. He is one of the most famous composers and conductors in the United States, and it was never about him. He would stop the musicians at a particular measure, and he would say, "You know, this is not what I think the composer is trying to say here." He then asks, "Can you capture that and bring it across?" And then they tried it again. When they replayed it, you could hear the difference. I wouldn't know how to do it since I'm not a musician. But, you could absolutely hear it.

Are all these top musicians "competing" with one another? Yeah, in a way, but they had actually checked their egos at the door. They were trying to perform music, they were trying to accomplish that mission, and they were all working together as a team. When that happens, everyone is in the game. There's always competition, but competition can be a detriment if it is solely focused on the individual and their desire to be better. If it is focused on the team and the mission where the performer states, "I want the team to be better, I want to accomplish the mission," it raises everyone's ability.

Q: I want to address training and preparation, especially as a team. We break up training into three pieces. The first is fundamentals: skills of a job, the time on the marksmanship range, how quickly can you disassemble and assemble a weapon. The second is situational planning: how you enter a room, how you do bounding, how you do all those kinds of things in planned scenarios. The third is dynamic simulation: putting people in field training exercises, war games, or live fire. We found that a lot of people who don't perform well in real life tend to shy away from simulation, or they stop practicing their fundamentals once they get to a certain level of proficiency, or they just don't plan for all the situations. Can you talk about those three components and why they're important?

A: Well, you have to have the fundamentals, and you really have to go back to those fundamentals, in my opinion, throughout your career. In the Marine Corps, you go to the rifle range and you snap in, and you do your time. Now, you don't do it as often as you do it when you're in boot camp, but you go back periodically because after a while, you can wander away from it.

It reminds me of one of our more famous commandants who was a big poker player. He once said, "War is like poker. You really have to know the rules and the fundamentals. You have to know the fundamentals so well that you can bend and break them." So, fundamentals are important. Even Yo-Yo Ma practices his scales.

Some people have so much experience that when they see a situation, they don't even know why they come to the conclusion that they do, but they do it anyway. In a book I read called *Sources of Power*, the author used a number of firefighter studies. People who have fought a lot of fires would be in a new fire and all of a sudden they'd say, "We have to get out of here," and the guys around them would ask, "Why?" They respond, "I really don't know, but we've got to get out of here," and they get out, and the building collapses.

You can trace it back to experiences that they had had that were almost etched into them and they didn't even know it. They came up with these decisions that seem to be almost a miracle. But, it wasn't a miracle. The decisions were based on experience.

You put individuals in situations where something would come up, and they have to make a decision. Based on that decision, they made something else happen. Actually, we wanted them to fail, and we applauded when they failed. Because they knew that we would be trying to make them fail, they were much more relaxed when they trained. After a couple of hours, they would have fifteen to twenty different scenarios that they would have gone through, and they were building an experience database. They were understanding what they can do in various situations, and it was starting to become a part of them.

I think sometimes we put individuals into situations and we believe the really good guys are going to solve this and they're going to be successful, and we give them good grades. Actually, in those types of situations, it should be about learning, so if an individual is not failing, then something's wrong with the test; the tests and situations are too easy, because you want everyone to fail at first. As we've learned, individuals learned a whole lot more from failure than they do from success.

Q: One of the questions I had related to this concept is what we call "functional reserve." How do we get people to perform better than their past ability or what they thought they could do? When you're running a 5K with a friend, all of a sudden at the finish line you're running faster than you thought you could simply because they are challenging you. You mentioned that by failing, people learn and start to do better, and then the next time they do it, it becomes minimum standard. Are there other ways that you help people tap into their functional reserve to do more than they thought was possible before?

> A: You talked a little bit about it where you want individuals to fail, and most importantly, they know you want them to fail so they feel a little more comfortable about failing. Remember, we're dealing with human beings, and we're dealing with egos. You don't want to crush the guy or the gal. You want them to learn and to step up, and this is where the art comes back into it. Let's say you have a squad leader or a platoon commander and your sense as a leader is—based on your experience and your understanding of individuals—that this guy or gal has "got it." So, you give them a task that maybe they haven't done before and is a little more difficult. In that particular case, you probably don't want them to fail. You want to help them. You want to help them along, and you surely don't want to give them something that you know they're going to fail at because they are not ready for it. That is where the art of high performance comes back into it. That goes back to coaching. That's an important part of helping an individual realize his or her full potential.

Q: So, some people would listen to this and say, "Well, he's a marine; that's different. We're a law firm" or "We're a technology company" or something like, "That kind of stuff doesn't apply to us." But, what we see from domains like yours (that have terminal consequences) is that when things go wrong, we *can* learn quite a bit about how to prepare, and coach, and encourage high performance from people. Any kind of last statements related to that?

> A: First off, people who say that are wrong. They're absolutely wrong. We had, in the Marine Corps, individuals who are going through their MBA studies at the Wharton School. We took a group of non-marines who are in

classes with them down each year to Quantico as our guests. We would send them through one week of Officer Candidate School. The Wharton MBA students would remark, "What are we doing down here? This is crazy!"

Almost without exceptions, when they leave a week later, they get it. They're put into situations, they're deprived of food, they're deprived of sleep. When it's raining really hard and it's really cold and they're miserable, I will suddenly hand them a problem and say, "You've got to make a decision now." Hopefully, all of a sudden, they get it. They see: *This is about how I handle myself and how I take care of my team when there is a crisis.* They are smart enough to realize there are not only crises on battlefields. There are crises in the boardroom, there are crises on the stock exchange floor, there are crises if you're pumping gas. There's always a crisis that you have to handle, so the question is are you prepared to handle that crisis when it comes up?

I tell a story that happened to me when I first got to Vietnam, and I was a young lieutenant. I arrived in Vietnam at that particular point in time when we were supposed to come into Da Nang, and we were supposed to spend a couple days there to get acclimatized, get our gear, find out what's going on, and so on. I had been there about four hours, and this young marine came up and said, "Sir, are you Lieutenant Hagee?" I said, "Yes." And he said, "Sir, you are supposed to get your gear right now. The platoon you're taking over . . . well, the platoon commander has just been killed. They're bringing his body back on a helicopter, you're to get on that helicopter and go out and take over the platoon." And, all of a sudden, no more training, no more blanks, no more bang-bang. This is real.

So, I went out there, got the platoon, and had responsibility for a large section of road between two villages. We got the platoon up, and we started moving down the road. I could hear one marine complaining, "Man, are we screwed. We got this brand-new lieutenant. He doesn't know anything, and he's going to get us all killed." They kept mumbling and mumbling, and I knew that a lot of the things they were saying were right. I didn't know a whole lot. So, we'd moved down the road about forty-five minutes or so, and all of a sudden we started receiving very heavy fire—machine-gun fire included—from our right flank. I looked around to make sure everyone was down, and I was the only guy still standing up. Everybody was already on the ground! I got down on the ground, looked back up, and I'll never forget how every single marine in that platoon was looking back at me. It was no longer dumb lieutenant, green lieutenant, stupid lieutenant anymore. It was "Okay, shut up, everyone. Lieutenant, what do we do now?"

I have had that experience over and over again, especially after joining a new unit. Until they'd be comfortable with who you are, and know that you know your fundamentals, and that you know what to do in certain situations—only then do they think that maybe you know what you are doing.

The question that I have for squad leaders or CEOs is: When your company, team, or organization looks back at you when you're in crisis, are you going to be ready? Not only with the fundamentals and your knowledge, but have you built the team to handle it? Because in many cases, you personally can't do it. The team has got to do it. Have you built the team to where it can react to it? And if you have, then in my opinion, you are one of those really good leaders—elite if you want to call it that.

Q: That's excellent, General. Thank you so much for sharing that. That was great, actually. That's the end of my questions. Admiral Cross, are there any questions you wanted to ask?

Admiral Cross: We use the terms art, science, and grit (and some combination of those three things) as things that are necessary for a person to be a real high performer. And from my experience anyway, there are a lot of people who are pretty good at the science and grit part of that, but what makes people really stand out is how good at the art piece are they. Those intangibles like leadership, mentorship, and coaching that we talk about here—are, in my opinion, the art part of this. Although you are a great scientist, and a great, great guy, of course. But you know the art of leadership, coaching, and mentoring—and I really believe you've always been very successful. I compliment you on that, Mike, and I'll always admire you for it.

A: I appreciate that. One thing on the comment on Aristotle. I think chance plays a much larger role in how we end up than we like to think. In the United States, because of our background and our education and our culture, we believe that, "Man, if I just know how everything works, I can figure it out, and I can be successful." Well, I don't subscribe completely to that. I think chance plays an enormous part in it. And, it's how we handle that opportunity—either good luck or bad luck, and you're going to get both. It's how we handle it and prepare individuals to understand that you're going to have ... you're not always going to draw a royal flush, okay? How are you going to handle that? How are you going to be better? And individuals who can do that I think are more high performing and more successful than individuals who are stumped by that.

NOTES

Chapter 1

1. Fuqua, Brad. "Fosbury Takes Track and Field to New Heights," *Corvallis Gazette-Times* (March 29, 2014). Accessed January 15, 2017. http://www.gazettetimes.com/news/local/fosbury-takes-track-and-field-to-new-heights/article_17dcc0d8-b6cc-11e3-850a-0019bb2963f4 .html

2. "2016 Track & Field State Championships Qualifying Standards," Oregon School Activities Association. http://www.osaa.org/docs/btf/16standards.pdf

3. Jacobellis v. Ohio, 378 U.S. 184 (1964).

4. "Operation Nifty Package," Wikipedia. Accessed August 28, 2016. https://en.wikipedia.org/wiki/Operation_Nifty_Package

5. Dingfelder, Sadie F. "How Artists See," *Monitor on Psychology* 41, no. 2 (February 2010): p. 40. Accessed September 6, 2016. http://www.apa.org/monitor/2010/02/artists.aspx

6. Whyte, W. H., Jr. "Groupthink," *Fortune* (March 1952): pp. 114–117, 142, 146.

7. Janis, Irving Lester. *Victims of Groupthink: a Psychological Study of Foreign-Policy Decisions and Fiascoes* (Boston: Houghton Mifflin, 1972).

8. "Capitalizing on Complexity: Insights from the Global Chief Executive Officer Study," IBM (2010). Accessed September 26, 2016. http://www-01.ibm.com/common/ssi/cgi-bin/ssialias?htmlfid=GBE03297USEN

9. Rose, Barbara (ed.), *Pollock: Painting* (New York: Agrinde, 1980): p. 65.

Chapter 2

1. "Archimedes' Principle." Wikipedia. https://en.wikipedia.org/wiki/Archimedes%27_principle

2. Krzysztof, Mackala, and Antti Mero. "A Kinematics Analysis of Three Best 100 M Performances Ever," *Journal of Human Kinetics*, Volume 36. (2013): pp. 149–160. doi: 10.2478/hukin-2013-0015.

3. "Meet the New Men of Space." *The Salt Lake Tribune.* April 10, 1959. p. 1.

4. Slater, Matt. "Olympics Cycling: Marginal Gains Underpin Team GB Dominance," BBC Sport. Retrieved April 11, 2014. http://www.bbc.com/sport/olympics/19174302

5. Johnson, Steve. "Skills, Socrates and the Sophists: Learning from History," *British Journal of Educational Studies*, 46, no. 2 (1998): 201–13. doi:10.1111/1467-8527.00079

Chapter 3

1. "Milo of Croton: Greek Athlete." Encyclopaedia Brittanica. https://www.britannica.com/biography/Milo-of-Croton

2. Duckworth, Angela. "Grit: Perseverance and Passion for Long-Term Goals," *Journal of Personality and Social Psychology*, Vol. 92, No. 6 (2007): 1087–1101.

3. Galton, F., Sir. *Hereditary Genius: An Inquiry into Its Laws and Consequences*. (London: Julian Friedman Publishers, 1869).

4. Ericsson, K. Anders, Ralf Th. Krampe, and Clemens Tesch-Romer. "The Role of Deliberate Practice in the Acquisition of Expert Performance," *Psychological Review* Vol. 100, No. 3 (1993): pp. 363–406.

5. Fitts, P. and M.I. Posner, *Human Performance*. (Belmont, CA: Brooks/Cole, 1967).

6. Macnamara, B.N., D.Z. Hambrick, and F.L. Oswald. "Deliberate Practice and Performance in Music, Games, Sports, Education and Professions," *Psychological Science*, 25(8)(2014): 1608–1618. doi: 10.1177/0956797614535810

7. "Most Shoelaces Tied in a Bow in One Minute," Guinness World Records. http://www.guinnessworldrecords.com/world-records/most-shoelaces-tied-in-a-bow-in-one-minute

Chapter 4

1. Ericsson, K. Anders, Ralf Th. Krampe, and Clemens Tesch-Romer. "The Role of Deliberate Practice in the Acquisition of Expert Performance." *Psychological Review* 100, No. 3 (1993), 363–406.

2. "Multiple Integrated Laser Engagement System," Wikipedia. https://en.wikipedia.org/wiki/Multiple_integrated_laser_engagement_system

3. Jodlowski, Mark T., Stephanie M. Doane, and Randy J. Brou. "Adaptive Expertise During Simulated Flight," *Proceedings of the Human Factors and Ergonomics Society Annual Meeting*, Vol 47, Issue 19 (2016): 2028–2032.

4. Tauer, John M., and Judith M. Harackiewicz. "The Effects of Cooperation and Competition on Intrinsic Motivation and Performance," *Journal of Personality and Social Psychology*, 86, no. 6 (2004): 849–61. doi:10.1037/0022-3514.86.6.849

5. "United States Navy Strike Fighter Tactics Instructor Program," Wikipedia. https://en.wikipedia.org/wiki/United_States_Navy_Strike_Fighter_Tactics_Instructor_program

6. "College Football and Scholarship Opportunities," ScholarshipStats.com. http://www.scholarshipstats.com/football.html

Chapter 5

1. Summitt, Pat. *Reach for the Summitt* (New York: Broadway Books, 1999).

2. Crouse, Karen. "Pat Summitt Makes Tennessee a Cradle of Coaches." *The New York Times* (Jan. 4, 2009).

3. Nayar, Vineet. "Three Differences Between Managers and Leaders." *Harvard Business Review* (Aug. 3, 2013). https://hbr.org/2013/08/tests-of-a-leadership-transiti

4. Ericcson, K. Anders, Michael J. Prietula, and Edward T. Cokely. "The Making of an Expert," *Harvard Business Review* (July 2007). Accessed June 28, 2016. https://hbr.org/2007/07/the-making-of-an-expert

5. Team Bolt," usainbolt.com. Accessed June 29, 2016. http://usainbolt.com/team/

6. Sheinin, Dave. "Stroke of Genius," *The Washington Post* (June 26, 2016): Sports, p.1

7. "Google CEO, Eric Schmidt on Coaching," YouTube video, 00:00:41, Google CEO Eric Schmidt discusses the benefits of coaching, posted by MarkCannon202, June 29, 2016, https://www.youtube.com/watch?v=kIiwAcnSN1g

8. Larcker, David F., Steven Miles, Brian Tayan, and Michelle E. Gutman. "2013 Executive Coaching Survey," Stanford Graduate School of Business (Aug. 2013). https://www.gsb.stanford.edu/faculty-research/publications/2013-executive-coaching-survey

9. Turak, August. "Are You Coachable? The Five Steps to Coachability," *Forbes* (Sept. 30, 2011). Accessed June 30, 2016. http://www.forbes.com/sites/augustturak/2011/09/30/are-you-coachable-the-five-steps-to-coachability/#1a9b1d624761

10. https://www.td.org

Chapter 7

1. Knowles, Malcolm S. *The Adult Learner: A Neglected Species* (Houston: Gulf Pub., 1990).

2. Paul, Richard, and Linda Elder. *The Thinker's Guide to the Art of Socratic Questioning* (Dillon Beach, CA: Foundation for Critical Thinking, 2006).

3. Rogers, Carl. *Client-Centered Therapy: Its Current Practice, Implications and Theory* (London: Constable, 1951).

4. Prochaska, J.O., and J.C. Norcross. *Systems of Psychotherapy: A Trans-theoretical Analysis* (New York, Thompson Books/Cole: 2007): pp. 142–143.

5. "A Leader's Guide to After Action Reviews," Headquarters Department of the Army (Sept. 30, 1993). http://www.au.af.mil/au/awc/awcgate/army/tc_25-20/tc25-20.pdf

Chapter 8

1. Marsalis, Wynton. "Tackling the Monster: Wynton on Practice," directed by Michael Lindsay-Hogg. 54 min., Sony. ASIN 6-3035-8902-2, 1995. Videocassette.

2. Battista, Judy. "It's in the Play Cards," *The New York Times* (Oct. 27, 2006). Accessed July 10, 2016. http://www.nytimes.com/2006/10/27/sports/football/27coaches.html?_r=0

3. Hawk, A.J. "Interview with A.J. Hawk on High Performance." Telephone interview by author. June 27, 2016.

Chapter 9

1. Kroening, Shannon, LCPL, USMC. "Marines Learn Underwater Egress at Helo Dunker," The Official United States Marine Corps Public Website (Nov. 23, 2015). Accessed July 11, 2016. http://www.marines.mil/News/News-Display/Article/630878/ marines-learn-underwater-egress-at-helo-dunker/

2. Hebblethwaite, Cordelia. "Presidential Debates: Top Tips on How to Prepare," BBC News (Oct. 3, 2012). Accessed July 11, 2016. http://www.bbc.com/news/magazine-19791450

3. Zenko, Micah. *Red Team: How to Succeed by Thinking Like the Enemy*. (Basic Books, 2015): p. 135.

Chapter 10

1. Vandewalle, D. "Development and Validation of a Work Domain Goal Orientation Instrument," *Educational and Psychological Measurement* 57, no. 6 (1997): 1000. doi:10.1177/0013164497057006009

2. DeShon, R. P., and J. Z. Gillespie. "A Motivated Action Theory Account of Goal Orientation," *Journal of Applied Psychology* 90(6) (2005): pp. 1096–1127.

3. Button, Scott B., John E. Mathieu, and Dennis M. Zajac. "Goal Orientation in Organizational Research: A Conceptual and Empirical Foundation," *Organizational Behavior and Human Decision Processes* 67, no. 1 (1996): pp. 26–48. doi:10.1006/obhd.1996.0063

4. Horn, Thelma S. (ed). *Advances in Sport Psychology* (Champaign, IL: Human Kinetics, 2008), p. 344.

5. Horn. *Advances in Sport Psychology*, p. 357.

Chapter 11

1. Katzenbach, Jon R., and Douglas K. Smith. "The Discipline of Teams," *Harvard Business Review* (March–April, 1993). https://hbr.org/1993/03/the-discipline-of-teams-2

2. Russo, Joe, Larry Landsman, and Edward Gross. *Planet of the Apes Revisited: The Behind-the-Scenes Story of the Classic Science Fiction Saga* (New York: Thomas Dunne Books/St. Martin's Griffin, 2001).

ABOUT THE AUTHORS

DARRYL W. CROSS
CHIEF PERFORMANCE OFFICER, HIGHPER TEAMS

Darryl is the Chief Performance Officer and founder of HighPer Teams, a high-performance training company that unleashes the incredible potential and amplifies the results of the world's top individuals and organizations by leveraging team-centric performance development and culture.

Darryl combines thirty years of experience with research on proven scientific methods to offer a unique approach to improving performance. He is a *business* coach who has worked with organizations in dozens of countries, a USA Rugby-certified *athletic* head coach for the Virginia Rugby Football Club, and one of only 100 Master Fitness Trainers in the world certified by the National Academy of Sports Medicine.

He holds a master's degree in business administration and is a graduate of the George Washington University's Law Firm Management program. He also has numerous certifications in change management, human performance improvement, and performance enhancement.

As Vice President of Performance Development and Coaching at Lexis-Nexis, Darryl developed, coached, and trained the world's largest, full-time sales force of lawyers. The 1,500 lawyers and executives under his instruction generated over $2 billion in annual sales in the legal, corporate, and government sectors in North America, Asia, Australia, and Europe.

Darryl also served as the chief marketing officer and member of the executive committee of an international law firm, where he was awarded the most prestigious national award in legal marketing, the Marketing Partner Forum's Excellence in Marketing Award, for "creating a sales culture at a law firm."

Darryl is currently on the international board of directors of the Legal Marketing Association. He is a past board member for the Association of Talent Development's AG Forum, a collection of the top fifty training executives from companies such as Facebook, Intel, Delta Airlines, Hilton International, IBM, and Accenture.

An internationally known expert on the art, science, and grit of high performance, Darryl has spoken to more than 10,000 executives, professionals, and athletes from more than one hundred countries on four continents about how to continuously maximize performance and results.

REAR ADMIRAL WILLIAM V. CROSS, US NAVY (RETIRED)
PERFORMANCE COACH AND OPERATIONAL EXPERT

Bill Cross enjoyed an active-duty US Naval career for thirty-three years, retiring as a two-star rear admiral. His military experience included combat tours in Vietnam and Operation Desert Storm and four operational commands, including an F-14 fighter squadron, amphibious assault ship, nuclear aircraft carrier (CVN-69, USS *Eisenhower*), and an aircraft carrier striking group.

He was the navy's first Program Executive Officer for Aircraft Carriers; as such, Bill led the initial design of the advanced command and control system for the navy's newest class of aircraft carriers. His other military positions include navy test pilot, test pilot school flight instructor, engineering manager (US Navy's F-14 programs), director of plans and policy (US Transportation Command), and director of operations (US European Command).

Following his retirement from the navy, Bill worked for eleven years in the corporate world (Vice President of Engineering Systems and Navy Business

Development for CACI International, Director of Global Defense Sales and Chairman of the Defense Advisory Board for BearingPoint Consulting, and Defense Leader for Deloitte Consulting). He is currently a member of the Board of Advisors for Electronic Warfare Associates.

Continuing education has played an important role in Bill's life and career. He holds a master's degree in management and is a graduate with highest distinction from the Naval War College, Naval Nuclear Propulsion School, Navy Test Pilot School, and Defense Acquisition Management College.

Bill has extensive knowledge of the art and science of military and business war gaming and has broad experience as a participant, Red Team leader, and sponsor in numerous strategic and tactical games. His philosophy on success and high performance is based on the principles of hard work, personal responsibility and accountability, constructive competition, innovation and creativity, and compassionate leadership.

Made in United States
Orlando, FL
21 April 2022

17062771R00182